Dale Spender is an internationally known scholar and feminist writer. Australian by birth, she lectures all over the world and has written many books including the bestselling *Man Made Language*, *Reflecting Men* and a series about seventeenth-century women writers.

By the same author

Edited by
DALE SPENDER

# The Diary of
# Elizabeth Pepys

Grafton
*An Imprint of* HarperCollins*Publishers*

Grafton
An Imprint of HarperCollins*Publishers*
77–85 Fulham Palace Road,
Hammersmith, London W6 8JB

A Grafton Original 1991
9 8 7 6 5 4 3 2 1

A catalogue record for this book
is available from the British Library

ISBN 0 586 06735 3

Set in Times

Printed in Great Britain by
HarperCollinsManufacturing Glasgow

FOR MY SISTER
LYNNE SPENDER

# Contents

# Acknowledgements

There are many people I would like to thank for the help they have given me during this extensive editorial exercise. First of all, my agent, Tessa Sayle, who has been especially supportive over the years: and Judith Kendra, my first editor at GraftonBooks, who has shown great patience, and provided me with considerable encouragement: and Nancy Webber who has proved to be the most delightful audience and advisor.

Elizabeth Crawford has found me many literary treasures and Candida Lacey has given me advice and assistance, and kept me supplied with useful books. George Spender has traced Spender-Pepys records. I am also grateful to Dieter Pevsner and Judith Miller for their counsel and comments on my editing practices. Frances McHarg and Glynis Wood have transcribed and typed, and, I trust, have not incurred any serious eye damage. Catherine Wearing has checked references and recipes, Christine Zmroczek has provided details on housework, and Kirsten Lees has done some of the library/archival queueing and deserves a medal. And Carole Hayman has enlightened and entertained me with a very good impression of Elizabeth Pepys.

The staff of the Fawcett Library have provided me with invaluable assistance and I am sure that Elizabeth Pepys would have been appreciative of David Doughan's contribution to the publication of her journal. The staff of the London Library have also been more than helpful, and I am very grateful for their courtesy and cooperation.

I would like to acknowledge my debt to some of my friends who have, of necessity, become familiar with Elizabeth Pepys, and the place of women in the seventeenth century. For knowing when to ask, and when not to ask, about the state of the Diary and my emotional wellbeing, I would like to thank

Renate Klein, Susan Hawthorne, Cheris Kramarae, Anna Coote, Pippa Brewster, Sally Cline, Margaret Bluman, Shere Hite and Helen Thomson. For providing me with new insights, much fun, an attentive audience and a balanced diet, I am grateful to Robyn M. Daniels.

When I have been immersed in the Diary over the last few years, I have sometimes found it difficult to return to the conventions of modern English. To all those with whom I have corresponded and who have found my phraseology unfamiliar, I offer my apologies. My parents, Ivy and Harry Spender, will no longer receive letters written in seventeenth-century-ese.

All my family have developed an affection for Elizabeth Pepys who is now a regular presence among us. And while she has taught us much about herself, about her husband, and the position of women in seventeenth-century England, she has also helped us to realize that there is a great deal about human nature which does not change. Elizabeth Pepys has become another voice, another reference point in our understandings.

For their emotional and financial support, as well as their forbearance, I would like to thank my parents: for the faith he has had in me and the security he has provided me with, I would like to thank Ted Brown. For the joy we have had even when the task has been difficult and demanding, I would like to thank Lynne Spender, who has not wilted under the weight of the thousands of pages of Diary manuscript which she has read.

Dale Spender
March 1989

# Bibliography

*Diaries quoted*:

Lady Grace Mildmay's Journal and Papers (1570–1617, Unpublished), Northampton Public Library.

*Diary of Lady Margaret Hoby 1599–1605*, edited by Dorothy M. Meads, George Routledge, London, 1930.

*The Diary of Lady Anne Clifford*, edited by Vita Sackville-West, 1923.

*The Life of Mrs Hutchinson Written by Herself*, 1806.

*Memoirs of Lady Fanshawe*, edited by Sir N. Harris Nicolas, 1829.

*Natures Pictures drawn by Fancies Pencil to the Life. Written by the thrice Noble, Illustrious, and Excellent Princess, the Lady Marchioness of Newcastle . . . 1656–1671*, Margaret Cavendish.

Fanny Burney, from *The History of Fanny Burney*, Joyce Hemlow, Oxford University Press, 1958.

# Introduction

Elizabeth Pepys, the daughter of Dorothea and Alexander St Michel, was born on 23 October 1640. Her father was a minor noble of Anjou; disinherited after he converted to Protestantism, he was a man of intense religious passion. He had crossed to England from France to join the household of Queen Henrietta-Maria – as a gentleman carver – but religious argument led to his dismissal. Later he moved to Ireland where he married the widow Dorothea Fleetwood, in about 1639.

Born in 1609, the daughter of Sir Francis Kingsmill who had acquired Ballybegg Abbey while serving in Ireland, Dorothea claimed kinship with the noble Cliffords through her mother's side of the family. She was left in comfortable circumstances on the death of her first husband and she also inherited property from her father, at Bideford, where her children Elizabeth and Balthasar were born. But the resources she brought with her to her second marriage were soon dissipated by her husband: throughout her life with Alexander, Dorothea was plagued by financial worries and she soon determined that her daughter should not have to deal with the same problem.

Alexander St Michel was a tall and striking man, with courtly French manners which were very impressive. He was persuasive and passionate – and he had a very chequered career: from gentleman carver to soldier (he fought in Flanders in 1648–49 and under Cromwell in Ireland) and then to inventor. The later years of his life were devoted to his inventions, for which he always needed more capital but which he was always convinced would make him his fortune. He had great faith in his perpetual-motion machine and took out patents for curing smoking chimneys, for keeping pond-water clean and fit for horses to drink, and for manufacturing ornamental bricks in moulds.

Elizabeth's father, however, did not completely abandon his

hopes of restoring his fortunes by regaining his lost inheritance: visits were made to France expressly for this purpose. Then in 1652, Dorothea took her two children to France to meet their noble relatives, but not even the grandchildren were reinstated as beneficiaries. But in Elizabeth's terms the trip was by no means a waste: she became fluent in French (a skill for which she was later very grateful), and she developed a fascination for Catholicism, which she later 'revived' – particularly when she wanted to vex Samuel Pepys who was frightened that popish associations would be damaging to his career.

When Elizabeth and Samuel Pepys met, the St Michel family were living at Charing Cross in the Parish of St Martin-in-the-Fields, in very reduced circumstances, with only one maid. Elizabeth was considered a great beauty, and somewhat exotic, with her noble and eccentric connections and her French background. Samuel fell in love with her immediately – and then proposed marriage.

This was unusual. Not just because this was a time when love matches were rare but because by anyone's reckonings, a woman without money or influence was an unsuitable choice of wife for a young and ambitious man. And Samuel was ambitious, and extremely money conscious: it was really quite out of character for him not to count the cost – although later, this did not prevent him from holding Elizabeth's lack of dowry against her.

Samuel, of course, had many relationships with women without wanting to marry them. His own explanation for his rash behaviour on this occasion was that Elizabeth was so beautiful and that he was so passionately in love with her, he was made quite ill. And for Elizabeth, marriage was the only 'solution'.

And as she made clear in her diary, she thought she was lucky to get him. There had been other expressions of interest, but they had come to nothing: the son of Lord John Somerset, for example, with whom Elizabeth had been 'familiar' in France when she was *very* young and, later, Captain Robin Holmes who obviously found her very attractive. One of her fears was that no good man would want a wife who had nothing but beauty and breeding to bring to the union. And not only was Samuel good-looking, but also there was the promise of a good career in front of him and, with a little luck and latitude, a very good life for her, too. She was pleased at the prospect; she was also aware of some of Samuel's weaknesses and realized that she was taking quite a risk. Quite how big a risk she did not understand, until after the wedding.

She knew Samuel was mean with money; she knew he could be bad-tempered. She was forced to acknowledge that he was probably unfaithful, that he had relationships with other women even though he fervently denied this. She also knew that Samuel was not one to be pushed – not about marriage, monogamy, or money. So Elizabeth would not press Samuel to enter into a financial settlement.

For her mother this presented something of a dilemma. It was partly because of her own financial predicament that she was determined that Elizabeth should have some formal arrangement made about money; *before* she was married. She was most distressed, and her stance was later vindicated, when Elizabeth resisted and refused to have her love reduced to a 'business agreement'. But Elizabeth had her reasons for not following her mother's counsel.

First of all, she knew her man and his money habits; she was frightened that any pressure to make him sign a settlement which would guarantee her a certain allowance would not only make him angry, it could also well drive him away. He could look for someone else who had more money and made fewer demands. Elizabeth may have only been in her fifteenth year but she was quite astute when it came to relationships and, with Samuel, she knew that she was not in an advantageous bargaining position.

She also *wanted* to believe that once they were married Samuel would be – if not generous – at least fair. She wanted to have faith in him, rather than to prepare for the worst. So she adopted the stand that she did not want to despoil their love by consideration of base money matters.

No financial arrangement was made, a failure which Elizabeth later came to regret

Samuel knew of Dorothea's counsel and didn't like her interference. Their differences over money and the responsibility for Elizabeth led to much bitter feeling. Once married,

Samuel would not visit Elizabeth's parents and would not have them visit him – though Elizabeth and her mother still met: husband and wife often quarrelled over his attitude to her family.

But although Dorothea St Michel cautioned her daughter against an early marriage and urged her to wait another year; although she warned her about financial difficulties – about the problems of marrying the son of a washerwoman and a tailor-man, who was mean and moody – she also recognized that the handsome Samuel Pepys with his position and prospects was a fine match for Elizabeth. They were married with her consent, on 1 December, at St Margaret's in the Parish of Westminster when Elizabeth was only fifteen. Later, Elizabeth and Samuel disagreed about the day and the year of their anniversary; this could have been because the couple were separated for a period and Elizabeth chose to celebrate their reconciliation and their 'new life' together. This is more likely than the conventional explanation – that one thought it appropriate to celebrate the civil ceremony, and the other, the religious one.

Before their marriage, Dorothea – herself a dedicated diurnal-keeper – urged her daughter to keep account of the significant events of her life, along with any useful information she might need. At this time it was not uncommon for some women to keep a 'closet'[1], a written record of events, of advice, of housewifery practices and of recipes. As no distinction was made between recipes for the table and recipes for physic, these closets could contain instructions on the preparation of poultices and herbal brews alongside those for venison pasties and the making of sack-posset. It is a mark of Elizabeth's culinary and housewifely interests that there are very few recipe entries in her written records. With her concentration on the details of her life and the exploration of her own emotional state, Elizabeth's accounts are better placed within the emerging genre of diary rather than among the women's closets.

During the seventeenth century 'personal chronicles' became a popular literary form among a cross-section of women. Grace

[1] See: *The Queen's Closet Opened: Incomparable Secrets in Physick, Chirurgery (Surgery), Preserving, Candying, and Cookery, As they were presented to the Queen*. 'Never before published. Transcribed from the true copies of her Majesties own recipe books, by WM, one of her late servants, 1655.'

Sherrington Mildmay (1553–1620), for example, who was taught to read and write so that she might study her Bible, kept her unpublished diary from 1570 to 1617. Begun three years after her arranged marriage to Anthony Mildmay, it is written in the style of the period with records of meditation, advice and autobiography, along with collections of cures and recipes, and other items of household interest. Lady Margaret Hoby (*c*. 1571–1633) also kept a diary – not published until 1930: it comprised 118 folios, each written on both sides, and covers but a few years of the diarist's life – from August 1599 to July 1605. Some of the entries are about visits to York and London in pursuit of law and physic, but nearly all contain devotional material.

Then, of course, there was the great Anne Clifford (1590–1676) to whom Dorothea St Michel claimed kinship. Leading a much more 'courtly' life than Lady Mildmay or Lady Hoby, Anne Clifford's diaries contain information about family and personal details, along with the records of great events: the death of Queen Elizabeth; a conversation with Queen Anne; a complaint about the lice which attacked her party when they attended the court of King James I. Interestingly, Anne Clifford wrote two accounts of her daily life: one in the first person, and one in the third person. When Elizabeth Pepys contemplated keeping two versions – one for her own private use and one, with household accounts, for Samuel's perusal – she was well within a family tradition.

Other chroniclers of the period are Lucy Hutchinson (1620–1675), who was unusually well educated and who wrote among other things *The Life of Mrs Hutchinson Written by Herself* which – like *The Diary of Samuel Pepys* – was not published until a much later date, in 1806. There was Lady Anne Fanshawe (1625–1680), who wrote her *Memoirs*, full of fascinating detail about the Civil War and her own adventures, and not published until 1829. And, of course, Margaret Cavendish (1623–1673), later Duchess of Newcastle, who wrote her autobiography and had it published with *Natures Pictures Drawn by Fancies Pencil to the Life* (1656–1671). All these journals give some idea of women's lives, the social and political context of the time, and the development of the diary and its significance for women, and it is regrettable that they have not enjoyed the same popularity and prestige as their male counterpart, Samuel Pepys.

When her mother first suggested that she keep a diary, Elizabeth wasn't at all enthusiastic. She saw it as a chore, but one she should undertake to please Dorothea. But once she got into the habit, diary-keeping became a central and satisfying activity throughout most of her life. There were exceptions of course; for example, during the period when she left Samuel she wrote little, but this was partly because she had so little time and was so tired by the effort to support herself.

Although she was enjoined to start a diary as a written record of significant dates and events, Elizabeth soon established the practice of using her diary as a 'confidante' – an audience to whom she expressed all her hopes and fears. Fanny Burney at much the same age – fifteen – a little more than a hundred years later did much the same thing; ' – to *whom* dare I reveal my private opinion of my nearest relations? my secret thoughts of my dearest friends? my own hopes, fears, reflections and dislikes? – Nobody!' she wrote in March 1768, and then proceeded to address her diary as *Nobody*.[2]

Elizabeth had soon moved so far from official record-keeping to personal revelation – about herself and those around her – that she became quite concerned that no one should be able to read her entries. Particularly not Samuel, who would not take kindly to some of her assessments of his character and capabilities. This is one reason that Elizabeth often wrote in French, a language which Samuel could not readily read. In this edition of the Diary the passages in French have been translated into English (and are appropriately marked in the text); their purpose is self-evident when it is noted that they almost always contain unflattering comments about Samuel, a state of affairs he would not have been able to tolerate.

Samuel could be a bit paranoid. He often believed that people were saying things about him behind his back and got very distressed. To find that his wife was keeping a regular written record on his shortcomings, on his bank balance and his peculiar personal habits, was sufficient to send him into a frenzy. As Elizabeth unfortunately found out.

[2] See: *The History of Fanny Burney*, Joyce Hemlow, 1958.

In her early days of diary-keeping she could generally find safe hiding places for her pages, particularly in her parents' household. But her home upon marriage was small and sparsely furnished, and as the diary grew it became a recurring problem to find a hiding place for it. It says something about the conventions of housework at the time – and of Elizabeth's housewifely standards – that when she was married she believed the best place to hide her diary was in the covers of her bed. But the pile of pages outgrew even this form of protection and once more Elizabeth faced the problem of finding a place where her husband would not come across them.

Another associated problem was that of procuring writing materials. Paper and 'pen' were expensive and not readily available at a local store. As a woman and a wife, Elizabeth, of course, did not have a stationer nor the financial resources to purchase all the necessary supplies. And this is where her friend Eliza came in. Married to Richard Harvey, a ship's chandler, Eliza had access, limited and surreptitious, to her husband's stores; to a certain extent she was able to keep Elizabeth in paper and ink without her husband becoming suspicious. This was in contrast to Samuel who, when he took up diary-keeping, did store stationery at home, but who kept such a close watch on the number of sheets he possessed that Elizabeth would probably not have been able to remove a single one, without risking discovery, and Samuel's wrath.

Eliza Spender was born on 8 March 1623 and had married Richard Harvey at St Giles, Cripplegate, on 17 October 1652. Richard Harvey was a prosperous business man, and the couple – with their two children – lived at Holborn. While it is not clear whether the initial friendship was between Eliza and Elizabeth, or between the two men, a close relationship developed between the two couples – with Richard Harvey being the bridesman at the Pepys' wedding. From some of Elizabeth's entries it seems that the two women had known each other for quite a long time. And though it can only be speculation, the fact that Richard Harvey is never mentioned in Samuel's diary – and that there is no evidence that he maintained his acquaintanceship with Richard Harvey when Elizabeth left him – does suggest that the friendship between the couples was based on the relationship of the women.

Quite a few years older than Elizabeth, Eliza was much more experienced about the world and the ways of men, and she tried to give Elizabeth instruction on the duties of a wife and the management of a husband. She too urged Elizabeth to obtain some form of financial settlement – 'before love dwindles'. But on these matters Elizabeth does not always take the advice of her friend seriously: while she acknowledges that things have not gone always well with Eliza, in her own case with Samuel, all will be different.

But Elizabeth does follow up some of Eliza's warnings about Samuel's 'affairs'. She wonders about the week he was supposed to be in Cambridge and when Richard Harvey reported seeing him in London at 'the low Rhenish wine house' on 5 November 1655. She questions Samuel about his past amours and is deeply distressed when she sees him enjoying himself on his 'liberty night' – in the company of whores. Given Samuel's own admissions of his philandering, it is not unlikely that he was deceiving Elizabeth and having relationships with other women from the time he met her, though, of course, things might not always have been what they seemed. For example, there is the possibility that the gloves Elizabeth saw Samuel buy on 8 January 1656, were not for the 'baggage' he was with, but were a genuine errand for Lord Montagu who routinely instructed Samuel to purchase items for him and his family. But, of course, Elizabeth had no way of knowing this.

However, Elizabeth does not push these incidents too far: partly because she is insecure, partly because she is not sure what to do. And partly because she is convinced that Samuel will be faithful after they are wed.

Aside from the fact that she doesn't want to lose him, one reason that Elizabeth does not put pressure on Samuel is that he has such a bad temper. From her diary entries it seems that at first she is not frightened of his fits; rather she finds them embarrassing, a sign of low behaviour, and she doesn't want to be reminded of his lack of breeding. Before they are married, when Samuel 'gets in a pett' and gives vent to his unjustified attacks of jealousy, Elizabeth manages him so that he doesn't make an exhibition of himself, and doesn't spoil the celebrations on her birthday when she receives a present from 'someone else'. But she always files away these occurrences of unreasonable behaviour which later fuel her own retaliation.

Elizabeth Pepys is by no means a foolish or fragile female. When we first meet her in her diary she is young, inexperienced, even something of a romantic. But she is also witty and wilful. She is clever and runs rings round Samuel Pepys when it comes to arithmetic (especially to division) and accounts. She speaks fluent French, is quite a talented writer and is an excellent mimic (the last often being put to use to mock her husband's 'low-born' family).

She is proud of her beauty and is prepared to spend both time and money maintaining it. Quite rightly she sees it as an asset – neither Samuel nor perhaps any other man would have wanted to marry her without it. While she wants to live in a style commensurate with her birth – while she wants to have finery and be a lady of fashion, she is not just a snob, or a social climber as some of Samuel's supporters have pompously suggested. Both she and Samuel liked clothes and aspired to the good life, but while Samuel acquired the means to indulge his tastes, he was nothing short of miserly to his wife. Even *after* they did have a financial agreement.

But if Samuel didn't always provide, neither did Elizabeth always keep order in the house. The greatest source of antagonism between them was Samuel's meanness and Elizabeth's household carelessness. She wasn't interested in the cooking or cleaning, only the entertaining. And it must also be noted that Samuel was so obsessive about order that it's doubtful whether anyone could have ever accommodated his demands for tidiness. A hanging slightly off-centre, a book not precisely placed, these were sufficient to send him into a rage about the disarray of his establishment.

Elizabeth clearly believed that some household chores were beneath her: she bitterly resented the fact that Samuel expected her to lay the coals and do the wash – with her own hands! She looked down on her mother-in-law, who had been a washerwoman, and was incensed that her husband expected her to descend to the same level. That she refused to do the menial chores – rather than that she omitted to do them – is a much more likely explanation for her supposed slothfulness and incompetence.

She never led Samuel to believe that she could or that she would clean. On the contrary, she always emphasized that she was of noble birth and she genuinely believed that it was the quality of her beauty and breeding that Samuel prized in her. So why would she sacrifice them?

There was much she could put up with in Samuel, but not his attempts to 'debase' her. It took enormous spirit to become independent but she determined it was better to preserve breeding and dignity than to be so badly treated. In leaving him she demonstrated she really was 'a Clifford'.

One of the most frequently entered items of complaint in Elizabeth's diary relates to chamber pots. Samuel filled a lot of them. Because they had always been emptied for him – at home, in lodgings, in Cambridge – he wasn't aware of how often they had to be cleaned and how awful the work could be. He simply expected chamber pots to be washed without thinking much about the reality – that it was Elizabeth who would have to provide the service. And she found this exceedingly galling.

Toilet habits were very different in the seventeenth century. Internal plumbing was the exception; Thomas Povey, a friend of Samuel's, had a bathroom at the top of his country house, but with all the renovations Samuel made to his home in Seething Lane, plumbing was never among them. Bathing was by no means a normal occurrence; Elizabeth sometimes went to a Turkish bath, 'a public hot house', but Samuel only ever immersed himself in water at a spa, and on very rare occasions, and was convinced that one of the most injurious things he could do was get his feet wet. Without bathrooms, toilets, or running water, sanitation practices were very primitive. The disposal of 'swill' was frequently out of the window and into the street below. There are even instances of members of the aristocracy having filled their chamber pots only to have the contents poured all over the 'unfortunates' at public gatherings.

But this method of disposal wasn't available in Whitehall where Samuel and Elizabeth first went to live. Many of the chambers did not have windows on to the street below and the pots had to be carried downstairs and along passages to the drains, where they could be emptied. This could not have been a pleasant pastime and it is not surprising that Elizabeth should have found this constant chore abhorrent and degrading.

Even allowing for the differences in standards in the seventeenth century, it was still very distressing for Elizabeth to have to endure some of Samuel's toilet habits. Cohabitation in one room, with Samuel indulging in regular purges to relieve his constipation, must have given Elizabeth great offence. Even without the knowledge of the relationship between germs and disease, Elizabeth was still justified in objecting to her husband's behaviour. No wonder she kept carping about this awful aspect of married life in her diary.

And this wasn't the only part of their life together which upset her. Elizabeth was also distressed by Samuel's sexual demands, which she associated with his drinking. For her there was little pleasure in their sexual union, and there was a great deal of pain. Soon after their marriage she developed an abscess on her labia, which made sexual intercourse excruciatingly painful. Understandably, she tried to avoid it.

But she also found Samuel's lack of consideration about her health or her happiness deeply hurtful. He could show anger and impatience, and could still demand his conjugal rights, even when she was racked by period pains or the tormenting throbbing of the abscess.

That Samuel had no progeny – despite his many affairs – suggests that he was sterile. This could have been the result of his operation for a kidney stone – where the ducts to the testicles were impaired. But as he had many sexual liaisons before this date, Elizabeth among them, without recorded offspring, it is possible that his sterility preceded the operation. It is also possible that it was the result of syphilis, that he had 'the pox' and that this was the origin of the abscess on Elizabeth's labia.

Both Elizabeth and Samuel made regular use of 'physic': Elizabeth records some of the cures she tried for period pains, 'privy problems', toothache and, later, barrenness. And Samuel suffered from a variety of ailments which called for pills and medication. His kidney-stone problem – which would not have been improved by his alcohol consumption – led him to try numerous treatments: he often sought soothing ointment for his eyes, and he regularly took his 'clyster' (enema) for his bowel troubles and 'wind-cholique'.

During the first months of their marriage, neither Samuel nor Elizabeth had a particularly healthy lifestyle: if Samuel over-indulged, Elizabeth was distinctly undernourished. In a contemporary context their relationship, and Elizabeth's predicament, can seem extraordinary.

That Samuel did not want to hand any money over to Elizabeth is patently clear. His meanness meant he didn't want to part with his money: his jealousy meant he didn't want Elizabeth going about the town – not even to market. Yet had he kept her properly, had he bought her food and given her some finery, theirs might have been a workable arrangement, if an unsatisfying one for Elizabeth. She had not worried unduly about the absence of a financial arrangement before their marriage, partly because she had planned to save money from the housekeeping, which she would then have for her own use. But her plan for the way she would conduct her married life was completely dashed when she didn't receive any house-keeping allowance.

Elizabeth found herself in a shocking situation: a cold, hungry, sore and sorry young wife. Plagued with 'the burning piss-pain', (she also seems to have had thrush), she was unwilling and some days unable to leave her bed. So Samuel went off to make some money and to join his friends, and Elizabeth was left alone: generally without coals, candles or any form of sustenance.

Of course, if Samuel had *not* gone out 'to increase his crumb', they would not have had any income. While he worked a little for his father and was a steward for Lord Montagu, when they were first married Samuel only received payment for services rendered. He didn't have a regular salary. His way of adding to his purse was to make himself useful to his lord, and to arrange meetings for those who wished to do business with him – for men who would then give Samuel 'expressions of their grati-tude'. As most of this business was organized in taverns, coffee houses and other meeting places, Samuel had good reason to go off with his friends to eat, drink and be merry.

But he didn't have good reason to deprive Elizabeth of the necessities of life. Whether it was meanness, mindlessness or malice which was responsible for his appalling treatment of his wife, it is difficult to tell. Meanness certainly prompted his pretexts for not providing her with any money. And there was some malice in his response to her sickness, her despondency – her inability to be the constant beauty who catered to his every wish: some malice, too, in his determination that he would not be the means of her independence and enable her to go about in the world – and be prey to other men. But overall it was probably mindlessness that was most to blame. Samuel simply hadn't thought about keeping a wife. As he went about his activities he was warm and well fed, and when he came home each night and found a miserable and complaining wife – who wouldn't even happily sport with him – he started to think of her as bad-tempered, difficult – even a shrew. What had she married for if she was not going to keep the place tidy, look after him – and play the wife?

He stayed out later, drank more, and became more abusive: Elizabeth became more upset, resentful and bitter.

In today's western world where young couples are likely to have their own kitchen and where it is customary to prepare and cook meals, some of the problems faced by Elizabeth and Samuel would not have arisen. In our times, neither the husband nor the wife can remain oblivious to the demands of money and time for shopping and cooking, though there may be arguments about degree, and about the division of labour. But in the seventeenth century it was easier to ignore these items, because cooking was not customary. What has to be remembered is that in Elizabeth and Samuel's day, it was more common for ordinary people to eat 'take-aways' than to cook family meals in their own homes – if for no other reason than that they had no cooking facilities.

Elizabeth Pepys didn't have a kitchen: just one room. She didn't have running water, or an oven: just a fire and a pot on a hook. She could make soups, puddings, stews, but it wasn't easy and besides, these chores did not appeal to her. She had envisaged their married dining habits as eating out, or else eating in with food purchased from the cookshop – it being possible to buy cuts of meat etc., and to take them to the shop to be cooked for you. This was how Elizabeth had planned to combine her marketing and entertaining.

Samuel *did* eat out. Sometimes he bought food from the cookshop and brought it home. But without the facilities – or the fashion – for the home-cooked family meal, Samuel could ensure that he was well fed without giving any thought to Elizabeth's fare. And she was very hungry.

What Samuel did think about, and felt to be unfair, was the transformation in Elizabeth. Not only had she ceased to be the constant beauty and the caring lover, on marriage she had also become a sharp-tongued miss with a will of her own. From the pretty and pleasing ways she had shown during their courting days, this was a development Samuel had not expected.

But the more he complained about the household disarray, about the comfortlessness of the room and the shortcomings of her company, the more Elizabeth railed against him. When he became angered by her sickness and surliness, she blamed him for everything. Which is one reason he stayed out later, and drank more; and one reason she became increasingly disillusioned and distressed. And determined to make changes.

Both Elizabeth's mother, and Eliza Harvey, urged her to manage Samuel better. And she did make an effort. But he so infuriated her with his attitudes, offended her with his personal habits, humiliated her with his refusal to give her any money – and outraged her with his jealous and violent behaviour – that no matter how often she resolved 'to handle him', her good intentions were doomed. Within a few months of their marriage there was no loving couple: things were so bad that Elizabeth took the extraordinary step of leaving her husband. She became a disobedient wife: had he wanted to, Samuel could probably have forced her return but this would have exposed him to further mockery from his friends.

How long Elizabeth intended to stay away can only be a matter of speculation. She might have wanted just to frighten Samuel, even to teach him a lesson. And had she been pregnant, she might have acted very differently. But when Samuel discovered part of her diary, followed her to Eliza's, and became so abusive that he had to be restrained, he pre-empted an early reconciliation. It was no longer a private quarrel: his base treatment of her had been witnessed. Elizabeth decided at that stage that virtually anything would be better than going back to Samuel.

Elizabeth and Samuel were separated until December 1657. During that period Elizabeth supported herself, mainly by translating and interpreting, and presumably with a little help from her family and friends. But she struggled to make ends meet and was always trying to think of extra ways to make money. She even thought about publishing her diary – her 'life-story', like Margaret Cavendish, the Marchioness of Newcastle – but decided against this on the grounds that she would lose all respectability, and there was no guarantee that there was any profit in it anyway.

While she was separated from Samuel, Elizabeth appears to have spent most of her time with the Palmers, at Charing Cross. But because this period is poorly documented in her diary, it is not possible to draw any definitive conclusions. However, Elizabeth includes sufficient entries to show that life was difficult. She worked hard, she was poor, she was lonely: she still went without candles and coals on occasions. And there was no compensation in the form of a dashing young man to take her around, offer her a respectable and rewarding future and make her the envy of all her friends. There had been problems with Samuel, but there had also been some advantages.

As a 'disobedient wife' Elizabeth was in an awkward position. No man could look upon her with the honourable intention of marriage, so she either went without male company, or risked dishonourable intentions.

The dashing Captain Robin Holmes, who had shown some interest in Elizabeth prior to Samuel's proposal, appeared on the scene again. He was good-looking, very impressive in his marine's uniform, sensitive and yet sophisticated, and quite sought-after by the many young women whom he managed to avoid marrying. He suggested to Elizabeth that she become his mistress, and offered her material comfort as well as warmth and companionship at a time when she was in need of all of these. Tired, lonely, and in financial difficulties, it would not have been surprising if Elizabeth had been tempted by such an arrangement, though had she been seen in this role she certainly would not have been envied. It would have been her 'downfall'.

Whether or not she did have an affair with Captain Holmes,

it is not possible to determine. She makes virtually no diary entries during this period. But some of the later entries which imply that she had evidence that she was not infertile, and that it was not fair to lay the fault of childlessness at her door, could refer to this experience.

What is clear is that she was still seen as decent and respectable – that she had remained 'true' – throughout her separation from Samuel. Otherwise it would not have been likely that she would have been able to return to her husband. And even while they were apart, Elizabeth had never entirely ruled out the option of a reunion. She didn't walk away, and not give him another thought. On the contrary, she was always interested in what he was doing, what he had to say about her, how he was managing. And it was a sign of her emotional involvement that the few times she had come across Samuel by accident, she had felt faint. For the most part she kept herself informed about his behaviour through her brother Balty, whom she paid to check up on her husband.

And the longer she stayed away from Samuel, the more her attitude mellowed. She forgot some of the fury and the fights, and started to be amused at the memory of some of his foibles. So that when brother Balty told her that Samuel was seriously ill with a kidney-stone complaint, Elizabeth was full of concern and sympathy – and ripe for a reconciliation.

This didn't stop her from thinking about any other possibilities. Samuel could die. This would bring to an end her ambiguous position as a separated wife: it would allow her to think of marrying someone else, and there might even be some money available for the widow. This was how her own mother had acquired property, though it was unlikely that Samuel Pepys had any to leave.

But Elizabeth didn't hold long to this line of reasoning. She was soon convinced that it was Samuel she wanted, and in good health. She began to think of a life together again – under certain conditions.

However, there was one area where Elizabeth did not change her mind: she didn't show any greater kindness or tolerance to the Pepys family. She thought them mean and boorish, and she was particularly incensed when it was suggested within their family circle that *she* was responsible for Samuel's poor health.

She was very hostile to Samuel's sister, Pauline, whom she later employed as a servant and triumphantly found her to be unsatisfactory. Only John Pepys, Samuel's young brother, found any favour with Elizabeth.

While Elizabeth nursed Samuel through his bout of illness in August–September 1657, it became clear that Samuel also wanted them to be together again. But Elizabeth had learnt her lesson and was in a strong position. She would only return when there was a signed, official agreement which covered everything from money matters to wenches: Elizabeth wanted a fixed sum for her allowance, and an undertaking that Samuel would not engage in wenching.

But Samuel had some conditions too. Among them, that Elizabeth would not even think of another man, and that she should visit his family every Sunday.

At first Elizabeth resisted the regular visits to the Pepys household. And she was also very wary about having the agreement lodged with Samuel's father for safekeeping. She considered Mr Pepys senior ill-bred and untrustworthy and she was frightened that others would see the undertakings that she had given. She dreaded to think how the appalling Pall – Pauline, the sister-in-law whom Elizabeth thought oafish, ugly and nasty – how Pall Pepys would use the information if she ever read the document and came across some of the silly conditions Elizabeth had agreed to. The very prospect was mortifying.

But when Elizabeth realized that Samuel was even more frightened at the thought of prying eyes and would not consent to the document being kept anywhere else, she gave in. Their agreement about allowances, fidelity and family obligations was signed and witnessed and, in December 1657, the couple began life together again.

Things were different the second time around. There were still problems, but both had had a hard time during the separation and were determined that this time it would be better and there was always the agreement to refer to, to settle disputes.

Samuel's recovery from the kidney-stone attack was only a respite, unfortunately. At the beginning of 1658 the pain became so constant, and excruciating, that he decided he could no longer endure it. He had been afflicted by attacks since childhood, but they were becoming more frequent and unbearable, no doubt aggravated by his considerable alcoholic intake. It was a desperate measure to undergo a major operation and to be 'cut for the stone', but the suffering had made Samuel a desperate man.

There was no anaesthetic of course. And with none of our contemporary knowledge about the nature of infection, the chances of the patient dying from shock, or sepsis, were high indeed. Elizabeth and Samuel talked realistically about all the possibilities but when Samuel decided he was going ahead with the operation, Elizabeth controlled her fears and was very supportive. She even stayed with him for part of the awful surgery. In Samuel's case a three-inch cut was made between the anus and the scrotum, down to the neck of the bladder, which was then opened to allow the kidney stone to be removed. Although it has been surmised that this was when sterility might have been caused, as Samuel soon makes clear, his potency was not impaired.

Samuel knew how lucky he was to survive this surgery: this is one reason he had an annual stone-feast where he expressed his gratitude for his recovery – and for the part that his cousin, Jane Turner, played in nursing him through the ordeal.

With Samuel's return to health, the Pepys' life style also improved. There were not so many financial problems to contend with when, in 1658, Samuel got the job as 'mean clerk' to George Downing at the Exchequer. For this he received his first regular salary, the princely sum of fifty pounds per annum. It was enough to make a move from the garret and to lease a small house in Axe Yard on the west side of King Street, Westminster.

Elizabeth and Samuel continued to live in their Whitehall chamber until their new home was refurbished. It was quite impressive: as well as its own garden, it had a bedroom, a dining room, a room for Samuel's books, a dressing room and a maid's room. Soon, they also had a maid. For the sum of three pounds per annum, they were joined by Jane Birch. Elizabeth was delighted. While Samuel still had his failings, she was beginning to feel that there were compensations.

At this stage Elizabeth's diary starts to take a different form.

The style of her entries was generally a reflection of her circumstances and this is but another example: when first married, and unhappy, she had written daily and felt better for the emotional release. When she left Samuel, she wrote very little. But the habit of keeping diary entries reasserts itself when Samuel is sick, and Elizabeth is in need of a confidante to help her through a very difficult period. Yet when they move to Axe Yard and life is very satisfying, Elizabeth virtually abandons the daily entry in favour of the longer narrative. She almost takes to story-writing as a mature woman and it is easy to see that she enjoyed this literary occupation.

There are overlaps of course: some 'short stories' appear among the daily entries, and vice versa. But the clear shifts in style have helped to determine the division of the Diary into five sections. Each part represents a chronological period, as well as a stage of development in Elizabeth's life with its own particular emotional and literary characteristics.

After Samuel is 'cut of the stone' – a gripping short story which reveals much about surgical practices of the time – and the couple move to Axe Yard to the comforts of a pleasant home, a reasonable salary, and a maid, a series of short stories flows from Elizabeth's pen.

There is the story of her barrenness, where Elizabeth seeks every possible cure for her unhappy predicament. And while some of the 'cures' are quite extraordinary, and revolting, some have a ring of familiarity: in an age in which panty-hose have sometimes been seen as a contributory factor in infertility, it comes as no surprise to find that Elizabeth was advised to wear loose cotton drawers, which allowed for circulation.

There is also the issue of who is at fault. When there are no progeny, attention usually focuses on the wife, even though as Elizabeth points out, there are two parents. She leaves a few clues which suggest that she suspects it was Samuel, and not herself, who was sterile. And by this stage, she has become sufficiently wise in the ways of the world to know that Samuel's operation, as well as 'the clap' and 'the pox' could all be linked to infertility. But even if Elizabeth had definite proof that Samuel was the source of the problem, she did not confront him directly with his deficiency. Like many of his counterparts, then and now, he would not have taken kindly to aspersions

31

being cast on his virility. He might also have interrogated Elizabeth about the nature of her evidence, which could have been damning.

As well as the recipe for physic that is contained in the cure for childlessness story, there are recipes for food included in the birthday story, which reveals a great deal about diet and entertaining. And there is the washing story, which is quite a gem.

In 1660, Samuel Pepys follows Elizabeth's example and starts to keep a journal. It is in cypher, but that is another matter. And on 16 January, it contains the following entry:

> To the Greene Dragon on Lambeth Hill, both the Mr Pinknys, Smith, Harrison, Morrice that sung the bass, Shepley and I, and there we sang all sorts of things and I ventured with good success upon things at first sight and after that played on my flagelette, and stayed there till 9 a-clock, very merry and drawn on with one song after another till it came to be so late. After that, Shepley, Harrison and myself, we went towards Westminster on foot, and at the Golden Lion, near Charing Cross, we went in and drank a pint of wine, and so parted; and thence home where I found my wife and maid a-washing. I sat up till the bell-man came by with his bell, just under my window as I was writing of this very line, and cried, 'Past one of the clock, and a cold, frosty, windy morning'. I then went to bed and left my wife and the maid a-washing still.

While Samuel includes detailed information about his own life – right through to the vagaries of his various drinking companions – it is astonishing how little comment he makes on Elizabeth's daily existence. He has no idea how she spends her day: like so many diarists he records only what interests him, and what suits him. This was why Elizabeth believed him to be such an unreliable reporter: and the 16 January entry supports her allegation. For Samuel makes no mention in it of his inebriated state and the problems he caused for Jane and Elizabeth. His account is spectacularly different from *hers*.

The washing story, however, does more than highlight some of the discrepancies between the accounts of Elizabeth and Samuel: with its descriptions of doing the washing, it reveals some of the realities of seventeenth-century women's daily lives. While it would be impossible to tell what women did, and how they felt, from Samuel's diary, Elizabeth fills in the gaps and gives us a picture of woman's place.

It takes Elizabeth some time to assess Samuel's ability as a journal keeper: though she is quite pleased when he follows her example and takes up diary writing she is quite upset when he hides his personal detail from her by writing in 'code'. And she determines to 'bottom it'. It's not just that she's curious about his talents as a writer: she wants to know more about his habits. She wants to find out more about his financial situation and his 'wenching' from his entries. So she is quite excited when she manages to get hold of Thomas Shelton's *Tachygraphy*[3] and is able to learn the shorthand that Samuel uses.

But if she doesn't like Samuel having any secrets from her, she doesn't mind having some from him. She thinks nothing of hiding some of her pages, of writing in French, or even of keeping a double set of accounts. And there was some justification for her double standard. She stored up what she learnt about Samuel: she used it to strengthen her own position rather than to confront him with accusations. But if Samuel read anything of hers that he didn't like – or which aroused his jealousy – he could become violent and try and destroy her diary. No matter that he had agreed to her keeping it. Sometimes Samuel even includes such accounts of his behaviour in his own diary: on 6 January 1663, after reading some of Elizabeth's pages, Samuel records:

> . . . I was vexed at it, and desired her and commanded her to teare it – which she desired to be excused it; I forced it from her and tore it, and with all took her other bundle of papers from her and leapt out of the bed in my shirt, clapped them into the pocket of my breeches, that she might not get them from me; and having got on my stockings, breeches and gown, I pulled them out one by one and tore them all before her face, though it went against my heart to do it, she crying and desiring me not to do it.

It's not surprising that Elizabeth did not leave her diary around for Samuel to read at his leisure. Even when he really had no cause for complaint, he could still get in a rage and make

[3] The *Tachygraphy* was used by Samuel Pepys to master shorthand and write in code.

problems for Elizabeth. Many of his outbursts were about money; he might have made an agreement about Elizabeth's allowance, but it certainly didn't grant her the right to spend her own money as she pleased, and without his interference. He was consistently critical of her expenses, constantly complaining that she would bring about his 'fall' (bankruptcy); yet the evidence seems to be that it was Elizabeth who could manage money while Samuel was something of a spendthrift. Except when it came to handing money over to his wife.

In order to keep the peace, and to preserve a modicum of independence, Elizabeth – understandably – elected to keep a second set of records for Samuel's benefit. They were fictitious, and despite Samuel's experience and skill as an auditor, they seem to have satisfied his demands for Elizabeth's accountability.

The advice that Elizabeth's mother had given over the financial settlement was that Elizabeth should insist on being paid a fixed sum; her rationale was that Samuel could not then evade his responsibilities on the grounds that his income was variable and that there were some weeks when there was no money in the coffers. But if this protected her from non-payment, the fixed allowance also precluded Elizabeth from participating in Samuel's increased wealth. So while she enjoyed a guaranteed sum, it became small in comparison with Samuel's growing resources. The precise amount of this allowance is not known but what is known is that for many years Samuel did not increase it, despite his own prosperity.

Samuel could almost be said to have been perverse in his dealings with his wife. Apart from his outrageous stinginess which almost resulted in her malnutrition in the first months of their marriage, there was the contrast between his meanness to her and his relative generosity to others. It has even been suggested that Samuel gave more money to Elizabeth's brother, Balthasar, whom he insisted he did not like, than he gave to his own wife.

He gave generously to his own family, to his brothers and to Pall: as he became more affluent he supported his parents, though there was never a penny for his in-laws! He gave Elizabeth very few presents and even those he did give her were often either of little value or procured for nothing: such as the ring he gave her in 1665 which was valued at ten pounds but cost him naught.

But that was before the Deb Willett incident. This incident is not included in the current edition of the Diary but, from reading Samuel's journal, it appears that Elizabeth set up a trap and caught Samuel breaking their agreement when she found him in the arms of the maid, Deb Willett: after that Elizabeth's allowance was increased to thirty pounds per annum which she was 'mightily pleased with', and which suggests that the original sum must have been but a pittance. Even the sum of thirty pounds looks paltry alongside Samuel's stockpile: he reckoned himself worth £6,200 at this time. Elizabeth would have known this – from his diary entries – and it shows that she wasn't greedy.

No doubt there is much missing about Elizabeth's life: there is not even any guarantee that all the diary manuscript has been collected. But the information which Elizabeth provides here about herself, and Samuel, and seventeenth-century life, is invaluable.

# Notes on the Text

Elizabeth St Michel began keeping her diary on 13 October 1655, and did so until her death in November 1669. This edition of the Diary opens with her first entry and concludes with the entry on 24 April 1661; and this represents approximately one third of the manuscript which has been recovered. Further volumes could follow. At this stage however, it is not known whether the pages collected constitute the entire diary. Perhaps when the floorboards require replacing in another establishment in Clapham, there could be another diary 'find', and the possibility of an even more extensive collection of the papers of Elizabeth Pepys; she so much enjoyed writing that it is likely that she engaged in much more than diary-keeping, despite the fact that she recounted many 'stories' in the Diary itself.

Why Clapham should have been the place to have yielded such a significant literary and historical reference is not such a mystery. Samuel Pepys' heir was his nephew, John Jackson, the son of the unfortunate Pall. John Jackson followed in his uncle's footsteps, attending Magdalene College, and when he gained his degree in 1690 he began working for Samuel, assisting him with the acquisition and classification of his library. On Samuel's death, John was charged with the responsibility of completing the collection and the cataloguing and he moved, with the library, to Clapham; presumably he took many of Samuel's papers with him and perhaps the diary of Elizabeth Pepys was among them. It was certainly not among the approximately eighty volumes of Pepys' papers which were lodged in the Bodleian Library in 1755.

No doubt it is too much to hope that further Elizabeth Pepys' jottings should materialize. But of those which are currently available, all those which are intact, and legible, up to 24 April 1661 have been included in this edition. While there are some additional manuscript pages in a decayed and indecipherable state, it is fortunate that they do not seem to be an integral part of the Diary. Rather, from what can be deduced they appear to have been accounts, or letters (not in Elizabeth's hand), or even incidental papers which have been used as a protective covering for the diary pages themselves, and not necessarily anything that Elizabeth had an interest in.

Many of the dates in the Diary are editorial inclusions. With the first entry each month, Elizabeth Pepys generally noted the day and the month, but for most entries she simply marked the days, with the result that the month and the year (about which there is virtually no confusion) have been added for ease of reference. Wherever the writing or the meaning of the text is obscure, footnotes have been used for clarification, and a glossary has been included to aid in understanding some of the seventeenth-century vocabulary.

Spelling was a much more 'creative' activity in Elizabeth Pepys' day. (The playwright Ben Jonson, 1572/3–1637, decreed that it was a dull person who could spell a word only one way.) Because Elizabeth followed the fashion and was quite innovative in her representations, the spelling in the Diary has been standardized and modernized. Punctuation is also primarily editorial. This is because Elizabeth used very little apart from dots and dashes. So in order to facilitate comprehension, contemporary conventions have been employed. Current practices have also been used in relation to capitalization as there seemed to be no rationale for Elizabeth Pepys' use of upper (and lower) case.

Given the cost of stationery it is understandable that Elizabeth should have wanted to put as many entries on a page as possible; rarely does she divide her writing into paragraphs. Most of the paragraphing therefore is editorial, in the interest of easier reading.

Elizabeth Pepys did not often use abbreviations but where they did occur, they have been printed in full in the text. Passages that were written in French have been translated into English and are duly marked.

What has not emerged is the second set of accounts which Elizabeth refers to in some of her entries. She did not always want Samuel to know what she spent her money on, how much certain items cost, or even what she could save from economizing on the housekeeping. This meant that she had to keep a separate balance sheet for Samuel which sadly appears to have been lost. (It is of course possible that these accounts were in Samuel's keeping but not lodged, or identified, among his pages.)

Elizabeth did not subdivide her diary into the sections which appear here. But the five divisions are suggested by the particular periods of her life, and by the nature of her entries. As a maid, and a novice diary-keeper, her entries are short, and generally romantic. In the early months of her marriage, the entries are usually longer, and more plaintive; Elizabeth Pepys used her diary writing as a means of finding some relief from depression and bitterness during this time of distress. Part Three covers the period when she was separated from Samuel, and when she wrote very little in her journal. But in Part Four, when she is trying to decide whether to resume married life, the diary becomes a place for setting out the pros and cons, and for reflecting on the range of possibilities. Part Five contains some of Elizabeth Pepys' mature writings. So long and self-contained are some of these entries that it is quite in order to see them as 'short stories'. They reveal Elizabeth's skill as a recorder and writer; they also reveal some of her characteristic qualities of warmth, wit and humour.

Dale Spender

# PART ONE

# Maid

# 1655

October
Saturday 13

My mother does urge me to make note on this solemn occasion, and then to give her show. For tomorrow are to be read the first banns for my marriage to Mr Samuel Pepys at the Church of St Margaret at Westminster. 'Tis the custom among great families – such as the Cliffords, of which my mother be a member – to keep records which do set out the family history and character, so does my mother charge me with this duty.

Hard is it to think on the seriousness of all when my mind is wont to wonder on the fine frame and face of my good man. Better to write the love letter which should flow unbidden and could match the endearments that my love does send me. Not even my mother should I allow witness the promises that Samuel Pepys does make of the great tumbling there will be when he does bed me.

To my trusted friend, Eliza Harvey, I show some of my Samuel's love letters, but little is she impressed. The married woman of three years, this very week, she does say that to men the words do come easy but much do their actions leave to desire. 'Tis her mind that soon enough I too will make these comparisons.

Something of the cynic is there in her. Well may her husband Richard prove unsatisfactory, yet do I see it as the nature of the man. For he has none of the amour which does show itself in my Pepys – yet must I admit that her Richard does spend the money more freely. Eliza Harvey does wear more the badges of affection from her husband than Samuel does give to me. Yet all this should change when I am the wife and have better means to persuade him with.

To be sure this is not what my mother did intend for sober entry. Yet she should understand that there is much excitement in me as I do give myself to thinking of the pleasure there should be in the playing of *Mrs* Pepys.

'Tis not such a bad name either and gives no hint of the common stock it does come from.


## Sunday 14

Most subdued I did stay when the banns be read this day, though truly does Mr Pepys give me the eye, and tempt me to mirth. Yet did we wait till the service end afore we did say sweet things, against which I am sure there is no law, even though it be the Sabbath. Time enough later did my mother say for us to make the billing and cooing, for she does want me to put my mind to more practical matter, and so too does Eliza urge me.

No liking I have to be contrary, yet no use is some of their counsel for me. 'Tis Eliza's view that too soon does love turn sour, so the earlier the monies are arranged, the better it should be. To this I give my ready answer that my man and I have no thought to come to difficulties. And it does hurt me that my word should not be taken serious. I did tell Eliza that no more of her company I should seek if she does continue to make the mockery and to laugh at what she does call my innocent existence.

No better is my mother, who does say I am blind and foolish too. Frequent does she point to my father to make me see that he does fritter away all, her dower too, and that 'tis no treat to be without sustenance. Yet 'tis even possible that his new invention for the curing of smoking chimneys should have success[1], then would there be no troubles.

Did I but think I should go without the necessaries, then more should I heed these warnings. But nothing of this should happen to me. 'Tis true that no riches will we have to begin, but great faith do I put in my man's future. And readily does

[1] This was just one of the many costly inventions of Alexander St Michel: none appears to have enjoyed great success, or made any profits.

he promise that I should have all, and the finery, and the maid too, though some time it might take to fix this.

Does he not constant bow to my beauty and breeding, and write me the letters of love which vouchsafe always to serve me? Enough is this for me. If he be a little slow to part with the contents of his purse, all the more should there be for his family, and a good thing it is.


## Monday 15

Eliza Harvey does have a bawdy mind, and nothing is there she could say which should turn me from my marriage. 'Tis wicked on her part that she should try. And I defy her. No fear have I to question my Samuel about one Betty Aynsworth, who does keep a drinking-shop in Cambridge and teach lewd songs. Mr Pepys does say that fitting it is for the wife to place the full trust in the husband, and I too hold this to be right. So I believe not Eliza's tale that my lover does put his hand up or down any doxy he does have the stretch to.

No cause Eliza has to put the disappointment of her wedded state upon me. And no excuse it is that 'tis done only for mine own good. Though the truest friend she may have been, yet I do solemn swear here to heed her words no more if she does not forestall this mischief-making.


## Tuesday 16

'Twas sweet this eve when we did stroll along the Strand. E'en the weather did favour us, and many there were who did pay the compliment to Samuel. Such good humour was he in, that I did brave all and put to him that in the past he did play loose, and that he should not deceive me.

Swift does his brow change. As all do watch on, he does stand and call to know who does mouth such false and foul charge against him. Though I did not want to tell, yet no other way could I think on to still him. Reluctant, I did confess that 'twas Eliza Harvey who would have it that he does make too free of himself.

Then Samuel did order that no more I should see her. That though Richard Harvey be his friend, yet is his wife a shrew. And much effort did it take for me to smooth all over till Samuel did calm and say that no more of Eliza I should see but in his presence. To which I did give the placating nod – which could mean anything. No plans have I to dupe my man, yet to keep from Eliza would be too difficult, and no reason is there in him to ask it of me.

## Wednesday 17

Last night did my mother make request to see how my record does progress. But little is she impressed by my entries. If it be not the usual way to keep account, yet 'tis one which does please me. No burden is it to me to do the daily notes, e'en though to my mother they lack the right import.

Then for my learning she did show me some accounts she did keep from her early days as wife, and all about monies, and journeys, and legalities it was, and the jangles she does have with my father whom she does charge with wasting all on folly and inventions.

And while I did take the point that only that which is of great import should take the space and the cost in my record-keeping, yet did I think my own hand and style greatly superior to that of my mother – though this I do not own and would not have her see.

Perchance this is a form I have a talent for, and certain I am that I could teach others this method of journal-keeping, which does prove to have much satisfaction in it.

One problem only do I see. That of keeping the privacy. For it would hurt my mother most deep to sight what I enter here. And it should give my man the apoplexy. 'Tis not just that he should take offence at the words which do not flatter. 'Tis also that he does have such great fear that anyone should write down account against him. To put all in French would be to play safe for no skill does Samuel have to decipher that language, and difficult too it should be for my mother, yet it does come easy to me. And to Balty[2] and my father, yet no interest would they have in it.

[2] Balty: Balthasar St Michel, Elizabeth's brother.

## Jeudi 18

[3]As 'tis held by my mother that only momentous events should have space herein, so do I register that this day did lapse my 'agreement' with Samuel. Three days have I kept from Eliza, but most dull everything is. And too, my mother did call on me to help with the scrubbing and no liking did I have to do this. So my conscience should be clear, I did tell that the basket which my mother did seek, be left with Eliza on my last visit, and I should fetch it. Then if I be found out to have been with Eliza without Samuel's witness, readily can I say that 'twas my mother who did send me. And all do know, and none dispute, that the daughter does owe obedience to the parents till such time as she is wed! And then still too if necessary.


## Vendredi 19

No falseness was there needed. 'Twas Samuel who last night did suggest that we should celebrate the three years since Richard Harvey and Eliza Spender did wed, and no good way was there to keep Eliza from such event. Most foolish would it have been to add confession that earlier in the day, Eliza and I did share each other's company – when I did deliver a piece of my mind and caution her against the trouble-making.

Yet sorely did she try me again last eve. For while we did make merry in the tavern, she did prime me to watch out for Samuel and a piece of baggage who did sit nearby and leer. But firm did I say to her that no law there was against politeness and that 'twas the mark of a gentleman that he did smile at her. (Is it that she does try to gull me, or should there be some truth in her taunting? Which does have the worry in it.)


## Sunday 21

Is it a sin to keep the journal on the Sabbath? If it should count as work then it should go against, and if it be pleasure, then too would it be the wrong thing. But if it be duty – as my mother does decree it is – then it should be most fitting Sabbath activity. So do I say it.

No good should it have done me to make entry yesterday though some things there were to report. But all day did I spend in my mother's employ and though I did constant complain, yet she would have it that 'tis but practice to make me the wife that she does so use me. And I do tell her that she does risk her daughter as the comforter of her old age should she not desist. Which I did pray that the Lord did not hear. But all these who would vex me then give as excuse that it be but for mine own good, do well test my patience.

So then did I tell my mother that no plan is it of mine to work so hard as a wife. I did wager that soon should I have a maid, or more. But this pleases her not.

My mother does do the lofty manner with me and bid me to give account of where such monies should come from. For do I not *descend* to marry Mr Pepys?

Never did I think to hear such unkindness, particularly not from her who did bring me into the world. Full well do I know that she be of gentle birth and that Mr Pepys does have the family members who give no pride. But no good purpose should it serve to state far and wide that his mother be no other than a common washerwoman, and her brother nought but a Whitechapel butcher. And base was it of my mother to declare for all to hear that my man is no more than the message boy for his father-tailor.

Quick did I name all his assets. Be he not the Cambridge man, the cousin of Sir Edward Montagu of Hinchingbrooke, and trusted servant of his employ? But my mother stopped not her scoffings and did predict that Samuel Pepys be of low birth and have but poor prospects for the future. Then too did she unleash her tongue 'gainst my fond father, for he does fail in his duty to make examination of the purse of Mr Pepys. Which be true. All my father did want to know was what items his new son did invent, and whether he did have monies to put to the perpetual-motion machine which now does take my father's fancy.

But Samuel does have no time for these schemes which he does say have no profit in them. And more should he know than my father, for the Cambridge scholar he has been. And though my mother share it not – and will have it that education is no match for breeding – yet I have faith in Samuel to make his mark, and the monies with it.

The steward Samuel may now be, and true it is that he run the errands for his father and my Lord Montagu, though few there are to know for all measures does he take to conceal this. But no contentment does he have in the occupation and to me does he tell all his fine plans for the future. He does see a grand establishment with maids, and man-servant and waiting-woman, and coach and coachman, and all to do my bidding. And no objections do I make, but do encourage this. Well should I wear such service.

Yet no place is there for the daydreams here. Bed should be the proper place to dwell on such pleasantries.

## Tuesday 23

Today is the anniversary of my birth and does warrant register here. Full fifteen years does make my young days now behind me, and eager I be for the next stage which does have much of promise in it.

This day did we celebrate and Samuel does make the fine speech and give the toast to my charms, but no addition to them by way of finery. More kindly did he treat himself – with new doublet – and much talk did he make about the importance he now does have, for is he not given the turret room in Lord Montagu's lodging in the Whitehall Palace for when he does wed?

And while 'tis all very well to give public boast of good fortune and the plentiful purse (though in truth, 'tis without breeding), yet no joy do I take in it if there is nought in the purse for me. And no consolation either that 'twas the great expense of our coming wedding which he did confide did leave him short so that no birthday gift he could supply. Though what it should be does puzzle me.

Yet did I get mine own back. A fine bracelet I did parade, and give imply that some gift it was from an admirer who should go without name. Which be true in essence for certain I am that Eliza Harvey does admire me, and too does she know well my game and make not the slip. So did Samuel Pepys suspect that I did have some beau, and does make much reference to Captain Holmes. So monstrous vexed was he that he did risk the ruin of all our pleasantries. Swift then did I soothe him, which does become the nawit. And did I add in voice so sweet that more content I should have been if such fine bracelet had but come from him. Then did he seek for me to swear that no gifts should I accept in the future, except that they should be his. Which does seem a foolish undertaking and is a promise I do avoid giving.


## Thursday 25

After much thought I did this day make known to Eliza that I did do the daily journal entry. And most surprised I was that no surprise there was in her. All this time it does seem that she too does make the secret scribbling, yet she shares not this confidence with me. We do promise that one day we will show each to the other the records we do keep, though many there are who would disapprove of such entry-making and would put it with mischief so not to all would we make exposure.

Eliza would have me know that diary-keeping does become the risqué fashion now, among the highborn. Regular accounts do they keep of their duties and days – which is not how my mother does have it. But Eliza does quote her aunt – whom she does set great store by for she has the trusted place in the household of Lady Willoughby – and her aunt does swear that 'tis the noble thing to do to keep the diary.

'Tis her aunt's word that the good Lady each day does write when she does rise, the Bible verses she does read, the prayers she does say, and the viands she does eat. Which does seem a very waste of quire and ink to me. What satisfaction would there be in it for me to note that this very day I did rise, break my fast, and wind yarn for my mother? That I did threaten my brother Balty should he try to wheedle any money from my lover, and did soft-talk my father who does brave the disappointment with his brick-moulding machine.

Yet if my mother should think that the entries be about

marriages and births, and deaths and other grave events, and if Lady Willoughby should think that they be about devotions and diet, and if I should think they be about the thoughts I do have – and the wrangles, and the joys – that do make up the day – then only one conclusion should there be. That this diary-keeping can be on anything.

I wonder what content Eliza does put in . . .


## Saturday 27

Tomorrow the last call of the banns be made, then no impediment is there. Dear Lord, I do vow to be forever good, if you should hasten time till I do wed. This be my prayer for this day.


## Sunday 28

After service, publicly did I present myself with one Mr Pepys, who does make a fine impression. And full grateful I am for his wooing. Great standing does it give me (and some do envy me) and well does all this please me. For many there are who did warn me that to be without dower was to go without husband. Yet have I proved them wrong.

Though truth to tell, I did not always have the assurance. Nights there have been when I did lie awake afear'd that with no riches to bring to a marriage, no good man there would be who would have me.

No natural woman is there who would want to go to the grave without even the *offer* of marriage, though for some it must be said that they find satisfaction in the refusal. But not for me.

Always did I think to find the man of fine figure who did have some wit, and who did seek some enjoyment of living and truly have I been blessed. For though he does have more years than I could wish for, and sometimes the poor health and the kidney stone, yet the signs of the gallant are in him still. Already he does show the distance he does set himself apart from his tailor-family, and his washer-mother, and much further should he go with me at his side. And this do I let all know when I do stroll forth on the Sabbath and show my prize.

Oft does my mother urge that we should wait the year till we do wed but no mind has Samuel for such postponement. 'Tis for love he does marry me, and eager is he for me to know it. To make further delay would lead to my journal entry of a birth before a marriage!

## Monday 29

Strange incident do I record. Each time today I did Eliza see, she did pour penny-royal into herself till I did think she would drown in it. Most puzzling this be, for the penny-royal has the bitterness about it, and none there are who would for pleasure sip it. And I know of no peace or play to the mind it does bring. Yet when I did press Eliza for the reason she did swill such bitter brew, no love did she shew me. 'Twas the sharp side of her tongue that I did feel.

Our voices we did raise and my mother did hear and ask the cause of our controversy. No harm did I think was in it to say that Eliza is the fool to fill herself brimful of penny-royal – though Eliza did hiss at me for this. But then did I think that some signal did pass between my mother and Eliza and my mother did pet her. Yet when I did want to know what was going on, no satisfactory explanation did they give. And 'twas me who did finish in the bad mood when *both* did do the wifely-bit, and say soon enough it would be my turn to understand.

Which does make the devil of me. And try though I might, still I have not bottomed their meaning. All that I do understand is that Eliza does spend her day 'apissing', and that she does make like the child who does fill at one end to flood at the other, and no sense is in this for the grown woman.

November
Friday 2

'Tis the more exciting life I need, the better record to keep.
Dull life it is till I am wed. So do I enter here, in proper Lady
Willoughby fashion, that this day I did rise and make my way
to Clare Market, in Lincoln's Inn Fields where my mother did
prevent me from giving show of mine own bargaining skill. So
did I charge her with poor preparation to make the housewife
of me.

Brighter should the day have been did I but see Samuel, who
is gone from town in the service of my lord.


Tuesday 6

Most serious talk today there be betwixt my mother and me,
and some confusion does it give me. For 'tis her wish that I
should make the visit to the wise woman who does know the
secrets of the soothing herbs and who does have all concoctions
that do bring relief for brides on the night they do wed. Most
awkward this does make me. All manner of strange feelings I
do have, and wish not to think on the prospect.

Yet does my mother tell that all should prove unnecessary,
but better it be to take the precaution, for no joy is it to have
the pain and nothing to use for it.

So more to please my mother do I agree to go and make
copy of the recipe which it be in order to set down here. But
her offer of company I did refuse, for no liking do I have that
she should be with me when there is talk of such things. Eliza I
did seek out and she did promise on the morrow that we should
call on the wise woman in Cripplegate who does do all the
broths and balms.

And again does Eliza make to tease me. For she does say
that Richard, her man, does vow that he did look upon Mr
Pepys at the low Rhenish Wine House in Wise's Alley, this past
night. But know I what face to put upon this and I do call
Richard Harvey the fool or else the liar, and I do have it that
*he* be in his cups again, for well do I know that Samuel Pepys is
gone from here. Yet why should Eliza use me thus when we do

solemn swear to be true friends? This puzzling does take the stuffing out of me.

More shock was it to me to have Eliza tell the reason that she does drink endless of the penny-royal brew. For does she say that two babes she has already, and more than enough they be. So the remedy to keep from more is to fill up with penny-royal, a measure I have heard not of before. (Only the prod that does pierce, pushed up by the old women who know of these things, and which does then empty all; and much pain am I told is there in it.) So, considerable improvement should this herb drinking be, bitter though it is, and though it does make for water bursting. And does it look to work. This day Eliza does have her courses and much relief is there in her. True she does have the heavy flow and weary weakness, and burning pain too. These monthly trials, well do I know them. And much would I give to be rid of the bleeding and the ache that does pull all down around me. To be with child is to be without the coursing pain – though which does have the advantage is hard to choose. No matter, all do make a dreadful time of it for woman.

So much does rush forth from Eliza that the long trail there is aft her, and worse besides. But she does have it that 'tis worth it, for not only does it keep the babe from coming, but does stay the man too. For he does keep from her bed and make rude comment, which she does brush aside and say that to have him leave off does well suit her. And though this does seem desperate, yet certain I am 'tis only her manner of speaking for do I see softness in her too, and think that under all she does love her man. Perchance.

But no appearance of the good wife is there in her. And I would have it that no wish should it be of mine to keep my husband from me. To which Eliza does look knowing but does let the matter rest.

No word is there from my man as to when he should return.


## Wednesday 7

Much do I have this eve to set down, for this day did we make our way to Sarah Perkins who be the woman who does know all about the curing nature of herbs, yet not enough to put

52

some cheer in Eliza who does have the ague about her. But it did increase her bawdy talk for all the while we did make our journey she did instruct me in what the young wife should know of the woman and man between the sheets. More should it please me to learn the degree of truth she does put in her lessons, for certain it is that some strange things there are in this bedding business. So should I set forth her claims here, then can I compare when my own knowledge I should have to go by.

And do I prefer that I should learn these ways from my friend for much embarrassment is there for both of us when my mother does try these explanations. And while I do have some idea of what does go on around me, 'tis very different when my mother does try to put it into words. Always is the picture of my father afore my eyes, and no easy matter is it to keep the solemn face when my mother does discourse on the way he does put in his pintle. But no desire do I have to offend so better it be that I talk not with my mother on this than that I should be forced to stop up my mirth on the thought of my father as he does put up his bum.

Yet this is not the record I did set out to keep.

The entry of this day is to serve reminder of my visit to the herbal and all that I did learn. And first was that Sarah Perkins be no wizened woman whom I did think on, but the great beauty with fair complexion and most white hands. And close careful did I study her, for much there is in her that I should want to be.

Should I have had the purse, many purchases would I have made. Eager do I await the time when I am become the wife and mine own monies I do have freely to spend.

Yet did Eliza give me no indulgence. Ready should I have been to use what purse I did have to take the sweet water for my hair and the petals for my cheeks (which be my good feature) but Eliza did look to more serious uses. She did stern say that my monies should go on what I did come for and did bid me speak. Yet did my tongue astumble o'er it, for who of breeding is there who would want to say that it be the healing physic for the wedding night that they do come for? So did Eliza push at me and make bold the request and does claim it is for me that she does put aside false modesty, which I do gravely doubt.

But Sarah Perkins did take my hand and turn it about and look steady to my eyes. Then did she ask of my habits afore she does decree that 'tis the use of Amara dulcis and tormentil which should be most efficacious for my needs.

While we did await our instruction from the learned lady, many there were who did come in search of remedy and no great beauties among them. Some did have such mighty misery that I did sorrow for them. Yet one old crone there was who did make the moan that 'twas women's lot to suffer and the sure way for the soul to go straight to Heaven. Clear it was that Sarah Perkins had no liking for such a crier in her midst, and more reasons did she have than that it were bad for business. Plain did she announce to all that 'twas the Christian duty to give care to the body, and sinful was it for those who did willingly seek to suffer, for wherefore did the Lord provide such cures in the herbs and potions, if not to use them? Which did not please the old crone though it did serve to seal her mouth. And the good Sarah Perkins did have some comfort for her, and did make the powders for the weeping sores which did mottle up her legs. The old crone did go forth much calmed, and some pity was there in me.

More was it plain women's trouble which most patrons did come on. Eliza did do the constant commentary on those she did think who did come for babes, and those who did come to have them not, and either way it does seem that this be the thing in women's lives. And some there were who wanted charms, and some who did want to set a curse. All in turn did get recipes for their purpose, and much it was that I did learn.

So on the morrow, when less tired I should be, then will I set down my own recipes for safe-keeping, though 'tis my strong prayer that I should have no need of them. And I do think on the satisfaction there should be to have the living from their preparation. Certain I am that I should cut as fine a figure as Sarah Perkins. Were I not soon to be the wife, then would I think to teach myself all manner of herbs for the complexion and beauty – and for ailments, too. I did tell Eliza what sweet life it might be.

But the bleak side she does always see. Swift does she tell

that those there have been who did burn for knowing such things, and not so long past, and most dangerous profession it could be.

So does marriage look the better fate: much peace and protection does it provide. On the morrow does Samuel return and many a thing is there to tell him.

## Thursday 8

Early morn, it is, and the first time I do wake to ingross here while all else do sleep, which I could not, though no sense there be in it, but that this day my man I should once more see. And while I did lie abed, my mind did dwell on what changes there should be in these next weeks. Much there is which does promise well, but much too which does put the fear in me.

'Tis the cold with which I now contend, for no fire is lit and considerable discouragement is it, yet timely does it seem for me to make record of the recipes I do have note on, else should I forget the fine points and then no cure would there be in it.

Still do I have the prayer in me that all should be but for play and no necessity for the use. Sarah Perkins did wisely say that not all do have the rupture of the marriage bed, and no problem did she see in me. Yet little comfort do I take from her words that most usual is it for maids to tear and bleed, but much may be done aforehand to keep all from great soreness. The thought of all this poking and renting does truly terrify me.

So the cleansing medicine she does recommend and she would have it swallowed in preparation for the day a maid is brought to her husband's bed. Then does it preserve all sweet and ready, and with such ease no rent should there be which would be preferable. For this purpose Amara dulcis is there and too she does bid me know that my own supply later I can replenish for it goes also by the name of woody night shade and felon wort, and common it be though a sure physic to do all the work.

Great care should there be in the preparation of such bittersweet drink, for does the good Sarah Perkins warn that this be mercurial herb of most subtle part, and easy it should be to destroy its cleansing properties. Strict were the instructions she did give for my foule copy which she did check and which I do now faithful inscribe here.

So should this my housewife closet also be and all my receipts within[4].

To take one pound of wood and leaves together is how to begin. Bruise the wood, then place in a pot and put to it three pints of wine. After, put the pot lid on shut close, and set to infuse over the gentle fire, for twelve hours. Then should it be strained and the most excellent drink it does make for the cleansing. One quarter of the pint each morning in the days afore a maid be wed, does purgeth the body very gently, and not churlishly, and no badness is there to come out in the coupling.

When I do think on this brew, not so vile does it seem that I should gag upon taking it, for I know the nature of the woody night shade and the felon wort and not so very malodorous they be. Perchance I should imbibe if it be prepared and I had need. More do I think on its virtues than on the balm though, which should be used for after when there is more of the fire in the soreness.

Here should I confess that I did feel a tremble when Eliza bold did ask for the cure for the rending of the flesh in the marriage bed, but no pucker did it bring to the learned lady's brow. She did calm say that 'twas the use of tormentil that should soothe best, and that the plaister of it give the most efficacious measure. And Sarah Perkins does stand close and supervise the writing of this down in my by-book and Eliza too does make her own copy which the wise woman does peruse for the accuracy.

Grateful I am to learn that tormentil does stay all the many kinds of fluxes of the blood, and more besides, for does it still the pain of the hollow tooth, and that too do I oft need. Among the cures that Sarah Perkins did recite of all its properties – which she does get without book – is that it has the prevention of abortion in it, and too that it is the regular recourse of the sluts who do suffer from too great exertion of the company of

[4] In recipe books (receipt books) which were sometimes called *closets* no distinction was made between recipes for cooking food and recipes for making physic/medicine.

56

men. Though this does not make the best recommendation and does bring the colour to my brow. Yet did I listen attentive.

And tormentil too does thrive close nearby, and simple preparation there be with the roots. Strong potion does the juice yield, but to grind for the powder and to make ointment is the more common. Also the roots may be boiled to make the pints of nicotique though the boiling pot should be well scrubbed thereafter, else it does have consequences for those who do eat from it.

Whether it be juice or the powder, or the concoction, then do I have note in my by-book that it should be mixed in the plaister which should be applied. For the maid who does have the tearing soreness, 'tis in the privy part that the tormentil be most effective. The good Sarah Perkins does counsel that if there be great pain, then the fluid does have stronger properties if put in a syringe and flowed in by direct injection. Though this should be done with caution for 'tis a most drastic method and 'tis advised for stopping only the worst sort of sickness.

No appeal does all this boiling up have for me. But my money I will not waste, so must I give a day over to the mixing and brewing and physic. And perchance all that should ever be needed is the paste for the sore tooth. But no contest will I have this day with the fire which does rob me of all complexion. Samuel does return this eve and with fair, and not raw skin, should I welcome him. Yet some mind do I have to frize my hair, so 'tis well that a fire be lit though I have no hand in it.

## Saturday 10

Much of this day did I spend with my lover, who be the most handsome of men, and not e'en Eliza should dispute it. And all fair should it have been but that Samuel did vent his spleen, and no lover's cause did it have and no excuse either. More than sennit it be since we did meet together, and no good way be this to treat the bride to be, yet no grudge is there in me. For 'tis on important business Samuel has been, to which he does give some mystery. Which could be but the manly prating for well do I see that he does advertise his importance abroad. And willing do I give the sop, and foretell he will rise in the world – and show my amour – but short does his bonhomie last.

True, 'tis on account that I did see these vapourings in him that I did think to tease him light, and take him down the measure. So did I say that while he did give out that he was gone from hence, yet did Richard Harvey this Monday past see him in the low Rhenish Wine House where only those who do seek to towse do make appearance.

Nothing of the joke did he take from my words, though quick did I try and soothe and make sweet talk on the pleasures we soon together share. Yet did he pull a crow and lay all manner of charges 'gainst his good friend Richard Harvey – and 'gainst me – which does cause me to chafe for what trouble should I make? And many were the insults he did have for Richard Harvey, which does have something of the puzzle in it: for does not my man constant seek him out, and give credit for the way he does work and rise in the world, and call him friend? So what should bring this sudden change and cause complaint that Richard Harvey be naught but tattle.

And does this shift in mood serve to vex me, for no liking should I have to be wed to one who is a froward and no plea would I have that 'twas what he did eat which did put the acid in him, for no mors there was which should lead to this, though the drink be another matter. And this does all confuse me and bode not well.

## Tuesday 13

All *is* well. Today did Samuel call and most truly make amends. He did tell me I was his doty and swear that no cheer would the world have for him, yet I be his love. And to this does he add the favours of purple ribbands, which be welcome and do assuredly help his case. And now should I think on how best to shew them, for none there are who should have the likeness of them.

I but count the days till we do wed.

## Wednesday 14

Complete exhaustion does take me. And full ruined be my skin from all the brewing. All day I did grind and beat and mix and boil, and too did I contend with more than I did plan for. This day too my own courses did flow, and great need did I have for the letting of the pain and first did I try the physic which recipe does come down through my mother's family of the Cliffords. Though so little does it stem the flow and fierceness that I did think to try the tormentil when it did cool, but it too had no relief. Yet should it stand afore I pronounce Sarah Perkins to have no improvement in her brews.

But this eve I do look the boiled one, and I do swear that many days should pass afore I should stand o'er the boiling pot again. Yet none else is there to entrust such a task for my mother does have it that too much is there for her to do, and as the wife I should skill myself to make mine own medicines. Which does have some truth in it, though hard work it be, and worse when there is the flux of blood and all the pinching pain that does go with it.

So tired I am that I did come here to rest without my supper, and no more e'en can I push my pen.


## Friday 16

Oh Lord. Oh Lord. What to do. Would that none should read herein and know my sin. All around me are sick and should I think the cause be me. My father does hold his self and moan, and my brother Balty does gripe and cry out and move not from his bed. Brave be my mother who does give some comfort but most unwell she is and the maid is not to be seen.

First did I think to feign the illness, for no liking did I have to be in health and the one to scrub and clean, for most foul be the effluvient that they do unwilling bring forth and no willingness in me to empty all the shyte. But when I did close mine eyes and think on all, then did the good use of my dissembling full appear to me: so did I moan and make ill like the rest for no wish should I have for the discovery that the sickness does not strike me.

For why should all else be ill, yet not me, but it be the supper which I did not share.

And with guilt I do remember the clear caution to scrub well the cooking pot in which my medicines I did brew. But too tired I was when all were boiled and bottled, and though I did put all in order – which be my mother's first concern – yet the cooking pot I did leave to clean another day. And then surely did my mother make the supper in that same pot, while I did take my rest.

Oh Lord. Oh Lord. Yet do I hope that none should die for never should I confess and the harsh secret it would be to take to the grave with me. Anything would I willing do if they should all be spared, and none should know my part in this. Wise does it seem to keep up the appearance of my illness – and to keep these my records in the safest place.


## Sunday 18

Thanks did I give this day that all my family did get back their health, and no suspicion is there on me. Willing to service I did go and with no care on me, did take a turn in Lincoln's Inn Fields with my man. And the rain did hold while my new purple ribbands I did parade, for what point should there be to keep them hidden.

In gay humour was Samuel as I should call him and which I do try here. We did talk over our plans of our big day, and the wedding feast there should be at The Swan Tavern in Old Fish Street. 'Tis all set that the magistrate Richard Sherwyn should make of us husband and wife at the Church of St Margaret's at Westminster.


## Tuesday 20

Time does take its time. Dull is all. Nothing be there for me to do but mimic the Lady Willoughby.

Leave my bed
Break my fast

Read not the Bible
Wind yarn
Watch rain
Study my glass
Refuse loan to Balty
Naught to read
No callers

Did bicher with my mother and talk some time in the French language.

Then to bed and to write this.

Yet should marriage have none of this dullness in it.

## Thursday 22

Many days has it been since Eliza and I did meet for Richard, her babe, does take the cold, and the maid, Alice, does plead such tiredness from the night-care that she helps not during the day. So this morn Eliza does bring the young one with her and he does wet and squawk and come close to spoiling all. And no sweet smell is there about him.

As we did seek to have the private conversation out of the hearing of my mother, we did set forth down King Street towards the Palace Yard. But with the demon Richard. No liking did I have to carry the child, for he was heavy and I wanted not the puke or the piss on me. But much mirth there was when Eliza did tell of the way babies are made.

'Twas her way to set out what the bride should know. Yet what truth there was in her words I cannot test, for who would vouchsafe them for me? But solemn did Eliza insist that 'tis most necessary that the maid should be able to know the sign of the pox. For many there are who have it, and truly, the most foul illness it be. And if it be discovered, 'tis sufficient to bring all marriage plans to an end.

But surely my man would have it not. Surely Eliza does but jest with me? Yet does her counsel have the ring of truth in it, so that I know not whether to make merry or sober, to think on the marriage bed. ('Tis too much all this talk of yards and pintles and poxes and tearing . . .)

And all the while Eliza does say that 'tis easy to tell – and that swift could I put my mind to rest if I did but make inspection. She does instruct me that the man's tool does have the eye in it – which in part I do know, yet do I hesitate to write it all here for 'tis awkward to give such report – but Eliza does say that when the tool does rise up from its resting place, then does the eye close up if the pox it has seen. And should the eye stay clear and open, 'tis plain that it has not seen the pox.

Eliza does hold it to be the sure test, and 'tis her view that all maids should have the close look at the tool of the man afore they do take him to wed. But no pretty inspection ceremony should it be. My mind does go aboggle to think on requesting Samuel Pepys to put out his pintle for careful examination as Eliza does urge me.

Yet 'tis true it would give me great distress to have the pox put in me. To the fears I have already, Eliza does this day add more when she does foretell what should happen to the privy part if the pox does make it home. Much is there to deter a maid from the marriage bed.

Yet when I do quiz Eliza on how she does come to know all these things, little will she tell. And I do detect the mopish in her. But then on the gay note we did end our discourse on the delights of coupling. If it be not the poxy one, then is there the chance to be bedded by the Fanfarron who has naught but the talk in him. Or else the fumbler who has not the way to make his parts do his bidding. And when I say I know not which one of these Samuel should be, Eliza does wager that he be the braggart, yet will I not take her bet. 'Tis true that there be much of the windfucker in him though no pleasure does it give me to have her say it.

So would I think on other things – and on my pressing need: how should I obtain sufficient paper to keep these lengthy records? For many folios do I need and no money that I should choose to spend upon such purpose. So should I ask Eliza if she could provide me from her husband's store, for much does he have and no way of knowing if but a small lot goes missing. And I do wed, and have mine own monies to command, no more need should I have then of Eliza's devises, though very grateful I am for her consideration.

## Saturday 24

This day did I have a plan but no satisfaction in the execution of it. 'Twas my intent to hear from Samuel Pepys what he did think our marriage night should be, and to this end I did persuade him to a quiet room in The Angel in King Street[5]. By the fire we did snugly sit and he did partake of a pint of wine while I did lull him. When most propitious all did seem, then did I put my question. But no answer was there in him which did set my mind to rest.

True he did tell me of his great love – and the proof of it that he does take a maid without portion – and most insistent was he that as 'tis what we are made for, no pain should there be. Yet no assurance did I have that he did take my meaning or think on how it should be for me. And when I did try to press it, the loving words did soon give way to the peevish frown, and no point was there to continue. So would I risk it not to then make enquiry of the pox – though I know not when the right time for such an enquiry should be!

This time next week I should be wed: Oh Lord.

## Sunday 25

Midnight it is as I make entry here. And this day in Church as I did thank the Lord for my good fortune, strange thought did come to me. How should it be that my man does know so much about the ways of the world, and yet claim such single love for me, for truly 'tis not with me that he does learn this. And I do give my mind to other possibilities.

Something do I know about his favour to Elizabeth Whittle[6] for he had told me of the devotion she did inspire. But naught there was in it, for only the boy was he then and no rankle is there. Yet were there more on his list, and without such innocence, well would my blood boil and my man should feel full force of it.

[5] *The Angel*, King Street, Westminster: tavern and eating house kept by William Wells.

[6] When a boy Samuel had a great crush on Elizabeth Whittle, a London neighbour: the nature of their relationship is not known.

During service my thoughts did go to any there may have been who Mr Pepys did know, and I know not. And I did ask the Lord to forgive me for such base concerns on the Sabbath yet should my state be understandable.

This eve did I spend with the family of Pepys, and so awful it was that I think it should be my mistake to join with them. Nothing do they know of breeding, or of buying, or of playing host. The poorest meal do they make so that the hunger was with me when I did leave there.

And this is not the first time that such fate should befall me. When earlier I did visit – when Samuel and I did think to wed – no food did they supply us with though we did stay within long past the dinner hour. That time was I piqued and did play the mischief and when the Bible I did see before me I did leave it open to show the story of the multiplication of loaves and fishes, and later I did tell Samuel that it should take such a miracle to provide sufficient at the Pepys table. But no humour did he see in it.

Yet truly 'twas the meanest fare that ever there could be and no good plate, either. Caudle is all they do well supply, but no means is there to make clear what the lumps in it should be.

This time did I talk much of fine foods, and give account of the grand dishes my mother does prepare from the rabbits and the pigeons, and the beef and mutton too, and all the pies and the puddings I should make when we were wed. Yet no sign there was that they did take my meaning, 'less it be the talk that did flow on the way a man should be ruined by the extravagant wife, and dark looks did get directed at me. But no bending was there in me. Even did I think to hold forth on the wickedness of the miser but for the silencing look my man did give me.

No *vivante* my new mother should be, but the timid mouse who does take afright at everything, who does turn hither and thither to do all the bidding. Shaded is she by her man who clear does put the fear in her and so loud does he command her. Then too is there the oafish Pall[7] – who would shame me if I am forced to public call her sister – and who should be the

[7] *Pall*: (Pauline) Samuel's sister whom Elizabeth found boorish and an embarrassment and with whom she openly feuded.

64

best argument against the bringing forth of children so ugly is she, and greedy.

Even the little food that I did see spread, not one morsel did pass the lips of the wash-woman for Pall does put her paws on all and full feed her face, which has no surprise in it for 'tis the way with those who are constant hungry and trust not the coming of the next meal. Yet what sustenance does my new mother have? 'Tis not beyond belief that all are served afore her, and that nothing is there left for her to eat.

No comfort does it give me to see how she does live. Sooner would I die than endure such fearful treatment. For no kindness in the house is there to her, and 'tis true that the coarseness of the washerwoman does constant show. And this does give Samuel offence. Very fusty is he when 'tis plain for all to see that his mother did once work as the washing woman, and that he be low born.

We did stay what politeness did call for and most civil I be, but no pleasure was there in it, and much relief when we did leave. But no time was there for me to make complaint, or e'en to point to the poor ways of his kin and the worry of his mother's thinness, afore Samuel did suggest the visit to Eliza and Richard. For was not Richard the bridesman, and was there not much to settle? Which did somewhat shake me for 'tis but a short time past since he did have only abuse for Richard Harvey, and no intention to seek his company again. But no protest did I make for it did please me to make such call.

But playful did I tell my man that I should mimic all the manners of his family to our friends and soon does this put Samuel in such a pett that I do wonder in truth how much I do know him. For hard does he hold me and make the threat that quick should I rue the day that I did tell of the intimate habits of his family. To which I do agree and then can we proceed to pay call on the Harveys.

Yet do I know one thing I have over him, and should I tell of his poor parentage if there is necessary advantage in it for me.

And what contrast there should be at the Harveys, for there we were received as honoured guests. So many fine things they have therein, and so many that I do wish for. But such rich hangings and such solid plate take more than the steward's purse[8] to purchase. Richard Harvey makes business as the ship's chandler, and much profit does he have in it, though 'tis true that he does not dress as well as Mr Samuel Pepys – though this does not compensate for being the tailor's son.

Still did I manage to give Eliza some idea of the trials I had undergone, and the want of regard I had for my new family. So did she ply me with all manner of delicacies and wicked ask out loud whether I should be weak from lack of nourishment, though no attention did my man give this.

Yet all the while we did tune to the conversation of the men and so we did hear that Richard Harvey does plan a merry making for Mr Pepys, to mark the end of his liberty days. Though when upon the marriage the man is made the Lord and Master who the wife is meant to obey, does seem strange to say 'tis the man who does have the end of liberty.

And Eliza did read well my intention when I did seeming-innocent ask if we should join them in their revelry, and so keep them from any form of foolery. But no liking was there in them for my suggestion. No refusal, either, just the cool discouraging and the patting, that no pleasure would we find in such coarse company. And Richard Harvey does make the fuss and has it that too many duties does Eliza have – with *two* babes – as she does constant complain to him, and so no possibility would she have to attend both the wedding revels, and the wedding, *and* as the mother still be true.

But Samuel does try another tack, which he thinks I see not through. He does have the gall to try and colly me into the need for my beauty sleep, so close to the day we wed. And no moving them was there. So Eliza and I, we did give over with good grace and did give the appearance that we were beaten. Yet our looks did belie our meaning. No need did we have of words betwixt us to look to the making of our own event to mark *my* end of liberty, and the beginning of the wifely duties. But no chance then to settle what form it should be.

Too tired now am I to contemplate; time enough on the morrow to plan our secret.

[8] *Steward's purse*: a reference to Samuel's lowly job.

## Thursday 29

Late is the hour and fortunate I am to have the private place to write herein, for much mixing does go on in my head and dearly do I want to sort it. For true to our intent, Eliza and I did have this night upon the town, and the good start we did make of it from the Charing Cross. Daring did we paint our faces, and few would there be who could know us.

Then without protection we did make our tour, and much did I see that was new to me.

No want of company should there have been, if that is what we did go seeking. The catt-call did we get from some coquins and fond words from the gallants who did want more close acquaintance. And some apprehension did I feel when one young blade there was who did have harsh words for us and play the hector when we did give him refusal. Yet always did we stay in public view and 'twas Eliza's insistence that no danger were we in.

High humour did we have as we did make our way round through the low life and see how it is that many do live, and play, and die. So many cookshops that I know not of, and new dishes which ne'er before did I see[9]. And music, and mountebanks, and singers and tumblers, and meschants too and a great flowing of ale, and much else besides. Though it did have some of the lewdness in it, yet did we raise up our skirts for most bedaggled they be. And a disgrace it is that so many there are who do pour in the wine at one end and straight does it come forth at the other, and no great consideration do they have for where it should flow.

Yet such strange sights did have their fascination for me, till past The Bell in the Strand we did go. Then sudden did a sweat break upon me. For in the midst of this great bawdy crowd, whom was it I did espy? Mr Samuel Pepys! And no double should it be, and no credit to him either.

So much was I afear'd, that immediate did I think on how to

---

[9] So many new foods were introduced into England during the seventeenth century that it is impossible to determine what these new dishes might have been. Even the commonly available beans, cabbages, carrots, peas and onions underwent a change during this period as new and better strains were introduced from Holland.

stay concealed, for no partialness should my man have to see me gad abroad with painted face, and skirt ahoist, and with but Eliza for my companion, and great basting would there be for me on my discovery. So not to risk his wrath did I motion Eliza to stay back with me, so we should go undetected.

But soon did I surmise how little danger we were in, for unlikely was it that Mr Pepys had enough of his senses in him to know his surrounds. And mine eyes did see what mine eyes did see.

As I did start by 'twas clear that my man did have his cups and this way and that way he did sway in the arms of some great doxy who did treat him as the droll. And forced was I to witness his shameful foolery, and it does feed the rage in me when he does make big eyes at the baggage. No charge does he have o'er hisself, and no liking do I have that all should see him without honour.

Yet more tossed I be to see how Eliza does take it; no kindness nor sympathy does she show me, but delivers the stinging words for me to cease my scene, for 'tis time I should know what to expect of the man. Which does truly shock me. Yet has she not forewarned me, she does demand? Is not Samuel Pepys the effeminate? And all straightness does go from me so that I think not to walk in the world again.

Then did I see Richard Harvey, and the great bufflehead too was he. And for Eliza, no surprise did this seem to be. Oft does she tell me that her man comes home aswill, and with no mind to mark where he has been. Yet did I think it but her way to make much of little things and most wont she is to complain of the brute husband and his boorish ways. But here it was all afore me. To see with mine own eyes what he and Samuel should do. And awful for Eliza, but worse for me. What shame is on me. For while we did keep watch, no encouragement to the bawdies did Richard Harvey give. All it does come from Samuel Pepys. 'Tis *my man* who does have more of the knave and the fool in him.

And confused I am at what it should be when Richard Harvey does press but a bowl of broth on my man, and all about do jest and jeer, for what is there to make such mirth and mocking in the broth-bowl? Eliza too does note the mystery in this but soon does set all clear. Though it does put my heart apace, still does she move in close to make out the meaning of the talk, only to double up and shake with laughter which puts more of the panic in me that we should be uncovered. Then does she return and betwixt the laughing bouts inform me that 'tis nettle porridge which her husband does urge on my man. Which for me does still have the mystery in it till Eliza does betwitt my ignorance and tell that whores do feed the nettle porridge to men to make them more amorous and to help them part with their money.

Most churned up I be – and too I should like to know where Eliza does get all this learning – and why this sight makes not her gorge rise, as it does mine.

No excuse should there be for my man to take his pleasure of other women, and much does this rile me. Though whether to challenge or to later seek my revenge, is an issue which does burn in me. For the banns be read, and all is set, and great confusion there should be if the wedding plans should come to an end.

And though Eliza does say 'tis liberty night, and does not signify, except that Samuel should risk the clap in such company, much does it mean to me. Did we not to each other make the vow of faithfulness? And is this not now broken? But not by me. And such different rules this does now mean. For what is there to hold to, if the trust does go?

And more too, in the clap. Which be no pretty thing I have heard tell.

All does come down around me. For must I trust what I did see with mine own eyes. And how could this be the man I did look to for some wisdom in this world? What awfulness is this, and how should it pass? What to do? 'Tis hard to make up the pacquet of happiness to entrust to another's care, when no faith is there that it should be handled gently.

Samuel, how could you? All those assurances. What now does your word mean? What honour is in you? Such low breeding does make its presence felt . . .

But e'en when all this did strike me, still did we have to make our way from the scene. Though easy was it to move without detection despite my racing heart which all should hear, and my wild look which does mark me out, surely. The devil himself should have gone unnoticed by those foxed two.

But crushed were my good spirits when we did wend our way and all the while Eliza did keep up her cruel counsel that those who did wait for the temperate and true man, did die the spinster. And does she say that beggars be not choosers, and without dower, what else is there for me?

Yet more are there in the world than Samuel Pepys. There is Captain Robin Holmes[10] who does favour me and could be the better match. But too late should all this consideration be. The morrow does mark my last day in the single state – and no joy is there in me.


## Friday 30

Noon, on a chill and dark day and no plan was it of mine to have the melancholy wedding eve. And no good omen is it. All night did I think on whether to accost my man and fish from him his reasons. Yet to what purpose? That he should deny all, or turn on me, or that no wedding there should be?

While I know the cause of Eliza's dance no desire do I have to do the steps. Is this what the marriage should be?

I do feel that all the world does ride me and no peace is there. My heart does know my love but my head does bid me be wary, and no gain should it be to break my mind to my mother, though sorely am I tempted.

'Tis now the second entry I do make this day. Faith does that man confound my plans and no satisfaction is there in it for me. This hour a message I did receive from Samuel Pepys in which he does state – though not in his own hand – that it be considered ill fortune for the couple to meet the day afore they do wed. Which is the first I hear of this and mighty convenient should it be. Yet do I know it as the pretext for the heavy head he should have after putting so much of the drink in it. If fate be fair, no chance should he have to lift it from his pillow!

To sweeten all he does cunning add that he does have the ring to give, when on the morrow, Mr Sherwyn should say the solemnities o'er us. And though I see through such gulling still

[10] Captain Robin Holmes was a handsome soldier who re-emerged later in Elizabeth's life.

I will let it pass for it does suit me to have the ring and get it blessed. 'Tis but a week since Samuel did hold forth on the evil of ritual and against the place of a ring in the wedding service, and I did resign myself to doing without it. So does it please me, yet he buys me not with this token and I do bide my time to balance this account for much does he owe me. And I am afear'd. 'Tis a mighty thing to wed a man and have nothing.

## December 1

After the midnight hour it is, and this does count as my wedding day and sleep will not come to me.

Last eve did my mother sit upon my bed and tears we had when she did talk on the kindnesses we have shared. And does she wish me well and willing want to answer any questions I might have. But none there are for which the answer be satisfactory so I give her embrace and have her know that much sadness there is for me in our parting.

Then does she hold me and soothe – say that 'tis the way of the world. Though why it should be the custom for the maid to leave her mother and to set forth with the strange man does have something of the puzzle in it for me. And well did she remember that hard had it been for her when she did set out with the strange man yet it did bring her my brother and me for which she gives thanks, and some day should I have the recompense.

When I did show her that with my joy, I also had my fears, then quick did she say that even at this late hour there is still the time for mind-changing. Free was I to choose delay and she would bestir my father to give all notice. She did urge me well to listen to my doubts for after the service, then is there no going back. Which does have the awesome ring to it.

But all do seem to want the marriage path, so too should I follow it. And though my parading days be not at an end, yet no better offer have I received and I do know that if I should take not Mr Samuel Pepys, there are those who would eager have him.

So do I take my leave of my good mother. The next record do I keep as Mrs Elizabeth Pepys, and all should be different.

# PART TWO

# Marriage

# 1655

## December
## Tuesday 4

Poor preparation did I have for this and no warning. Nor should I want my mind to dwell on such frightful event. 'Tis too bitter. No strength is there in me . . . what disappointment is this. My first entry as *Mrs Pepys* and no satisfaction in it. 'Tis agony that I do endure, 'tis the burning pain and the burning piss that does not leave me, and not the least of it, it is . . . but I will not give way. I did calm myself to write this and so I will. But this is not how I did think it would be.

Is there no one to come to me?


## Saturday 8

One week a monstrous difference does make. When I think back the seven nights past, what cruel contrast there should be. Such content did I know on my wedding day, such promise for the future . . . all the fear I did put behind me and look on my man with trust. The good omen it should be . . . no better day could there have been, and the rain did hold back while we did merry make.

Right well did Richard Harvey do the part of bridesman and much mirth there was when the ribbands and garters were undone and they did throw our stockings to the hopefuls.[1] And great too my joy when Pall scored not, though mighty did she

---

[1] The bride and groom were ceremoniously 'undressed' as part of the proceedings; generally the bridesman and bridesmaid untied the ribbons and garters and the bridesmaid flung the groom's stockings over her head (for the hopeful brides) while the bridesman tossed the bride's stockings.

push for it, which has the sense in it, for much help will she need if she is to land a husband . . .

Yet why should I write this? That the husband be the prize for the lucky. And that Puss-Pall deserve it not. For more of the pain than the prize is there in the married state it does seem. Perchance the Plain-Pall should be the winner in all this which does jolt me . . . What changes there are wrought in me and such a short space of time to make them.

I do think on the distance that I have been in just one week. Only the warmest feelings were there in me when we did have our wedding-night ceremony. And to think that I did join in the jest when my handsome husband did take of the sack possett – that the sack should make him lusty and the sugar should make him kind. No foreknowing was there that too much would make of him the fumbler . . . what a fool I be!

E'en now I do recall that there was content and pride in me when we did make our way to our new living place, and though 'tis true that my husband . . . (*my husband*! so oft in my head I did say those words when we did make our way to our wedding bed) . . . my husband did stumble, but stayed hog high and would take no support . . . and much humour was there in it and no harm I could see. Though 'tis the case that Eliza did nod sagely all the while to me, yet – once more and in my ignorance – did I put it down to her loss of humour for her husband who does swill away and pay no attention to her . . .

But then after the untying of the ribbands when all did leave, and quiet did I survey our garret room, and most pleased I was with it. Though much more did I think to do and the housewife art was high in me when I did plan on the improvements – And all ready I was for my husband, and no panic did I feel . . . Yet my survey did show him to have the silly look upon him, and no sense did he have in him – and while he did talk big and be the braggart so too did he cease and take almost instant to loud snoring. So there was the disappointment in me that on my first night as a wife, no lover did I have but an ugly, noisome rumbler, yet too there was time for me to reflect on all, to offer my prayers and give thanks.

So did my mind turn to the events of my day. And with satisfaction did I think on my family who did all show their birth and breeding, even Balty did put forward his good manners, yet I paid him not, to do it. But no good claim could I make for my husband's family. There is much lowness and disagreeableness in them, and the women are such dowdies they do truly shame me. And none to pay shot among them which does mark them base and mean. But no scandalizing will I do of them, for no honour does it bring to my husband. Yet certain it is that one day I should tell them to their teeth how rude they be.

And will I bide my time before I do snuff that Puss-Pall-Pot. No kindness was it in her to point to one, the fair Betty Archer, and to sniggering say, that she was Samuel's great love in his student days.[2] From any other I might take this to be the serious allegation, but from Poison-Pall, who has so much of the malice in her, 'tis but a way to barb me, and no satisfaction will I give her. Yet always afore me I do admit is the suspicion that my husband be the wencher which is too burdensome to think on.

All else but Pock-Pall[3] did have pleasure in the display of finery, and I was shaded not. E'en Eliza who did parade in her fashion gown did not make the same figure as mine own paduasoy. Well did I smile when I did note the envy which did pull Pall's face when she did look on my stiff bodice. 'Tis all the mode though 'tis true that the more comfortable I have been without the pushing to my stomach.[4]

'Twas the beautiful kerchief of my mother's which does come down from the great Clifford family, which I did have at my neck and set all off. And too did I show the lace-trim front[5] and my only disappointment that I must wear my pattens for to save my shoes, which should be fouled by the mire of melted snow, yet no detraction was it.

But no smiles could I muster late on my wedding eve when I

[2] The Archer family lived in Bourn near Cambridge and Samuel had been very impressed with Betty in his student days.
[3] There is no evidence that Pall had had smallpox or that her face was marked so this is probably just one of Elizabeth's inventive terms for her.
[4] The fashion was for stiff bodices which were pointed in front and reached below the waist, and considerably hampered movement, particularly bending and sitting. (This fashion features in some of the Van Dyck portraits of the time.)
[5] Skirts were draped to display the petticoat and the quality of the lace displayed was quite important.

did look upon the man who did share my bed and with whom I had but short time vowed to share my life. No sign of loving was there from him, though much wind from him did emanate. And to think that I did feel failure then that so soon did he go into the stupor and not sport with me.

The great innocent I should be . . .

(A rest did I take afore I resume this pen, and so paltry my candle that no long period for record-keeping is there for me. What misery to stay alone, and no light, and much to torment me. No one is there worse . . . yet no good purpose should such melancholy serve, so shall I turn to what I do intend . . .)

To take up my history again. 'Twas not till the first day of our life together that my husband did have his way. Should I have known what splitting there was in such spoiling, long should I have delayed it. Hurtful even now it is to think on and no celebration was it for me to see my blood spilled upon the covers. What I should wonder is that there is not more, given the piercing pain, for truly it would not have stounded me to find that for hours it should steady flow forth, and not just the pissing pump I have become.

So. Six days do I stay here and none but my husband have I seen since I be wed. No move do I make outdoors, for the pain does shoot through me with but the smallest step, and no distance can I safe stay from the chamber pot, for the fiery pissing is constant with me till I should scream.

And as it is custom to leave new lovers alone to play their games of amour, and to await the call of the wife, none there are who do come to cheer me, which does bring this mopishness upon me. Readily could I think that none do care for me, and even the coals are low.

Such comfort did this one room give when first I did enter but now that sennen do pass and no change but that I stay within, 'tis not so soothing. One week and it should come to this. And not even the herbs should give relief. Company I have not, for this night my husband does lose all patience and go forth to the ordinary for to take his dinner; which may be very well for him, yet still do I go hungry. And none there is to hear me.

The only talk I have is the talk to paper which I make here.

And no more light to list my grievances, though many more there be.

## Tuesday 11

This morn when my husband does take his leave – I know not whereto – then does my mother come and much release in me is there to see her. And she does say that some worry did she have for me, till she did hear that my husband does put it abroad that no wish should I have to rise from my marriage bed. Which has something of the truth in it, but not the braggart way he does make it. And does my blood boil, for 'tis his fault that I should suffer so, and yet does he deport himself as the great lover which surely he is not.

So does he chouse me, but no more. 'Tis enough that I should go from my bed to undo him. Would that I could tell all that there is nothing of the fine-bred lover in him. When he does not fumble, then so swift is he led by his pintle that no loving is there in it, for all has been and gone by the count of three. Did I not have the cutting pain to tell me he does thrust it in, easy would it be to miss the sport so quick-passing it be.

And I did unburden myself to my mother and in rising voice I did make clear that badly have I been served by this unkind man.

Some comfort did she give as my tears did flow – though no water did I think was left in me – and bitter feelings were there in me that poor bargain I did make to exchange the love and companionship of my family for such a knavish man.

And my mother does begin to make light and bawdy of my state, which does show peculiar want of taste and sympathy, and she does have it that my pain soon should pass, yet not soon enough should it be for me. Difficult does she find it to salve up the matter for most worked-up, am I. And do I tell her that I like not this love making, that there is nothing of pleasure in it, and if it be the only way that babes be made, 'tis a wonder that so many of them there are.

Why is it, I ask, that no great discourse there is on the dreadfulness of coupling? And I do charge that some conspiracy there must be to stop the ears of young maids, for nowhere did

I hear tell of such pain and unpleasantness. To mine ears came only the promise of pretty sport and laughter, yet it does seem to me that multitudes of wives there should be who do protest such rough and rude treatment, if they do learn the same as me.

And when my mother does try to tell that 'tis the same for all, and soon used to it I should be, then do I do the great stir and make it clear that none there are who should have the great soreness and the burning piss which does plague me. All wives would soon find other means if each day did set their secrets afire, as mine do rage.

But do I confess that one niggle thought there is which does continual come to me. Though I should try to banish it from my mind, yet do I dwell on the warning that Eliza did give me. Could it be that my man does have the pox, and that this be the cause of my great agony?

Though I do school my mother for want of good counsel (which she does roundly deny) yet no liking do I have to ask her of the way of the pox. And no chance yet either to peruse the offending pintle and make test for the clear or the clouded eye. But I do resolve to make future early inspection.

No more this quick poke betwixt the covers and nothing do I see. So should I brace myself to take close look at this yard which does damage me. But naught of this did I pass on to my mother.

Willing did I have her do the nursing of me. And loud did I complain that no help was there in the herbs that the wise Sarah Perkins did recommend. But truth to tell, I should confess that little these last days did I use the remedies, for too ill have I been and no one to do for me.

And my mother does make the cooling cataplasm which is to place upon my poor soreness, which I do not allow my mother to see. For no sweetness is there in it, and I do want to mend my own. And the cataplasm does ferocious sting and draw, but then does abate somewhat, and grateful I am for my mother's attention.

And too does she bring order to our one room, which does have much atumble in it. Great improvement was it to have the bed made plump and the coals aplenished. And the chamber pots all emptied, and which I have these many days made to ignore, for if the swilling and scrubbing of them be the housewifely duty then no attraction should it have for me – and should it become the strongest cause for the getting of the maid.

My smock and drawers which were soiled my mother does take out to the whitester for unfit am I to do such chore and this time my mother does have it that Mr Pepys should pay. And from the cookshop she does bring me the delicacies which include the tansy that be advised for those who are the invalid and then do I know how ravenous I am and how little my husband does feed me. And no good omen is this.

Much better does my mother make me, and 'tis but one hour since she did leave, and I do write here. And does my sickness and melancholy return as my loneliness does increase. From this morn my husband has been abroad and no excuse should I have from him but that it should be to make money – which I should want to see. For none have I had as Mrs Pepys, and no future is there in this.


## Monday 17

Last night the first great bandy there be, betwixt my husband and me, and still I be tossed about it. And on the Sabbath too. And I know not what to do. But all week, my troubles I did store up, and till after service I did wait when I did think to find him in contrite mood. Then did I present him withall.

And did I steady list them as I do now recall.

No money do I have in hand, which be the worst. For though the pissing pain be with me still, yet should it be made more bearable if some distraction I should have. Even to have the romance for reading and to pass the time should help. But better still it should be if I could take my place among the married women – yet without money, not e'en to market can I go.

And no food. Nothing does he bring me. So should I starve were it not for the dishes my mother did provide.

No candles.

And the coals be perilous low and need replenishment if we are not to freeze.

And no liking to be Mrs Pepys. And no loving name for the coupling of husband and wife for the most barbarous behaviour it be. And I did say that should I have known this fortnight past what I know now, no wedding would there have been.

And all this did seem reasonable to me.

But no longer would my husband stroll forth and play the new weds. Swift does he well with great anger and rough did he pull me back to our room and make wild threat to scowre me – which did take my breath from me. And so hot was his rage that no sure way did I know how to make all smooth. So did I make to swoune which does have some solution in it.

And my man does make a-boggle afore he does succumb and seek to bring me round, for full well does he know how sick I have been, and no art of feigning has there been. And truly worried is he.

But no fixed answer should it be to my troubles to make the swoune and soon must I regain my senses. Then too does the concern and affection of my husband abate. No time before he is in a great pett and does seek to pick a crow and roundly does declare that no pleasure should this marriage be for him. And does he make it that he too does have the sickness – which is the first I should hear, and so he does make me know that he is greatly bound – and he does have no money either: which is a pretty thing.

On does he go. 'Tis a shrew of a wife he does claim he does get. And a place that has no order but does look like the bawdy house. And no light, and no warmth, and the great mistake he does think he has made to marry such a penniless slut.

Then do I find my tongue, and much release is there in it. Such shame he should suffer to come from the Lord's service and splutter and curse like the fool from Bedlam when I am the one who is ill used. Yet while I do berate full force, strange do I note that as my voice does rise, he does stiffen with the rage, and like he has been to the whitester does his colour pass quick from blotch to pale. And I do feel afright when he does stand there still yet savage afore me, and do I brace myself. But 'tis not to strike me that he does make his mark.

For then does he do the worst wipe of all. Right afore my eyes he does untruss and take a crap, and say that no choice it be of his but the opening medicine he did take. And that did end our bout. And much mortified I am to the depth of my soul.

But I did my self-charge keep when his breeches he did do up again and leave me with the chamber pot. And I did sob myself to sleep.

Monday morning now it is and still he comes not home. And stands the chamber pot which I did perforce cover, but which I would not empty. Even though the stench does end me, which is the possibility.


## Wednesday 19

When last entry I did make, no worse could all have been. But then to prove me wrong my termes did come – and early too – and did add to my distress. And there is the swelling and the stinging, and the burning piss, and now too my courses do flow as if they had been dammed, and the heavy ache does fill me, and the weakness too. And did I think to tell Samuel that all this sickness should be for the want of proper food and care.

Yet when he did return home Tuesday noon, much softness there was in him and free did his tears flow with ripe remorse. So did we make up and solemn swear that more kindness should we show. No complaints then did I make (and the chamber pot I stoic swilled) and all cries about my pain and poor health did I still. And most pleased I was with my good performance, though Samuel's should want more improvement.

For does he charge me with being froward (which does have the twist in it) and urge me to put on the smile, for 'tis his view that no man should have satisfaction in the constant-sick wife, which is what I be since we do wed. And this does show a want of true feeling, and does hurt me, yet no word do I pass on it so no bichering do we have.

But in truth it does seem hard. If this be the lot of the wife then 'tis clear that the life of the nun does have much to recommend it.

This day was I to pay call upon Eliza whom I have not seen for eighteen nights, and whom I do sorely miss, though many grievances too should I have against her. Yet I do think it might be too much for me to meet her for no liking do I have to drag myself through hurly streets when mine innards do make such a battle with me, and little relief is there.

And the toothache too. No more can there be sent to try me.

No dry money do I have, so no coals, nor candles, nor viands can I purchase.

And no kindness from my husband who does swagger forth and state that 'tis matters of great importance which do keep him hence. More reason is there for me to regain my health, for yet should I follow him and know his ways. 'Tis strange that in such short time a man should change so much for little evidence do I find now of the kind lover who I did so ready trust.

## Thursday 20

At last. This day did Eliza and I make merry and much has it done to put me back in temper. So much to enter – yet should I make it here? To this day my husband knows not that I talk to paper, for innocent though the practice be, yet do I know his ways, and no understanding should there be in him for my history-making. Great anger should it stir, for all he would see would be that I do keep score against him. And since his choler he does recent show, 'tis true that I do have some fear in me of him, which is not what it should be.

Eliza does regular say that the wife soon learns wisdom. And wise do I think it to keep hidden this book of days – though forsooth – the bigger my journal does grow, the more problem it has in it to conceal in such small space. So some sense there be in keeping all in disarray, for then naught is there which is easy to find.

Later should I make entry on what Eliza does say – and much roisting is there in it – but now my man I do await, and he did promise that we should take French dinner together this day.

My diurnal should I keep close beneath the covers.

# Friday 21

This morn did I wake tearful, and the splitting pain does make its presence felt. Great resentment was there in me when I did gaze upon my husband, who has still the effect of drink in him and does stay in such deep sleep – and the cause of all my suffering he be. And not even the best of food and drink, and company too, should be fair price for the misery I now endure.

Though 'twas not my wish, yet last night did my husband have his way and push his pintle in me – which he does say is his right – and long does he make his stroke, and much sense there should be to know how to quicken him.

Which does have the puzzle in it. For sometimes it is that the drink does make him fumble, and sometimes it should fuel him to flap away for what should seem eternity. And it would serve me well to know which wine it is that does have such cause for, truly, much the fumbler I should prefer my husband to be, for little endurance is left in me to cope with this mix of fire and water in my groin. And more does it itch[6] to my distraction.

'Twas the urge to piss which did drive me from my bed this night and cruel and cold out it be. And not enough to endure the chill and the dark for want of coal and candle, and to stumble forth to seek the chamber pot (for no close-stool is there). But then I find that all are full and foul, and 'tis not my crap that does cause them to swill to the brim, and my gorge does rise within me. Savage do I feel and I do think to tell my man that I was not born a Clifford to be soiled with his slops, yet all the while did he noisome sleep through my vexation and rage.

And why should sleep there be for him when I do burn from the piss pain and no relief? So did I tight screw his flesh till I did think to tear it, yet no alertness is there in him, just the dull mumble, and I do despair.

Through the night long I do lie there with the piss pain and more besides, and think on the sorry state I have come to. For now does it feel like the abscess that I do carry in my privities. All the while I do look to the fault of the man who does bring me to this, for who should know what monster the courting

---

[6] Elizabeth could have developed thrush.

gallant does become when he has turned into the husband and has no more need to form the flattering words and woo his way?

So some small consolation should it be for me when he does wake afore due time, with the heavy head and the stone pain and does moan and make the misery-face that he must pee or do hisself some damage. *And no room is there in the pot for him to piss.* And truth to tell, it does please me to see him hold tight to his parts and make that he should burst and spill hisself upon the floor, and not one pat of pity is there in me. Sweet revenge it did seem that he should blunder forth and trip upon the stairs, and all with much blowing and bleating, and the Lord knows where he did go to empty his stock but 'tis no more than he does warrant.

Brief-lived was my satisfaction. That I should come to this. 'Tis low and unworthy, and I do scorn it. There must be improvement.


## Saturday 22

This day I did with Eliza meet, though not to market we did go, for still no monies do I have, and greatly does this vex me. From Eliza I should not conceal that little dinner I do get as Mrs Pepys, and so she does quizz me; and feed me. Some pity did I shrink from that she should show, but naught did she give, and her sharp words did put the huffe in me for none did I deserve.

Yet does she say that I am the fool, for time enough has there been to learn how to manage the man, yet no sign do I give of how to do it.

She does counsel that I should cease to play the invalid and stay from my bed, that I should put aside my sloth and dress my hair – which truth to tell has no attention since the day I did wed. And that I should don my new gown for when my husband does make his appearance. In her words, this is how the man – and the monies – be managed.

Yet do I say that no effort does my husband make for me and unfair it is that I should do all for him. But Eliza does just cool-say that this is how it be. And she does add that the man has the purse and if it is to be opened, then must the woman please him.

Which is not very loving, but some sense it does have in it and certain it is that I should consult my pillow.

And while we did stroll and have such serious talk, yet did I note more. 'Twas Robin Holmes whom I did see was watching me, and most handsome he is. 'Tis possible that he knows not that I am the wife – and forsooth he does cut a fine figure in his uniform.

And too it does strike me that I be not at my best these past weeks. So do I resolve to get back my looks, and to unfurrow my brow, and think not on the pain that does cut into me.

As I do keep this record here, even more need is there to make it safe from prying eyes. For a great bout there would be if my husband did get to this and all effort should he make to stop me from my diary. And the veriest miserable creature I should be with no journal to keep. 'Tis the greatest comfort that it does provide me, and too do I think to pass these pages on to my daughter, so she should know what I did not. To preserve it, I must take all care to keep it from my husband's eyes and hands. And to think that but a few weeks past, I did seek to have no secrets from my man.

## Monday 24

'Tis not enough that I should make all endeavour to brighten myself. For no reward is there in it. No warm words does my husband give but turns his passionateness to our apartment. This day does he rage through and give cries as to the great disarray – which truly does have more of his making in it, than mine.

And then I do let forth that no money do I have, and no heat and no light, and no food but I must wait for him to feed me, and I swear that no more than five days do I eat since we are wed, and all soon should know that he does starve me in a garret and then who should trust him to be the steward? And all the while he does buy the books to fill our place and without order.

Swift does he make counter charge. That no clean apartment,

no clean drawers nor flannel waistcoats, no mending, and no beauty-wife, no sporting-wife and no companion-wife has he, which does make him the least fortunate of men. And to this he did add his fist and dry-beat me, though I did make the scratches and see some blood for *my* effort. So loud did we our voices raise, and so pump our feet upon the floor, that shouts did answer from those below who did threaten all manner of penalties, should we not cease. And I am shamed by such low behaviour.

In fierce whisper and without move, we did make to continue our great row, but soon did the sillyness of all start to come through, and unbidden did the mirth rise in us. So we did make-up, and sober think on how we should love each other and keep from such cruel usage in the future.

Yet should I set down here the pattern of my days and all there is that irks me. That each day my husband does late rise – and usual it is that he should have the heavy head and the ill humour – and first thing he should do is use the chamber pot, though no effort does he make to swill it, nor to set the coals, or make any order. Yet no servant do we have and rough red and raw my hands should be – and nothing of Sarah Perkins would there be to remedy this. Should I be the laundress, and set the fire, and do all the scrubbing, and keep scoured the chamber pot? None of this was our bargain.

And when he does have relief – which be no swift accomplishment, for my husband has the cruel kidney stone, and the great fluxes in his bowels, for which he does medicate, and these do cause him much strain and pain. And then does he don his breeches and his coat and make his way from hence, and sometimes with naught but the muttering that much is there for him to do, and not e'en a fond farewell do I receive.

So does he leave me abed. And not even the good book[7] is there for me (though I do note that my man does all the while add to *his* library). And our room is monstrous cold and no fire unless lit by me and not enough coals. And little that I should want to do. Better it be that I should go abroad and seek some light and warmth, which does send me to my mother, and Eliza.

[7] The good book: presumably a romance and not the Bible.

For dinner my husband does stay out. And I do know full well that he dines with many of his friends. They do take their pints and do their playing and a pleasant time they have of it.

When at these sessions too much my man does drink, then soon should I know of it. For he does return to our apartment. And sleep. And snore. And all manner of base things.

Then the evening there is.

Many plans we did have afore we did wed for the suppers we should have. And we did think to go abroad, and take supper at an eating house, or inn, and the gay life together it should be. Else would we sample the cookshop and return here for the tasty dish in our cosy nest. And so different should it come to be.

So much does he take at dinner that times there are when my husband wakes not for his supper. Or times when he does wake and say that he is not hungry, and though I shared not his dinner, by some magic feat he does think that no hunger there should be in me! And times too when he comes not home, or when he goes out again – alone.

'Tis but a few suppers out that we have shared, and much did I enjoy them. And only one supper did we share in our new home. 'Twas when I did give him the great fright that I should die of starvation and that all should know of it, so soon should he find himself up afore the court. Then swift did he bring home the leg of mutton from the cookshop, and ravenously did I set upon it. Yet even one leg – of which he had the bigger share – keeps not body and soul together for more than a few days. And 'tis true that since I have become the wife, I am constant hungry. And no plan did I have of this.

No conceit does Samuel have that a wife does cost the husband money, and no willingness is there in him to learn. All his monies does he keep for his own use, for his ale-house company, and his clothes and his books which he does continue to add to. Would that I could find his friend who did tell him that two could eat as cheap as one, for even he should concede that Samuel should not be the only one but that his viands he should share.

And do I think back to the warning my mother did give, though no reference to it do I make. For 'twas her counsel that firm agreement about monies there should be, *afore* we did wed. Yet then did I hold that love was sufficient and very hog high I was. Ready did I believe Samuel's soft words, and too his line that no room there was in our loving for base talk of money. But 'tis true that no good ground did I start from.

For I should confess that with no money of mine own, I did tread warily and make no firm call for the regular allowance. Grateful I was that Samuel should have me without portion and no consideration was there in me that he should prove to be so palterly. Though now when I do think back, some signs of the tight-fist perchance there have been, and the silver-tongue too, to make excuse. For when no tokens he did give me when he did woo, did he not promise to lay all at my feet when we did wed? The smooth talker he be and foolish I was to trust him. But what to do?

E'en now I do take his measure. When I do plead for the money to market – which well could I manage in mine own way – then does he make fabrication. He does urge me to give no thought to the drudge of marketing, but to stay the beauty. And this does unmask him for even the fool can see that it does take money and marketing to keep up beauty.

And more excuse he does make. Despite all, he does try to put it abroad that no head have I for the accounts, which is his veriest weakness. For all the world does know that no difficulty is there in them for me and 'tis Samuel who has little knowledge of arithmetic and whom division does defeat[8], and whom I do offer to teach. But not a bar will he have of it, though he knows not even his tables.

So should he keep me short and accuse me of seeking to rob him while he does play the great man who does lay out and though he does constant swear he should increase his crumb nothing is there that he does do without.

Too late it should be now for the money agreement, though 'tis clear that I must find some future strategy. Better to know what monies there are and what I should claim as my share. In this matter 'tis Balty who could further me: well would it suit him to make discovery of the payments for his errands my

[8] Samuel Pepys knew very little of mathematics and in July 1662 engaged Mr Cooper (a mate on the *Royal Charles*) to teach him arithmetic: they started with the multiplication tables. While Samuel mastered addition, subtraction and multiplication he was never very competent at division.

husband does receive, and where he does keep them. And this in return for a small fee when I do have my success. One thing which I do firm believe is that if money I had – then not so miserable would I be.

What length this entry be. And what satisfaction it does give. But late is the hour and no husband returns from the merry supper with his friends. And no order in the place have I made, which is my way to make all even.

## Wednesday 26

Where a new wife did dine this Christmas should be a notable event and worthy of record here. Much talk has there been of where to make merry, with friends or family?

For my mother would have that 'twas fitting that we should have the time with her, and much better would the fare be, but my husband did say that such arrangements would give *his* family offence. Always he makes the reason for staying from my mother's home and it does come to me that no meeting does he have with my family since we did wed, and something of the strangeness there is in this.

But no pleasure should it have been for me to present myself at the place of Pepys. So very brief I did entertain the solution that all should come and celebrate here, though no liking would I have for so much of the servant-work, and at least three maids and the cook I should need. But no patience did Samuel have for such a scheme. Wide would it force open his purse, though cunning-wise, this was not the reason he did give. No. 'Twas his considered view that our apartment is too bare and too small to have the entertainment. So must we dine elsewhere.

Bold did I suggest that *he* should visit to *his* family, and I to mine, which has the favour in it for me. Then later should we meet at the home of Eliza and Richard Harvey, who provide a good table, with food aplenty. And this did suit him, but not that we should beforehand go separately. For the twattlers would think that there is trouble betwixt us, which I do hold has the accuracy in it, and that no bad thing would it be to get abroad, though my husband has great fear of what people would say of him. And he did get fusty but it is nipped and no great violence is there in him.

And truth to tell I did taunt him somewhat and have my say that little enough food I have with him but even less should there be if we should dine with his family. Yet he did rise not to it but to say that none there are who could dine with us for such disarray there is and no place to put anything. Which is how he does have his little way. And 'tis this bouting which our married life does become, and who should have prophesied it?

Well did I dine with *my* family though the tongues do wag. Some excuse did I give for Samuel Pepys – that he does have the poor health, and be tired, and does work too hard, so too much would it be for him to attend *two* festivities. And that he does take the rest till I should meet him at the Harveys where Balty should escort me.

Much bad feeling there be between the husband and the wife, yet I did stand my ground and say that no law there be against the daughter taking dinner with her family. And if he should not choose to accompany me then 'twas not for me to go with him to his low family who know neither of good feeling nor good food. And the stalemate there was between us. But to my mother's I did determine to make my way. And 'tis certain that I did dine better than Samuel did. For she did observe the French custom and serve all separately.

Then to Eliza's where Samuel did come and though the pett was with him soon did it fade as he did eat and drink and be merry. And much kindness was there in me to see him sweet restored, though I knew not then what he did have in store for me.

Eliza too did have the turkey and most succulent but I should think my mother's plum porridge[9] and brawn[10] be the most superior. And all manner of pyes and tarts and sweetmeats and butter'd ale[11] and wine too, and all that I did eat that day did go far to make up for what I did late go without.

And just when I did know I had my fill and did think to make my way to the comfort of my bed, then did my husband take

[9] *Plum porridge*: dense soup of prunes, currants, raisins, and spices in thickened and sweetened beef broth: the forerunner of the Christmas pudding.

[10] *Brawn*: soused, pickled or potted boar's flesh, a Christmas speciality.

[11] *Butter'd ale*: made of sugar, cinnamon, butter: beer brewed without hops.

hold of me and make our excuses to our host. For further call we did plan to make, so he said. Then did I know that I should have no escape from the Pepys family – and most set was my husband's face.

But I did go with good grace to make my third dinner of the day, though no danger was there that I should over-eat at the table of John and Margaret Pepys. And I did resolve that our sojourn should be brief for much did I desire sleep upon all that feasting.

No merry making was there with the tailor-family who made not e'en the pleasant conversation, so many complaints there be about the lateness of the hour that they are forced to sup and such disapproving looks they did give me. And soon my good spirits turn to mopishness as I take my place among the sourness-brood. But some things do I learn. 'Tis clear that Samuel does take the measure of his mother to weigh what a wife does eat, for nothing did I see pass her lips, which does explain why she should play the fright'd mouse, for no hot humour is there in her.

And it does chill me that more of the Pepys family in Samuel can I see. For no grace is in them and very base they be. No gifts nor tokens do they make, but all is dour and talk of doom and what should happen in the land. Which as they can alter it not, why should they furrow over it? Tiresome it does become when all conversation ends in oaths on the great need there is for the getting of their crumb though what they should want it for I know not. If good plate the Pepys family do keep, then it is stored where none should see, and plain does it make itself to me that each day Samuel should put on more of his father's air. And naught does this please me. Yet worse should it be if I do follow the pattern of Mother Pepys. Lord preserve me from such end.

And too from Puss-Pall who does have the mischief in her. Many advances does she try to make intimate with me, but no encouragement do I give. Then she does sidle to me and say much information she should have for me, if I but be her friend – which does tempt me for much is there I should like to know. So with her do I step apart and hear her story which is that her brother does play with me, and gull me, and that many there are who do know that less than one month wed, and he does regular go awenching.

And sore tempted I was to strike that rude face. But no use would that have been to me. So I did keep my calm though all my inside does go the jelly on me.

'Tis possible though that this should be but the trouble-making in Pall – how else does such a plain one have any attention? But too I know enough to keep in mind that some truth there could be in it, which does most unnerve me.

Fair am I warned though, that no sister friend of mine should Pall the twattler be.

One thing only is there to do for it. To follow my husband and take note of his ways. And all that I do need to start is that this pissing pain should stay. Just when I do think it makes to mend, then does my husband take his right to stick his tool in again, and all flame and flood there is which does unsettle me. This be the pattern of the last night which did rob all the pleasures of my day. Though I can see it not – and some curiosity is there in me to know of its character – yet does the bubo make its mark and swell my groin so e'en the walking is painful, and all else cannot be comprehended.

## Friday 28

More should there be who do warn against the married state, and more ready the young maids to listen! Yet 'tis true, as my mother does say, that the maids think they do know it all and heed not the warning that the wedded state could be so soon the misery. 'Tis true my mother did her best to shew that love be not enough to guarantee the wifely bliss yet I did think 'twas more a measure of her own disappointment – and Eliza too – and not the same would it be for me. Yet I am made wise most quickly.

'Tis the pattern that I should never have made a prediction. Last night my husband did go abroad again without me, and gad about with fresh young blades whom he did swear he had seen not since we did wed, and most necessary are they to his business. Once more 'tis the cold and the dark, and no book either, which is my lot.

And time to think on how ill used I be and what I should do to have my time over. 'Twas the verdict of my past that Captain Holmes had not the stuff of faithfulness in him, and no security, which did turn my head to Samuel Pepys, yet the chance there is that I did judge both wrong, though too late now, and the Captain be much better bred.

But from my reverie I have the rude disturb. Rowdy comes my husband home with too much of the brew in him and the sore sight he should be. And to all this he does add insult when he does want to lie with me, and does state 'tis his right, and never has he heard that the wife does hold from her husband[12]. Which does put the ire in me for 'tis naught but the convenience I am for him, and no liking do I have for him, and for such ill usage. (And what sort of law should it be that does make the wife deliver, but not the husband for no food is there in the cupboard?[13])

And too does my abscess bell which I do have the certainty that he put on me, and the very last thing I should do would be make room for that popp'd-pintle to poke me. But easy task it was to stay him, for most unsteady he was and no strength in him, though much noise.

All night long did he sprawl, and most ugly. The wind and the drink do battle in him, and blow the loud noises, and give me no sleep. Sole benefit of the candle that is single and low for not so much should I see of him but enough to know he does slabber and no love can stay strong for such scurvy creature.

And I am become used to the ritual where he does wake afore the day and the ague is on him. And then he is with desperate need to make the water, and so he does struggle to the pot, which rare has the allowance for more to flow in't. *For empty his piss and his crap I will not.* And then the great bandy does again begin. And so regular the moves that all could be set out beforehand.

[12] Conjugal rights, or matrimonial rights, decreed that the husband had the right to the wife's body and the wife had no right of refusal; there could therefore be no rape in marriage.

[13] Frances Cobbe (1822–1904) pointed out that the law insisted that the wife be available to the husband but that it did not state the husband was obliged to feed the wife.

First does he hold hard his pintle and put a stop to it for to prevent the leaking, and then does he tightlip demand to know why he should keep the wife if she washes not the linnin, nor mends, *nor swills his pot* – though these he did not state clear to be my wifely duties afore we did wed. And no reference to them in the marriage service to my memory. Time past it was my white hands that he did hold up as my beauty and which he did vow to preserve. Yet now he does urge me to become the red-pucker-washerwoman, like his mother, and no more consideration for me than she does get. When he does start on this he deserves not even the answering.

When this part of the performance be done, then does he take to me. One hand does he still hold hard to his spout, but the other he does use to pull the covers from me, and low-like put it that I do spend too much time in bed. Days there are when he does call me slut and fool, and say that 'tis on my back that I should earn my keep, and I am become accustomed to his common ways when he does make the bawdy. Yet no way do I have to know beforehand which he should shout – that I do sport too little, or too much, or whether it be with him or some other. What I do know is that no balance is there in him and that he be dangerous when he does put himself in such a state.

But that it does hurt his head to raise his voice, all those who do close by inhabit, should hear the accusations and the complaint he does make of his wife. That she does try to rob him (which be always first on the list), that she does cheat on him (which be a regular grievance), and that she shews naught but sloth and sickness. That she does no wifely duties and should be taught the lesson with the salt-eele.

Then this morning he does make to give substance to his words. 'Spite his sorry state he does try to scowre me. And does he make to pull me by the nose though too quick I am for him.

But what to do? No way is this to live. And greatly tossed I am. But only mine own pot should I empty.

## Saturday 29

Balty does come this day and tell that good employment does my husband have and ample monies should there be. For my lord does have Samuel in his household, and several sums does he give him to serve as steward. By Balty's reckoning these do add all to thirty pounds each year, which is a handsome sum indeed and big enough for sharing.

Then too is what his father does pay for the tailor-errands, yet no princely fee should that be. But even the three pence here and there does have its attraction and this day should make the satisfied woman of me.

But Balty says much more is there besides. 'Tis not the yearly payment that should make a man rich but the chances of getting money while he be guarding the door. And he does swear that many there are who do pay Samuel Pepys to open it up to arrange the meeting, or bespeak the good character to my lord. Always is there the extra fee which does find its way to my husband's purse, and all this does have the substance in it.

Should it be that my husband does have receipt of upwards of seventy pounds each year, as Balty does suggest? And for which Balty does demand payment of an angel. Which I do tell him he should ready have – if he does find where Samuel does keep his store – for I will need to dip in it if Balty is to get it.

'Tis too much that my man should have all this and lay out on a base life when I do need the necessaries. And if I do find that other wenches there are who do reap from him, then should my passionateness take its course. No mention does Balty make of this – though 'tis the case that I did not direct ask him about Samuel's *amour* habits.


## Monday 31

And new close-kneed breeches which he does pass off as favour from his kin, and urgent does he say is his need of them, for no washing nor mending should there be done. 'Tis how he does chouse me . . . for nought do I see. And no recourse but to turn to Eliza and my mother for counsel though bitter it be to swallow all I did say and how I did make light of their wisdom.

Much of the charity is there in Eliza. No scoring did I see. Just the words to try the loving, which does have the sense in it, but the chagrin too.

All complaint did I put behind me and last eve – when my husband did return early – and shew some kind sign to me, our quarrel we did repair and make as lovers again. And well did I try to please him, and offer to read to him – from his own book, not mine – for he does complain of the tired eyes. (And too did I resist to say that those who try to read by but one candle and that burnt down to the faintest glimmer, should be asking for sore eyes, for 'tis true that 'tis his miserliness does bring it on him, yet did I refrain.) While I do still my tongue and say only sweet things all does go smooth and he does play soft on his flageolet, and together then we go forth to the cookshop at the Clare Market – which is the good place to be seen though not so good for the quality – and we did choose of a pot-venison to bring back here and quiet eat in, and together too. And I did smile o'er our supper and think on the pleasant life we should lead – e'en though it does depend on me to keep the peace and take no offence to aught that my man should do which does have the trial in it.

But all was as I did dream afore we did wed yet too the finger bowls[14] we should need if we are to partake of this again.

Much consideration was there in Samuel who did have concern for my privy parts which do plague me – and the offer of a poultice, and e'en the tears stars do come to him when I do tell him sincere of the stinging soreness that is always with me. And lulled we both are. So do we jest that both do have the pissing pain, and constant should the chamber pots have use, for the stone does undo the control of his water. And both of us do leak, and need the physic to stop up the piss, which does not make the same amusement when writ here as when we did discourse on it. Yet no troubles have we that the purchase of further chamber pots should not overcome.

Though 'tis true that soon should we be known as Chamber-Pot-Place if more we are to add. Already are there four, and the one for the bleaching[15] which should have no use but the

---

[14] *Finger bowls*: with no running water and few eating implements, finger bowls would be a necessity.

[15] *Bleaching*: urine was used as a bleach for washing.

piss, yet times there are when Samuel should be caught short and have the need of it for purging e'en though I do plead with him not to put it to such purpose.

But no complaint did pass my lips and all did stay in pleasant state till the issue of the monies I did raise. Which almost did put Samuel in a pett, yet this time did he show the cleverness in his evasion. Despite all my effort, 'tis clear that my greatest act be wasted. E'en though I did first consent to sport with him and not one cry did I make when he did bore into me and the scalding pain I did feel, and agony enough there was in the rubbing of the cankre to almost swoune me.

Still no protest-utterance I did make, but did promise that all care should I give to our apartment and all household order make, and be the pleasing wife as I had been – but that he should make me regular allowance to find the coals, the viands, the laundry – and the maid, to do the slops, which would have content in it.

Yet he does stop my mouth with kisses and tender say that some plan on the morrow we should devise.

So this scheme too does cake make of my dough and so much for the counsel of wise Eliza.

# 1656

## January
## Tuesday 1

The first day of the month and fitting time it be to make the money arrangements and again I must put my mind to it. All guile I know I have tried and to no effect. And better should I feel if I did cease my collying and let all loose though it should mean I fall most foule of my man.


## Friday 4

Brief did I wonder what risk this should be for as I make entry here 'tis with my husband abed beside me. 'Tis the first time I do take such chance – yet no consciousness is there in him and truly it were probably easier to wake the dead than to rouse him from drink-sleep. And this does bring me low for no good company is the drinking man.

'Tis now almost the daily habit. (And sure I am that this was not his way afore we did wed, which does put the questions to me – yet do I know that no daring would there be in Samuel Pepys to go to his father's place with so much brew in him, which does show his want of respect for me. Yet is this all that there be? Who does know what the man does transform to when he does become the husband! What mystery is this?)

But to my entry. What to do when at the latest hour, with full singing voice he does return, and great difficulty does he have with his parts, and much noise is there upon the stair so that most unpopular we be. And some nights there are when he does enter and just slip upon the covers, but others, in more cantankerous mood he be. From the hectoring (which I make to ignore) to the great threats he does deliver which have more of the harmfulness in them, he does do his disruption. And then too when he does have the fluxes and the slops that there are to mop clean, for times there are when he does retch as well as all other things which I do refrain from listing. And no pleasant life is this for me.

Yet what to do? 'Tis the gas from his bowels which does give the greatest offence. And all manner of assistance does it have from the posset to the purges and the physic. And no warning of this did my mother give. Truth to tell I think I should die from the poison air.

But I do know that great risk this is to put all down here. What if he should this second wake, and call to know what record I do keep? My heart does stop apace to think on it, and what he should do if he were to discover what is writ here. Undone would I be.

Yet if he were to get his senses now 'tis more like he would take to pintle-waving than peruse my penwork. For does seem that 'tis his way to be tool-governed. Times there are when he does call on it to rise, yet perverse it does shrivel, and the most poor sight it should be – just the small grub, and no instruction will it take of him, no matter how he does urge it to show forth. Then too there is when he wants it not, yet does it stand forth and command him. Quite the fright it should give when sudden-like, in the dark, his pintle does spring and summon him, for when it does get erect so does my husband follow it. The great fullness does wake him and he does declare that the damage there should be if the tool has not its draining. Which be not likely. For oft do I push it from me and soon does he return to sleep and no pain nor sickness do I detect in him from the danger to his yard! But no more prodding should there be till he does show more kindness to me, and money too. This I do resolve and no breaking of it.

So do I scold till my breath does go and the veriest shrew I should be. Yet 'tis for his own good too that I should call like the fish wife. For if the drink does cause him such great pain – why should he do it so continual?

This day did I say that if he does keep on, then the widow soon I should be. And no great regrets either, I did tell him. Many more there are who should have me – and next time, the better choice I should make (though I uttered not these words in my husband's hearing).

Again this morn he does greet the day with gouty temper and make to pay call on the apothecary. For badly bound he is. And he does think he takes the chill which be no wonder, for cold as death should this apartment be without the coals to heat it. But 'tis the kidney stone which should cause him the greatest pain.

## Saturday 5

Too much bulk these pages have. To conceal beneath the carpet each day does have the increasing problem in it. Yet no liking should I have for S.[1] to see this – forsooth it does scare me to my core that he should discover this account. Naked I am upon these pages and blown up I should be if S. were to know me here. 'Tis the veriest safest of places I do need to find – though where it should be does bottom me for no hiding can there be in here. E'en with no order – and the great stack of Samuel's books which do fill the place – too ready would such a pacquet be seen. But I do beat my brains to know where to screen this.

Most useful would my mother be, yet 'tis likely that with my father soon should she go abroad. Again my father does think to claim his legacy – and this time does want to borrow yet more monies[2] and my mother does tell that the veriest imprudent act it would be to let him go alone, so must she make to go with him. Which does not please me. For great need do I have now of my mother and kin, and not just for the concealing of my diurnal. Which 'tis true, my mother did first urge me on the manner of keeping and so does she have some duty to safe-keep it. Yet no solution is this.

And doubts I do have about Eliza's fitness. Ready reassurance does she give that all should be safe with her, yet do I know that no secresy this would offer for me. Though she might

[1] 'S.': Elizabeth begins to use 'S.' for 'Samuel' from this point when she starts to worry about discovery; she does not use it all the time.
[2] Elizabeth's father borrowed £1500 the first time he went to France to try for his inheritance; it still was not paid back.

swear to the world's end that she would peruse not my pages, yet I would believe her not. Nor even the decent tempting interval would she let lapse afore she did play me false and read all herein. As I would with hers.

But better Eliza should know all than that I should risk S.'s wrath. And no other way is there. To think is to do. This day will I deliver these pages to her guardianship.


## Monday 7

'Tis strange how I feel without all my pages nearby for comfort. And too do I shrink to know what Eliza does make of all. 'Tis true that some sheets I did remove and keep among the covers, for too naked did they leave me. And such shame that e'en Eliza should have all detail how low I do go with S. And not e'en the marrow bone for nourishment[3]. And while the good Lord does know that all this be Samuel's fault and none does rest with me, yet would those outside think that such ill-usage does cast the poor light on me. 'Tis the saying that no smoke should there be without the fire, yet what great fabrication it would be if the world did come to think that I be slothful, or the shrew, or even the shrill wife who has no interest but to rob her husband for the finery, and does cheat on him and make false complaint against the man. For not one particle of truth should there be in it, but Samuel's disorientation, and no justice would there be.

Yet I now can commence all my pages again and keep true record. The clean sheet this is. And first should I start with plans to sort me for none else is there to do it for me.

1. That no good life is this for me and so should I change it.

But where to? 'Tis the case that I would be the burden on my family who do make for foreign parts so soon. Yet perchance I could accompany them for the pleasant change it should be to see Paris again, and much contentment I could find in it. But no money for the doing.

[3] Marrow bone: a reference to the most basic form of nourishment that Samuel denies her.

More like that I should all cares of the world put aside and take me to a nunnery. 'Tis like in France a welcome I should find and that the Ursulines[4] do say that all trials are sent me to test my faith and keep me to the true state.

Yet should the religious life be the last and not the first solution I should find. And true it is that the Sisters might not have me. For no eagerness is there among them to prise the wife from the husband, or not so soon as the very months after they are wed. So while I should keep this plan open, yet let it not take my direction for more choice should there be.

2. Then should I leave such a husband and make mine own way?

But no joy would this be, and wise it is to know it. The young and beauteous widow might make the happy bargain, but no good prospects are there for the wife who is disobedient. A poor time I should have of it. For what way to earn the living yet stay among the honourable?

And no friends to turn to for shelter. For the short period it would be possible to spend my days with loyal Eliza, and even would she conceal me if required and no other roof I get for my head. Yet Richard Harvey would allow no permanent refuge in his place to the disobedient wife, for all the parish would ply him and no stomach does he have to make enemy of those who do purchase from him.

But e'en if he would have me, not till my old age would I have licence to stay on, so who would there be to care for me and keep the roof above my head? No one should there be. So worse plan is this than the nunnery, which does have the security for the aged years, if one should live so long. For 'tis true that no ancient nuns have I seen . . . and what to do with them or do they not see it to three score and ten?

Yet not to my purpose is this. The further choices do I need.

3. That I should stay and if I do, then 'tis money – and the slops maid – which are my urgent need.

[4] When in France as a child, Elizabeth had enjoyed a short stay with the Ursuline sisters.

[5]All reasonable manner have I tried with the miserly-man, and naught should I ever get willing from him, so the plan to milk him would be prudent to abandon for I should lose the use of my arm afore he should come to put his hand to his money belt. And while I do often think to relieve him of the excess which he does carry in his purse and which should truly be my share, when no fit condition is he in to keep charge of it, too much of the risk is there in it. For well about his person does he place it.

So then, if no monies I can find from my husband, to myself must I look. And what measures should there be for me? For no permission should Samuel give me to make mine own fortune. Which does have the vexation in it. For does he profess to want me living (though some doubt is there in me) and to look the beauty, and do him proud, yet no funds for this purpose, and no consent either to fare for myself. 'Tis true that men do have no logic, only pride which does contrive to make them askew.

So how do I set myself up with the monies? For having some to start does surely breed some more.

No extra jewels, or plate, or books do I have which I could pawn or vaunt so other option there must be. Perchance my services I could put out but few would I want to parade and no liking do I have to be the serving maid, or the scrubbing-swilling woman, or even the washer one, though too soon will it be that I do bear resemblance to Mother Pepys which does thin the very blood within me.

Some interest I should have in the dressing of hair – for most well do I frize mine own and all do comment on my art – and some disposition too for the preparation of beauty. But these are not wares which should ready sell and fill the purse.

Eliza does ask if I should teach the young, for 'tis well known that I speak well in the French language, that I do have the breeding and the manners, and the competence in most branches of arithmetic. Yet such has no appeal for me. 'Tis one thing to *learn* in the strict confines of the nunnery, and 'tis another to instruct, and to teach those whose parents do make much of them and give not the guidance of the religious order.

[5] Translated from the French.

Desperate I should be afore I would try my hand at this (though desperate I should almost be). But did I to Eliza make clear that such small monies are given to the woman-tutor that worse I could be to take the work for all the expenses that there are in it. And worse too if Samuel should detect me at it.

But just when no way I could see and melancholy were the thoughts that did come to me, then the inspiration we did have that made my spirits soar . . . of late, it seems that great need there is for those who can make the meaning of one language into another, and well should this work suit me. E'en the Montagus do oft have need of the interpreter, and most well would I fill the role, and certain it is that there is money in it.

So I did tell Eliza to put it round that the best translator from English to French does present vaunt her skills – and though I should come at the French to the English if commanded, much more difficult should this be. And not the same should I hawk it. And now must we wait to see if any there are who would want me.

Well could I go forth each day and do the hours, and have the money, and no inkling should Samuel have of it. 'Tis a good job, and much do I wish for it. And little patience is there in me.

Yet one task does take my time afore I have such offer. This week should I become the surveiller; my husband should I follow and keep the dossier.

## Wednesday 9

This day my menses do full flow and so I do lie abed and nurse my pain. Times there are when I do think that better it is to be dead than to suffer such sickness and indignity. For does it seem that all inside should draw from me, and nothing left there be – but the throbbing pain, and the burning piss, and the great swelling sore that I do feel agrowing by the day. And the wildpoppy[6] should I seek, for should it stay the flux of the belly

---

[6] *Wild poppy*: Nicholas Culpeper says of it that 'the black seed boiled in wine, and drank, is said also to stay the flux of the belly, and women's courses. The empty shells, or poppy heads, are usually boiled in water, and given to procure rest and sleep.' And '. . . it is also put into hollow teeth to ease the pain.' Translated from the French.

and the courses, and too does it bring with it the soothing sleep.

Yet much should I have to set down here. And I do will myself to record it – and to keep my wits which do threaten to give way. For yesterday my plan I did pursue and 'tis as I did have my fears. And some way should I devise to know what use to make of all that I did glean.

And if the habits of yesterday should serve as guide to my husband's duties then all day should I have to enter here what I did fish from him, for no appearance should he make before the darkness does descend. And full record of all do I intend to keep, for time there will be when to my husband I should put all this, and call him to account. For 'tis true that I but bide my time and be not under him.

'Twas well light this past morn when he did stir and still did I lie aside him. And though the ache he did have in his head, yet no connection did he give it to his carousing. But to the cold did he lay it, when he did have the wet feet and the chill of our apartment. Which it be in his power to attend to, but no taunting do I fall to.

Not so sick though that he does refrain from pulling for me, which I do meet with sharp words for no thought is it of mine to have his pintle push into me, and no liking either to be just the dish that he does empty in all his juices. And the great bandy we do have but no yielding is there in me. And the swift measures I do now take to foyle him, and put down his pintle, so that the fumbler he should be.

When he does reckon that no satisfaction should he have of me, then fusty does he take hisself from the bed, but not without he does call me many foule names and no jesting was there in it. But 'tis one thing for him to proclaim that the wife should submit and make sport with the man when e'er he so desire it, but quite another to make her bend.

(Yet does it strike me that perchance the sober life that Samuel should lead – then more his way would he win. So 'tis like his drinking does have the mixed blessing in it.)

Next does he take a crap. Still unused to it I be. And the purgatives which regular he does imbibe – e'en when he is taken by the drink – do add to the odour which does fell me. Quick did I learn that the best place to be when such event does occur, is well beneath the carpets[7] which do help stop up the fouleness. Yet this day no great burrow did I make for the need I did have to monitor and to see him leave, so one eye did I keep above to check his movements.

Then does he finish – and swill not his crap, but the chamber maid would still try to make of me! Then his doublet and wide breeches he does don, and great difficulty there is with the fastening hooks but no aid does he seek. Yet I do think that not all are done and the chance there is that his breeches should descend when 'tis not his intention. But no worry of mine should this be.

Next does he start on a long list to quarrel with me. That our place be too cold – and whose fault should this be? Though 'tis true that some coals do current lie there. But would he have me to rise afore him, and in the dark and cold, so to set a fire to greet him when he does finish with his sleep? No chore of mine was this while under my father's roof I did reside, and no fitting task now, either. True it is that no skill is there in me to set the fire for soon should the room be filled with smoke (e'en though my father does profess to have the cure of it).

Yet I do digress. And much more is there to add to this. But hard do I find it to face what I did see.

No easy time does my husband have to find his band for well covered it be among a goodly number of garments which unruly lie upon the floor, and do mix with his books, for which *he* makes no order. And then worse with the band strings which do total defeat him. But final touches does he make and stand ready to meet the world – though no kind adieu to me.

Alert do I listen for his foot upon the lower stair (which do squeak announcement of the comings and goings to our room), then swift do I rise and make to follow, and well prepared I be. Within the minute I go abroad to keep check upon him.

Down the stairs I rapid go, and no time to greet those who do stand around and seek the soothing talk. So should I catch him afore he does wend his way through this great Palace. So numerous the courtyards and passages be, that 'tis a veritable maze that all does make, and no wish should I have to lose him afore he does begin.

[7] Carpets: the term for bed coverings as well as floor coverings and sometimes hangings.

But the luck is with me. As I make my way across the courtyard which does situate near the bottom of the stairs, clear do I espy him in conversation. Some gentleman does seem to accost him and to implore my man, though what it should be I know not, for no hearing of them do I have.

Then do they saunter forth together, and slow should I follow and keep from their sight.

And down to The Bell, in King Street Westminster they did make their way. From those who did greet them 'tis plain that the regular my husband be, and that this should be the manner in which he does commence his day. There do I watch as Samuel does take his flagon of ale, and all is bon-homie with his friends though none there are of my acquaintance.

And little protection is there for me when the rain does keep up a steady pace. Long time is it that I do stand watch, and nothing amiss there should be. A weary business it is and the doubts do come on the benefits of all this skulking. Yet just as I do think to leave and pay call upon Eliza – for mighty cold are my feet and most welcome would the warm beverage be – then do my eyes discover what my spleen does fearful suspect.

For one bold wench there was who does come by and squeeze my husband, and no new sport does this seem to be for him. Playful does he hand her, and the nuzzle they do have, and hot did my blood rise within me to see all. Sudden was the urge to step forward and vent my rage, yet did I take charge of all my humours and stay aback, for full knowledge did I want of what the day would bring, and much of it was there left to follow.

Then did my husband take his leave of the company – though not the baggage that did hang upon him, and which I did detect the paint upon her, and the poor hair, and no fine figure did she lay claim to. Together did they set forth and did my gorge rise when gallant-like my husband did place her to take the wall, which rare he does with me and be most shameful.

And a great chill did spread o'er me as I did make observation and keep to those two who did defy the wet. To the haberdashers and booksellers at Westminster Hall, they did cross, and there did they dally.

And stounded was I to see – with mine own eyes – that the gloves he does buy for that hussy who does ogle him. While I did watch, clear should it be that he did hold aloft the prettiest gloves, and did match them to her hand. All smiles they were which does make my belly lurch to see, and then does he put his hand to purse and make purchase of them.

So sorely used I be. Not one farthing does he spend on me, not since we did wed. And nothing to fill my purse either which does reduce me now to but the few pence. No anger like this have I known before, and it does shake me.

Though next to blind I be with the frenzy that does brim within me, yet do I note that when the gloves are done that they do part. But not afore much cooing and tweaking – which be vile acts here and but courting memories now to me – and then the whore does set out while his eyes do follow, and fleet footed I should be to stay from my husband's vision.

And the hot anger and the cold rage each take their turn and which be the worse I know not. Nor even now should I know whether I should want the return to our loving state – or the fierce feeling of revenge.

No time then though should I have to think on what satisfaction there should be for me, for straightforward did Samuel start to make his way again. Back does he go down to the water and the struggle it is for me to keep apace. But not for long. Into the coffee house[8] there he does go, and so again must I stay sentinel.

All manner of men do go in and out, and the great hub of business it does seem. And but that someone should pay for his dish – which be not without cause for the great shirker he be – the more my husband must lay out, for the coffee be not less than 1d. So long did he stay within 'tis like that more than one dish should he drink.

Wet and miserable I be as I stand back and keep check, but just when despair almost o'er takes me and I should give in,

[8] The first coffee house was opened in London in 1650 by Jacob: in 1652 he moved to Holborn and by 1663 there were 82 coffee houses in the city. There were usually plain stools and tables, coffee at 1d a dish – and sometimes tea and chocolate were served. They soon became popular centres of business and newsletters and notices, circulars (advertisements) were made available. Women were not welcome and some of these coffee houses went on to become business institutions (Lloyd's) and clubs (Boodle's and White's). The coffee house Miles's was on the waterside in Westminster and was frequented by Pepys so this could have been the one on which Elizabeth kept watch.

then does Samuel Pepys step forth again and ayery make his way easterly, which does have the problem for me to keep with him. Did he not stay awhiles and converse with those who do greet him, yet should I have fallen far behind.

By the Strand we did go, and each great mansion he did pass did draw him to it. Well do I know that such fashion he does admire, and that 'tis his dream to live in such splendid style, yet none else but me would I have beside him!

No easy thoroughfare he did take but through the twisting alleys and past the Wall, and most wearied was I to keep such pace, and wet and bedaggled too, and oft should I stumble. And whether it be rain or tears that did flood my face, I know not, yet did it make my way more difficult.

Then down to Thames Street and the stench of stale mud did set on to me, and the veriest point it should have been to give up my mission. When London Bridge did stand afore me, then did I know how far I did walk – from one side to the other – and no heart was there left in me. Yet Samuel still did sprightly stride, and straight to The Hoop, in Fish Street Hill. Clear was it that he be expected, for many there were who did hail him and seek for him to join them.

So bone-tired should I be that little care did I have of discovery, so did I follow in from the rain, yet with some discretion to have no notice. By the hearth did I stand concealed from more than Samuel, and the Florence wine[9] I did have with me – though it did take my last coin (but one). There did I watch as my husband did partake of hearty dinner.

Many there were about him. Some business did seem to be transacted for I did witness the placing of coins in my husband's hand, though the donors be not known to me. And much drinking, and playing the music instruments, and singing – but no wenches.

(And I give pause now, for must I ask myself if better it should be that my man does sport with one, or with many? I know not which should make it the worst. All that I do know now as I write herein is that the sickness of my body does rival the sickness that does fill up mine head, and no future should I see.)

[9] *Florence wine*: a lady's drink.

Yet unfinished my history be and more is there to enter. For two hours or more my husband did make merry, and hard was it for me to keep my drink to stay such distance. Yet no more would I lay out. And when I did see the glower of the tavernman and fear that he should show me out, then did my husband make signs of leaving, so did I go afore and bide in Thames Street till he did make appearance. Soon did he step forth and all can see that the ale did warm him. Though I kept not the record of what he did eat or drink for his dinner, yet some quantity should it have been.

North then did he head and I did think that perverse enough he should be to set out for Highgate Fields – which distance should end me. But no. 'Twas the booksellers of St Paul's who did take his attention – and one among them who is the woman though no coquetting should I see her do. And then – *for one hour more he did seek among the books* – which does try me beyond all 'durance. Yet this far did I come and so should I see it to the finish. And one small volume he does purchase – which be no bargain for the time spent – and not for me it is either, for later did I note it and 'tis in the Latin language.

And darkness did make to descend, and the danger to be abroad alone did come to me. I did think on what to do, e'en to making myself known to my man for must he make his way to Whitehall. But while I did boggle it did become too late. Swift did Samuel stride to the waterside and it did take all mine effort that I did have remaining to be able to make pursuit. Not that I did meet up to him. As the stairs to Paul's Wharf I did reach 'twas time to see him hail the boatman and into the darkness he did disappear. And no money I had to follow him.

Then did I sit upon the stair and weep till some did gather round with offer of assistance. And though I did have the pretext that my purse did separate from me, and keep me from my husband, none there were who did lend me the coin that I should get the boatman. So though the night be dark and wet and much there was to affright me, yet must I make my way the long trudge from Paul's Wharf to Whitehall, and my best shoe ripped, and my dress amuddied, and my hair did hang about me. And the veriest most miserable night of my life it should be.

No comfort but to think what might have been, e'en to the

wish that Captain Holmes should come upon the scene and take me from all. For truth to tell, no smooth tongue would he have needed.

Yet none there were about but those who did take their pleasure in scaring the wits from those who do frequent the street. Some ballers there were who did harny me though I did bluff them and keep to the centre as Eliza does counsel. But the price be horse-shit which does cling upon me and take the last strength from me. 'Twas fear and hurt which does propel me homewards.

Weary to Whitehall did I make my way and climb upon the stairs. But no warmth should I find inside. Alone did I fall upon the bed and did I sob with all my might, till kind sleep did take me.

And then this morn do I have my rude awakening when all does come to me, and my menses too. And one harsh interchange with my husband.

No stomach did I have to turn him when he did wake me and demand to know where I should be when last night he did return to find me not in. And did he pin me to confess who should bring me to such a mess as my clothes did declare. And the jealous passionateness does possess him and he does accuse me of the vilest things and with some other man – as if I would have such inclination to give myself more misery! And usual would it be for me to lose all wits when he does brew up such a storm yet this time it was beyond me.

Yet e'en the energy for trembling does baulk me, and in stone silence do I think on how 'tis he who does warrant such questions and reprimand. And no matter that he should scold or beat me, no feeling should I know, and no answer give. And does he make the full mouth till he does take his leave.

And all this day do I stay here and make my entry. No company nor comfort there be, and the sickness does heavy lie. All the world does ride me and better it be that I should be dead. Oh Lord.

# Thursday 10

'Tis worse. This slide to despair. How far away my dreams to be Mrs Pepys do seem. And not one new piece of finery to show for it, and no blooming either. Just the pulsing abscess and the burning piss. And now these bruises on me. None there is who would envy me. E'en to be the paid woman of some gallant would have the better use in it. To be innocent, yet treated as the unfaithful wife does have no fairness in it.

This day past when I did have my monthly sickness, with all else that ails me, then did I think on what fearful mistake this marriage should be. No money and no coals, no visits abroad and no fine clothes, and the unwed life under my father's roof did show the advantage in it. And while I did think on the great blot I did make, and what family comfort should be left behind, then did my mother come and give brightness to my black day.

So pleased was I to see her, and most moved too. But I did make an effort to play the womanly part and keep my dignity, yet soon did my reserve go from me, and I did burst into tears and pour forth all my miseries. And soon too did my mother know of all my cruel usage, though no ready remedy did she have for me.

'Spite my worries, some cheer did my mother give me. 'Twas her belief that with management, many of my troubles would be mended. And much kindness was there in her towards my secret sickness. She did stroke my brow – which be not done since I did wed – and take the ribband from my box to fix my hair. All the tears she does wipe away and soft tell how she does care for me. With mother-love does she cosset me and change my night-geere, and gentle balm bring to all mine ills. Then when soothed and settled I be, brief did she leave me.

From the cookshop she did return with the warming broth, and the spicy wine. And some coals moreover, which with her own hand she does set and have the brazier burn, so even the room should have the comfort in it. Such pleasure was there in each other's company that moments there were when the pain did pass from me, and some laughter too we did have.

But when my mother did come to serve the broth, a fine time did she have to discover the place of the bowls. 'Tis true that much trouble it should be to find the items in all that disarray.

And the disapproval I did sense though my mother did not open betwitt me.

Fair it is to set down too though, that most angry should my mother be at my man. And fierce did she snuff him and mark his miserly ways. Yet too did she school me and soundly tell that 'tis the good wife who does cry-up her man and colly him, so that she does get her keep and more besides. And did she speak broad on my need to learn the winning ways. Which I do know is easier said than done.

Many stratagems did my mother set out for the betterment of my lot, and some there were that I did much prefer. For mine own part so choleric should I be when I do think on what my husband does bring me to, that 'tis the plan to put the poison in his porridge that I do put forward as the satisfactory solution. (And many the wives there are who have done it, as my mother is the judge.) More appeal did poison porridge have for me than the scheme that my mother did favour. For did she say when all be said and done, 'tis the rate of exchange which does govern. When the husband does want to take the wife, then should it be paid for. And the full purse there is in it.

And cross do I quizz her how this should be different from the paid woman who be considered such a ruined creature. Yet my mother will not be drawn. 'Tis how the world works, she does say, and 'tis for wives to do the best they can with what the Lord does give them.

No objection should I make to the wife being paid. 'Tis what should be allowed in exchange that is disagreeable. No easy matter for me to charge the payment from my man when no liking I have for the giving of the goods. Not even were my sore to heal, and the burning piss to cure.

Yet the problem this does leave me. Still should I need the coins to make merry so no two-ways is there in it. And my mother does give calm counsel. Her word it is that it be something the wife should get used to – and no great time does it take from her day. 'Tis just the push-pintle for the few seconds and no bane should this be. Then the money for the marketing, and the coals – and the finery – does flow. If all be managed skilful.

The start it should be for the wife to close-keep herself, and the husband should have only what he does purchase. My mother does say that this business does have the art in it and be the subtility of wise women, which should show the truth of it for it does keep to the counsel that Eliza did give me.

Yet reluctance is there in me to make this my way. And the cause be not that I think I should fail to learn such wifely arts. Simple should it be to take the money from my husband's pocket when he does seek to stick his pintle into me. No, 'tis not that which does have the difficulty in it. 'Tis that to take payment for the sticking is such a base act that it should shame all who are of good breeding. Certain I am that my Lady Clifford would not do it.

Then too there is the pain. So much burning hurt is there in it for me that I choose not to have this as my way of living forever after. So do I scruple about this way to keep a man so he can proper keep his wife.

But no patience had my mother. Stern did she enquire how else I should fill my purse for she has no means to supply me, though she should make all sacrifice. And 'tis true, no other way is there. So must I take her word that soon the weeping sore should close and the piss-pain pass, and all my disrelish, and like all good wives I should make no complaint about the sporting.

Too soon comes the time when my mother must take her leave and much toss'd I be. For near is the time when she should set sail to sort my father's legacy, and I do think to be lost, and lonely. But resignation did creep o'er me, and so soothed I be, that clear is my recall of the pleasure that did come to me as I did sink into sweet sleep.

But short peace should it be.

Frightened was I when first my husband did loud stumble in and jolt me from my rest. Dark it was, and the coals so low, and the great stir he did make with all his windfucking. And I did hear talk of how all now consult him and the big man he be, and sense was there in it for me to feign sleep and ignore him. But so full of foolishness was he – with the drink – that close by he did come to pull up mine eye and to enquire if I be within.

And hot is my spleen. No consideration does he give to my sickness. And 'tis true. No memory did I keep to aid me of the wise words of my mother – to rule with tender wifely ways.

And loud do I score my cruel husband – to some effect. Straight did he stand more sober, and fix to glower on me.

Great quietness was there betwixt us. Then slow did he turn and ready could I see that harsh thoughts did start to shape in him – though no cause should make itself known to me. And then, afore I could question or calm him – the shouting did again begin. And 'twas clear that it was his jealous sickness which did lay hold to him.

Who could know that 'twas the order and comfort of our room – and the *two* supper dishes – which do put the wrath in him? That he does see me night-dress'd and groom'd, and does add all this up to the entertainment of a man. Rough does he shake me and pull the ribband from my hair, and coarse does he charge me to confess the favours I did grant.

This it is that does touch the spark in me, and I do match his fury. Brief do I forget my soreness and vengeful hit back, and scratch as good as the blows he does give. Little of the affray does fix in my mind, but cause have I to remember that I did bite hard upon the hand that would strike me, for to this day I have the sore tooth as reminder.

No point should there have been to answer calm the falseness of the charge my husband did lay upon me, for so great was his fury that no likelihood he had to hear me. So much was my surprise, that naught could I do but fend off the frenzy, and give the curse to his very great stupidity, which did but serve to further enrage him.

And he did pursue me, but so poor his balance he did stumble at the obstacles I did place in his way, so did I keep from him. And soon did I think he should tire and fall into sleep, but no. Rather did he give call for the man who did cowardly hide therein, to step forth and front him.

All that was in our place could ready be seen so the veriest fool he did make of hisself when with slow step he did careful move to look where no man could conceal. With much deliberation in him he did push aside the hangings, and make to examine 'neath every book and clothing piece which does litter the floor. Till his legs do go, and he does tumble to the bed. Yet not to sleep.

For he did hold me fast, and with no caresse, and no contriteness in him for all the hurt he does cause, then did he force his way with me. No resistance did I give. The weariness was in me. And no more should I want to think on it. Does make the gentle time my mother did give seem but fancy in this hateful life.

Here should I give in to my sorrow. My tears do blot my page and make the mess of everything. Which is the nature of my life. And I do ache all over.


## Friday 25

(*Editorial note: written from the home of Eliza and Richard Harvey.*)

Much has passed since the last entry I did make, and all this does truly age me. Yet do I check my pages here and see that all should be complete – though some be teared apart – and all should be in order, afore I do begin, and yet what fondness it were to keep the loose and shameful pages in the covers when the most damning they should be and do bring my undoing. When I did think to be no worse then this does come upon me, yet does it make all decision for me.

My daily companion my journal is to me, and no liking do I have to be denied it. So did I consult my pillow and 'spite all, I did decide that 'tis my need to keep entry, for 'customed I am to it, and great comfort it affords me. When I do think what measures I should take, then do I need my quire and quill to guide me – else how should I know what way is best?

Yet I know not where to begin.

[10]That my husband did beat me and leave his mark and take his departure from me with no consideration. That no will was there in me but to stay amid the shambles, and ask the Lord what I had done to offend to warrant such miserable fate. And much of the guilt was in me, but bitterness too, and no cause should there be for me to stay with such a man. Though my mother should give counsel to the judgement day, yet did I know that no management could there be of such ungovern'd temper as mine husband did show. And no stuffing was there in me.

[10] Translated from the French.

So I did stay depressed and try to think what course to take, and ask the Lord to send the sign to lift me, when Eliza did come and be my deliverance. Distressed was she to look upon my sorry state and my bruising, and to see all confusion. And no coals and no fare for warming. And truth to tell when I did look on my surrounds and see all with her eye, then the veriest squalid place it did seem. No comfort bower where lovers play but a poor cruel place and most fervent was my wish to leave.

Eliza quizzed me not about my state yet her visage did speak plain. Not e'en the smallest demur did come from me when my second placket she did take to wrap my arm with the cut upon it. No talk there was between us, and we did together set forth. Eliza did help me down the stairs and be my shield from busy looks though the scandalizing be not prevented. All the world should know that the last night Mr and Mrs Pepys do brawl. So more of the stomachful it should show to leave, than to stay, when such wiping is the wife's treatment.

Though I did brave the curiousness of those who did watch, yet 'twas not pity but respect which be my desire, and my due.

No penny-pinching is in Eliza and soon – with maid – in carriage we hasten, for no walking could I do. 'Tis with the trust of a babe that I do give myself over to her, and she does take me along the Strand, and through Shoe Lane, to the quietness of her home in Holborn.

Poultic'd and dress'd my cuts and bruises be, though my hands still have the grazing on them – and then in clean linnins with the warm milk to sip on, and after all this the world does seem a better place, e'en if it be but temporary.

When the grief does look to recede, some discourse do we have on what did cause this great trouble betwixt my husband and me and so I do relate the full history. How my mother did do my hair, and fix the bed, how she did fetch the broth and put all in order but the two dishes she did leave. And that when my husband did roll in, he did mistook all for the sign that I had been with the man. Then did the wildness o'ertake him, and no reasoning was there in him. He did set upon me, and beat me, and force me, and a terrible night it was, and no more care should I have for such a scurvy knave, though he be called husband.

And no remorse does he show on the morn, and no amends to make.

Callous does he leave me to my suffering, and much there was of it, for no part of me did stay unhurt. And in that state – I did tell her – she did find me.

And full sympathy did she give me and say that rest I did need, and the few days I should spend with her till I did get back my health – and my looks – afore we did put our minds to the way through this trouble.

Yet did she seek my permit to send her maid to Mr Pepys that he should know safe where I am. But to this I did not agree. Perchance he should stay adrinking and note not my absence. Yet if this be not the case and he does get o'ertaken by worry, then no wish should I have to ease his mind. What is given to the goose is food for the gander. He should be drove to distraction afore I should agree to allow him e'en the smallest relief.

Eliza did not press me. Rather did we play like maids and do the mocking and tell tales of the trials of men. What boys they be.

And too did we look at many a book for some of the best do stand within Eliza's press. *Polexandre*[11] did sit there and ask to be read and *Cassandra and Cleopatra*[12]. And Madame Scudéry's *Le Grand Cyrus*[13] which I already know, though no hardship should it be to do again. This time more attention should I give when 'tis put down that for women, marriage be but slavery.

While we were at play, Eliza's maid my mother did forewarn, and she did put aside her preparations and pay me visit. Most loud did she bewail my poor eye which does close upon me, and which no glass I would have by to see it. Then does she say 'tis cruel she should be so torn betwixt my father and me. Dearly should she want to stay and see me through this trying time yet too great a folly it should be to leave my father to make his own way. For he is as open with money as Mr Pepys is tight with it.

[11] *Polexandre*, by M. Le Roy, Sieur de Gomberville, translated by W. Browne, London, 1647.

[12] *Cassandra and Cleopatra*, by G. de Costes, Seigneur de la Calprenède, Paris, 1649–63: English version Robert Loveday 1652–65.

[13] *Le Grand Cyrus*, Madeleine de Scudéry, Paris, 1653–55, London, 1653–55.

But in the quiet and easiness which is Eliza's place, the meaning does come to me and my resolve does steady increase. Full well do I know that all entreaty which would have me return to my husband, I should steadfast resist. Till the guarantees there are for my fair treatment. And the sign that all is well[14]. Though the conditions did still take some consideration yet did I determine that they should be set, and solemn oath to bide by them would be given. Only then would I think on the return to be the wife.

No yielding would there be. No tears did I shed as my mother I did bid adieu. Plain could she see that I do forgo the child-play and henceforth make mine own stand. Which does have the braveness in it, but the quaking too. Yet should I have the charge of my own life, and satisfaction and dignity this does bring me.

Afore she does take her leave, my mother would have me think on the good Palmers of Charing Cross. For Mrs Palmer long has been my mother's friend (like Eliza is friend to me) and to me too she does show much affection. Ready should they be to take me in – my mother does serious say – if ever I have need of lodging.

So does my mother take her leave and the great turmoil she is in yet does she know that this should be my own doing and all seriousness should I give to it. And the sadness is in me, for many months do pass afore we should meet again, and e'en then all dangers there are in't – for bandits, and pirates, and storms and so many possibilities of ill fate that no sense is there to dwell on it.

But no time there be for me to weep at Eliza's place – too many others there are who do it, and no rest do the babes allow. Some stirring I did hear betwixt Eliza and Richard Harvey, yet I know not if I be the cause. 'Tis Eliza's way that her man does make no objection to my presence here and that he does wish to convey to me his kindness, his wish for my speedy recovery, and the assurance of his protection till I should find solution; but not from him do I hear this, and some defyance of Eliza do I have in this matter.

[14] From later references this could be taken to mean as long as she was not pregnant.

And strange did it seem that first night when I did settle in the Harvey house. Like the invalid I did sit propped in my warm bed and take my butter'd eggs and anchovy, and my spiced wine, and when I did stretch within my bed and savour the ease in me, then did I know what great burden be lifted. No interruption should there be. No man to come arowdy home and put his self upon me. No moans and groans athrough the night, no chivvying with the chamber pots and no foul farting. No battle for the space within the bed . . .

Then I did lie and think on why Samuel did want to wed. And well do I recall that sleep did steal upon me as I did mull the break betwixt us and look to mine own conduct, and then conscience clear I could attest that no part did I play in our ending. My mind did wander to the courting man who so ready did sway me, who yet did play me false. And so to sleep.

Then does the world wake. E'en now the remembrance does afill me with fear. Instant did I know that 'twas Samuel's voice which does rise above all and afore I do find a light, rude does he burst in upon me. But Eliza did follow close by and the greatest relief her presence did give me. And from the candle she does bear I do see that Samuel does hold something fast in his hands – which threatening like he does shake at me.

And does my heart miss. For 'tis my diary. What a fool I be to leave all behind me, and too the pages that did most incriminate, and shew criticism of my husband. To be blown up so. 'Tis all now come to an end. And no more can I continue here. Too trying it is to think on these past events, yet should I need to record it here. But no stomach I have to put it down at present, though the time should come when I do not baulk at it.

## February
## Friday 1

Better this day do I feel and more settled my future does seem. And my journal pieced together again – though some damage it does sustain – and confront me with the record of my great unhappiness. On the morrow should I finish my entry which does close this chapter of my life.

## Saturday 2

'Tis a cold and bleak day and one which does set the tone for my tale. The veriest true friend has Eliza Harvey been to me, and this night past, with her I did verify all that did happen to me for my married life and we did agree that I did draw the lemon. And though for my sake she does say that still there are good things to befall me, yet I do know my life is ruined and the early death should be the welcome release.

Few good prospects does the world hold for the wife who will return not to her husband and do her duty – if he does call for it. And many there are who would force her, else she be damned. And 'tis true, that no pity did I show past-times, to the fond wife who did forsake her man, so none should I expect, just the tattle and twitter which be most galling. Yet must it be my fate for no other choice is there.

No quarter should I give. For no prospect either to return to Samuel Pepys who does public and private degrade me. Better the parish should pass judgement on my pride as the disobedient wife than that I should have the sentence to be scoured and scorned.

And better to starve by mine own hand, than by the neglectful husband.

So do I make my conditions. That not unless Samuel Pepys should sign the bond – for his word I should not take – that I do have mine own monies for the housekeeping, and that he should leave off the drinking, and the wenching too. For did I not see him with the doxies? And does he not know I know his game from my writing? And if he should keep these terms then perchance there should be some future in it.

Yet no substance does he give me. Rather does he make it that I be the wrong doer, that all the fault does lie with me, and had I but the energy, I should protest. The way he does cunning twist things and no looking to what this does do to me. For did he not make announcement that I did try to rob him, and that 'twas me who did try to gull him when it does seem that the full world does know that Samuel Pepys does go aregular whoremongering and keep not his part to his own person, but does purpose to put it any place that do pump him? And at the Harvey House did he not make the public scene so all should know his business and tell it abroad? And who should blame those who did forcible turn him from the house, if they should later turn the tattler? 'Tis his own fault and the mark of his betwitted state that he should call all else the problem and see not his own sign in what he does do.

And all did witness the great indignity. No liking do I have for Richard Harvey and all his household to see the gross way I do suffer, and the more, to watch me dogged dutiful like to follow home my husband for more such treatment. And there is resolve in me.

When I do think on how he did rant and rave, and hold aloft my diary and damn me for my disloyalty, there is still the sinking sensation in me. Every part of me did quake, yet whether it was for mine own safety or for my precious pages, 'tis difficult to separate. But truth to tell, 'twas the most afear'd I have ever been. And to jolt from such sweet sleep to brave such blows and bellows, 'tis the wonder that I did not swoune from the shock of all.

There he was menacing afore me, and with wrath did he claim to find me out, yet no clue to start to what he did mean. And then in the instant I did try to concentrate my thoughts to know what confessions I did record, that he did so set upon me.

All did gather upon the stair and when so many of the household I did see behind him and I did know my numbers, then did I take my turn and call him knave, and cowardly, that he should take my pages and keep them from me. 'Twas then he did make to tear them apart, and fierce did I strike upon his chest, and seek to seize them from him. But he did hold them too high up and none did then come forward to help me. Yet no great damage could he do with but one hand aflapping in the air, for the other he did need to fend me.

No abating was there of his frenzy. More and more did he work himself to fever as he did charge me with playing him false, and all manner of accusations did he lay against me. Constant did I clamour, and pull at him, as he did hold the papers from my reach. Yet all I did achieve was to tear some pieces from his grasp, and great vexation did it give me.

Truth to tell I think I did always know that a terrible sin my husband would take it to be to keep the record on him. For does he not have the constant fear that others do oft talk of him, and make the mockery? Bad enough he should be when he does believe that account is kept of him when none there is who makes it. But worse hounded he does feel when direct evidence he does have afore him.

And much was within my pages which did keep score against him. Not even the good angels should hold their grace if they were to come up against such lists of complaint agin them. So should Samuel show such passionateness that Richard Harvey did later say he was afeard my husband should fall down with apoplexy. Yet he did not. Though such anger do I feel come o'er me when I do stop and think on everything that some solution it would be if he had but dropt afore me, for then the sorry widow and not the ill used wife I should be.

And now no pity do I have for him. For all the score that I did make against him, I should give my oath to. And naught there was within my pages that did give substance to his charges of me. Now that I have had fair time to full peruse my entries, 'tis clear that no great sins did I confess to. No gallant in my bed has there been – only the record of the veriest stupidity and jealousy which would think it. No crimes of passion, and no other crimes of the spendthrift or the dupe. Just the account of the miserable life he does make for me. And the coarseness, and the pain. And much indignity. (And do I think to tell Eliza that 'tis likely he does give me the pox, but this is the last I have strength to admit to and I do shrink from such a list of woes.) Yet does my cankre improve. These weeks past when I lie not with Samuel, then does the burning soreness almost pass, and 'tis but another count I have to be relieved of him.

This he does read in my record. And does he hear it from me. And this does take away all his reason.

Base wretch, he did call me. And much more, which I should not enter here. And every accusation of disloyalty did he heap upon me. Then did he make to beat me, which did serve as sign for those who did witness the scandal, and grateful I was to see him constrained, though the choler was still high within him.

Richard Harvey and his man did take Samuel from my chamber while all the time he did loud protest that he would have his revenge of me, and truly did it chill me. Right down the passage I did hear his threats, and his cries that he did rue the day when he did meet me. Which does set my heart against him. No sight since do I have of him, and no knowledge either, yet Balty does offer to be surveiller.

Most strange does all this seem. For while I am the wife, yet I am not. 'Tis a limbo land, and weary I am of it.

Dear Diary[15]. 'Tis you alone who does know me naked as I do set down upon the page. 'Twas afore I did begin my life with Samuel Pepys that I did make of you my confidante. Much comfort have you been to me – and much trouble too. But now that I do plan to bring an end to this period of my life, so too do I think to end these entries.

'Tis too testing to contemplate. No future do I see for me, yet worse to return to the bitter garret days of my bridal time. E'en the few pence I should make from translating which my friends do find for me – and the lodgings the Palmers should provide – will keep me better than I did fare as the bride.

No more chances should there be for me to have a man, for no whore will I be. While Samuel Pepys does live, which does have the risk in it, yet do I lead but a half life.

One thing only should there be to take me from this path. The Lord should send such a sign[16].

## Monday 4

Nothing now is there to keep me aside Samuel Pepys. This day my termes did come, and 'tis true that pleased I be to see them. Yet such pain that puts me low. This I deserve not, though many are the blots which are mine own.

[15] There is no date for this entry: perhaps it was just another phase completed on the same day.
[16] This is probably a reference to whether or not she is pregnant.

# PART THREE

# Separation

# 1656

## February
## Thursday 14

No Valentine did I receive. Fool I was to think that he would use this day as pretext to persuade me to play the full wife once more. Better that I should have no false hopes and know that all is lost. And that is what I want it to be.

## June

This day did I see Samuel Pepys, and all alone, and no joy did there seem to be in him. So did I muse on all that does come to pass which does prompt me to break open this diary pacquet which I did seal and keep safe with me.

These hours past have I read this sad tale of mine own making, and most melancholy do I feel. For while 'tis true that some peace have I gained to end my wifely duty, yet added hardship is there in it. Times there are now when I must be without coals – and food – so not all does improve. And still there are long nights and loneliness too.

Yet do I wonder: does Samuel take a mistress? And if it be so, what should I feel? Balty does swear that he knows all my husband does, and that he does tell me all that there is. 'Tis his solemn word that no wenches does Samuel have. Yet I have no confidence in it. Well do I *know* my husband and that he does look to sporting.

So handsome did Samuel be that mine heart did sink within me, and almost did I forget what should drive me to my state. But I did turn away and firm press in my mind the hurt and heartbreak there had been. The list of grievances I did make in my head. Yet snoring and farting seemed no great sins when I did think on it. And more amusement than anger did come to me when I did remember the battle of the chamber pots.

And do I remember the satisfaction this journal keeping did bring. Some times I do look on my bride time with fond memories. Yet that stage be passed and no returning there is to it. This page does seal it.


## September

Sudden did the need for journal keeping come upon me this day and did I bring my pages forth again. 'Tis strange that when there is thinking to be done and a decision made, and I do try to add the pros and cons, 'tis the journal which helps me to make such measure.

Yet e'en as I do sit here this late hour, yet do I know there are no pros, and all is cons, and 'tis but the treat to make entry here.

True it is that I do make eyes at the gallant Captain Robin Holmes who does give me sympathy in my difficulties. No objection do I have to sup with him. And none there is who could survive without some sweet talk and words of praise. A silver tongue he does have to cry-up my charms and no harm should there be in it. And the trinkets too, he does generous bestow.

Now he does promise more. Though I should give more too, which be the bargain he does seek. The fine lodging house, and the new garments – and the Lord knows I should have need of them – and more besides. While he does fulsome speak of my beauty, yet does he know that it takes payment, which is the goodly thing.

Much worse could I do. No dispute there should be that he is the dashing man, and kindness too. Plain it is that he does want me, yet how long? And what should the price be? For truly the sporting holds no temptation for me.

My mother and father would tremble at it. No chance would there be to conceal it. Well do I know the answer and no great sacrifice it should be. Though 'tis hard to spend these warm days atied to the quill,[1] but no other means is there for my support and no assistance can my family give.

Times there are when I do think that to have learnt the needlework would have advantage in it: no more money should there be but perchance I should be better dress'd.

So must I say no to Captain Holmes, though 'tis with some regret. For will this change our friendship? No man does return for more when he is rejected.

Not even Samuel Pepys I should think.


## 23 October

Today is the anniversary of my birth. Full sixteen years I be and nothing is there left for me. Not even one present did I receive.


## November

This day did I take myself to Church and thence to Lincoln's Inn Fields, where I did chance to meet whoever might stroll in that place. None that I do know or care to see. No pleasure it be to go abroad alone.


## 1 December

No other amusement do I have but to read through this record again. 'Tis one year, this day, since I did wed. What dreams I did start with, and how short lived. And do I wish to have the time over again. Yet what should I do? 'Tis well to set it straight here.

First do I make the conditions. That regular monies there should be. And hours too. And no wenches. Fair too then would I play my part and do my wifely duties. So would I willing lie with him, and keep all ordered and clean. And well should I please Samuel so he be content.

[1] Atied to the quill: a reference to earning money from written translations.

Yet all this be but the wild dream. No chance there is for it. Not one word from Samuel does come to me. Not since those bitter days.

When from the Harveys I did send him hence, then all I did have from him was scoldings. Twice did he write and naught but hot words and threats. Eliza would have it that no man does believe the woman who does say nay and leave him, for they do all think we play but games for their entertainment. So no sweet words did come to woo me back. Rather did he say that I should tire and soon return, for who was there to keep me? Which did serve to make me stand firm.

And all who did close observe Samuel did see him come to sorry state. 'Tis told that many there were who did laugh and jibe him and say he could keep not the young and pretty wife. Afear'd he was too, that my Lord Montagu should hear, for only those of good character did my lord want to have as the guardian of his children.

Truth to tell, Samuel's pride did suffer the almighty blow. All the world did know that I did leave him for the very meanness of his ways. Yet 'twas his own fault in part, for did he not make announcement of it where e'er he did go? At the Harveys, the public scene he did make, and who should blame those who did forcible have to put him from the house and take my pages from him, if they should later tattle about the churlish knave?

Balty who now does serve as informer and keep me prised of Samuel's ways – though not enough, and too much of the expense is he for me, and much more would I know. Balty does quoth Samuel who did first try to mend his pride and put it about that I should have but the few days pique afore humble and polite I should apologetic return and mend my ways. And those there were who did give him counsel and steer him to this course, but they are all proved wrong. Nine months now do I make mine own way and will continue.

And when this did become clear then did Samuel sing a different song. That 'twas *he* who did put me out for my slothful and spendthrift ways, and making the cuckold of him. Yet none there are who would put the weight to this and soon did he know it and be the butt of the mock and jeer. For only the greatly-gulled would not see that 'tis more of Samuel's fondness than my ways that be the foundation of these fancies. Yet did he seek to keep brave his reputation as the wronged blade and not be looked upon as the miser man of rude temper.

But then does he make the serious change; no utterance does he give but keep all quiet and Balty does say 'tis moroseness now that does stamp him, and that private Samuel does have it that 'tis all up and never should he have me as wife again.

Though this should suit me yet do I feel the sting in it.

Yet times there are when it does seem that 'tis but the exchange of one dreary way for another and some sense there is in the saying that 'tis better to have one to pull a crow with than to quarrel with one's own.

'Tis Eliza's belief that the second chance there be, but I do doubt it. Naught is there left for me but to live out what small time does remain for me and to offend not further the Lord.

# 1657

## January

Balty does give out that Samuel does have more responsibility with my lord – and more money too. No monies are there handed to me.

Just the devil toothache. And it does rain, and harrowing cold it be.

## February

Good reason is there for me to put pen upon this page. Though fancy only, it should prove to be, yet should it bring some comfort to my dark day. 'Tis the money-worry which does plague me. For lodging, and coals, and victuals too. And desperate I be for finery. And all this does make me break, so do I confide in Balty, who does have the plan. Yet whether my father's footsteps he does follow with bright inventions which do *take* money, rather than *make* it, still I know not.

But 'twas his scheme that I should write the story of my life. With all my ill-usage, so to serve as warning to young brides. For others there are who do it and while the scandal there is, the profit is there too. Small price should it be to add to my reputation, and some revenge should there be. Much liking do I have for such a plan. So should I counter the twattling which does put it round that 'tis my husband who will not have me, when 'tis I, who will not have him, which is the veriest truth.

'Tis a great lady – the Lady Marchioness Newcastle – who does do this present book, and much talk there is of it. (My mother does say that 'tis the Clifford blood which is in her that does explain her daily scribblings, and so too it should for me.)

'Tis the story of her life which she does public make[1] and no ordinary tale it should be.[2] 'Tis said that her man, the Duke, has no mind against her printings though she does tell all the secrets of the marriage bed.

And well could I do this.

Should she get any profit from it, I know not. Such a grande dame should surely have no need of payment for her bread. Yet something for her there must be in it, else why should she court the jeers, and the jibes her husband does get for the wife he bends not to truckle under.

Some do say that if the story does have the art in it, then certain 'twas written by a man. No favour do I give to such a view. What reason should the Marchioness have to take the sting for some man who, unlikely, should seek to steer away from fame? More like it is that this be a lie put about by some man, for 'tis ready-noted that many men there are who shew great reluctance to allow women their true worth.

E'en this be the very point that does concentrate the mind of the clever Lady. 'Tis Balty's report that there is much scandal-talk about the book at St Paul's Churchyard. Bandying is there among the learned men who do charge the Lady with challenging God – and theirselves as well. They would have it that there is much of the madness in her, and that she knows not her proper place. And that she does offend the leaders of the realm.

And some women too. They do declare that the Marchioness be distracted, for she never could be so ridiculous else to venture at writing books, and in verse too, that any might peruse.

[1] 'The True Relation of My Birth, Breeding and Life' which is from Margaret Cavendish (Duchess of Newcastle), *Natures Pictures Drawn by Fancies Pencil to the Life*, 1656.
[2] The Duchess of Newcastle, (1623–1673) was born into a wealthy country family and educated at home. Poverty came with the Civil War and she went to serve the Queen – first in Oxford, then in France, where she met her husband. He was thirty years older than her, had also lost his fortune in the Civil War and much of their life on the Continent was spent evading their creditors. They had no children, and the Duke encouraged his wife's literary and scientific endeavours. They returned to England in 1660. There is a recent biography of Margaret Cavendish entitled *A Glorious Fame* by Kathleen Jones: 1988 (Bloomsbury).

So should they say there was madness in me if my lines I did put to public view.

'Tis true that all these entries I do make tell of mine own birth, breeding and life. Though 'tis not the high tale of the court, yet it is no common recital[3]. But if I should give my words to the bookseller, then should I be placed e'en lower than the whitester and prey to scorn. All should take it as the sign that I did have the loss of my senses.

Yet perforce Samuel Pepys could no longer ignore me. Bad enough that his own eyes should see what account I keep here. Worse to put it forth for all the world's meat. Sorely vexed he would be – though he should have proof that I did still breathe. Not that I have the interest in him.

And should I spell out to Balty what consequences there could be. That I might get no monies at all. That it might be me who does make the payment, with my good name, my senses – and my health if my husband does then find me. So no fair solution it be that I should make the book.


## 14 February

No Valentine I have. Not one. 'Tis a miserable life.


## 23 February

Today is the twenty-fourth anniversary of the birth of Samuel Pepys. I did look to send him the gift but then did think the better of it – for naught do I have from him.

What revels does he have this cold night? Certain it is that he be not alone.

[3] More likely a reference to her own aristocratic origins than to the nature of the story.

## April

'Tis well that the spring does announce its coming for the miserable winter it has been and no more of the cold and damp do I wish to see for truly it does add to my melancholy which does lay me, and more besides. And a mixed time I have of it.

Full well should I know where the sporting does lead and yet so many times did I lie with Samuel and nought was there in it. Yet just the once do I give way and the Lord does see fit to punish me and no liking do I have for the remedy and the fluxes which do make the most havoc and so hard to stem, and e'en now my good health comes not back to me – and all this consequence for the one night of warmth which – e'en should it prove to be the veriest ecstasy, which it was not – it has not the worth of the after price in it[4]. Yet all manner of questions does it give out for 'tis clear that 'tis not decreed that permanent barrenness be my fate.

But the lasting lesson I did learn from this and no temptation should there be. For no guarantees of protection are there for the disobedient wife, and no safety, and two mouths I could never feed. And no pleasure in it anywise.

## May

Shameful do I admit that this day I did follow Samuel Pepys to see how he does while-away his day. And 'tis true, that no baggage did I see him with, though one day does not a true test make. And when no whore did hang upon him I did brave it to step up and speak with him and first he does start, and then play the awkward part, and truth to tell I did think he did act pleased to see me which I did find pleasing . . . and would not have made prediction.

[4] This appears to be Elizabeth's reference to an affair, pregnancy, and a possible abortion – or miscarriage.

# June

'Tis well that my mother does return and did her presence make me think on these pages. Though much smoothing does she need for my father does spend all that he does borrow and more, and my mother has the want of ready money and none should I have to give her . . . and that I would have as the married one, who does have the thriving husband. Which my mother has not either . . . 'tis hard to treat my father with the respect that is his due when he does rave to make his fortune by the discovering of King Solomon's mine . . . and all treasure maps from the Bible he does make and seek to borrow more against the great find . . . which does vex me.

# July

This day I did go a-strawberrying and such a pleasant pastime it be, that I did think to keep the record of it. Many months has it been since I did write herein, for no time there be. Near all my waking hours it takes to earn my bread so e'en Eliza does say that 'tis the poor friendship when no time there is for meeting.

Much should I prefer the tripping we did have this day – and the man to earn the bread, and more besides. But it is not to be. So I must do the best with what there is, and grateful I am to have e'en one day for release.

All this does come about by reason of my toothache, which does constant try me. Two teeth I have which make threat to fall out and to any who should listen do I make the complaint. (And the worry is there too, for no liking do I have to see my teeth fall from me and to give off the sour odour from the softening of the gums. 'Twould be hard to be the beauty with the foul smelly breath and the gaps for the teeth, so will I try any measure for remedy.)

'Twas Eliza – or my mother? – I remember not which – who did first put forward the healing properties of the strawberry to this end. Though none there was to be had when it did come recommended. But now that the season does come – and the toothache and more – does grip me, so did we plan this excursion. And Eliza and I, and the three babes she does have with her (and who should be better left to the nursery) do venture down the river to gather the strawberries which do abound in the woods.

No tragedy was there, though sore was I tempted to make one when I did seek to still the child who does tax the temper of the waterman. And no task is it for babes to gather strawberries. Either they did bruise them, else they did eat them, and with dire effect. The *Herbal* does have in it the healing properties of the strawberry, yet naught on how it does make the young stomach-sick.

The sights I did see from the mouths of those babes did lead me to vow that ne'er should I eat of the strawberry again. Nor have the babes either, for that matter.

'Spite all, the sun did shine and the veriest fair day it be. Many a small reddish root did I gather to make up my medicine. 'Tis well known that without aid the strawberry does cool the liver, and the blood, and the spleen, and the hot choleric stomach (though not of the young). And when brewed, the tonic it does make to cure all inflammation, and stay the bloody flux of women's courses – which I do have the use for.

'Tis the cordial from the roots though which is the most efficacious for the fastening of loose teeth and the hardening of the gums. This should my mother make for me.

Eliza did know of the great beauty use – and clear it is that she does have some need of it. She is with child again and does it take toll of her complexion. Yet when she did list how to prepare this, we did have no enthusiasm for it. For when the berries are put into a body of glass – which can be well closed – then 'tis in the bed of horse dung which it be set. By this method do they make the mask which does end all flushes and wheals, and other breakings forth of hot sharp humours in the face or the hands. Or to bathe therewith is to take away the redness of the face, or spots, or other deformities of the skin, and to leave all clear and smooth.

We did think to get the horse dung to set it in, but I could not do it. When close I did get to some fresh clots, 'twas mirth which did o'ertake me. Eliza did want to know what it was which did shake me, and so did I tell. The stink did remind me of my husband.

'Twas a good day in all.

## August

Balty does tell that Samuel is struck down with severe sickness. 'Tis the kidney stone which does get him.

Who should nurse him? Should he die? What should I want from all this?


## August

Pall Pepys does come today and say her brother be most ill with the stone and 'tis thought that he should die. 'Tis the first time I did ever see her since I did play the runaway, and no improvement is there in her. The puzzle which is in't, is why should she come for no care she has for me. With curled lip and the sneer in it – which is her way – she does deliver her message and does add that my husband's family do hold that 'twas the worst blot he ever did make in his marrying of me. All fault do they pin to me for the scandal, and his ill-fortune.

Though no stone-maker I should be. 'Tis his mother, and other members of his family who do suffer so, and Samuel did always say that from the cradle it did beset him. So no blame to me.

Yet does my blood rise in alarm for the care of my husband. And is it he who does send Pall to inform me? But none of this in me should she see. Aloof do I hold till she does leave but then the panic does full force come upon me.

What would it be if he should die? What loss to me? Then should I be the widow – and perchance there would be some monies in it.


## August

Three days now I do have the regular bulletin from Balty who does feign to make eyes at the pesky Pall, so to get knowledge of Samuel. Flatter'd she be by such attention – which is all she does have though it be but a boy – that she does give up what she does know. And much danger should Samuel be in.

Nights passed I do consult my pillow on what this should mean. And should God judge me.

## August

This day did I visit Samuel Pepys and all that Pall did do could not prevent it. For did I call shame upon her head that she did stand between husband and wife. So, churlish she did leave her sentry.

And when mine anger did leave me, 'twas the strangest feelings I did have. To go once more into the room which once I did enter as the bride. Much is there still bare about it, and a cheerless chamber, for no woman's touch was there in it.

Soft did I tread to my husband's side, for no sign was there from him. Some help was this, for toss'd I was on what way to compose my features. And when close by I did get, 'twas well that he did sleep, else should he see my great shock to witness his veriest feeble state. Most ravaged was he and it did seem that not long should he cheat death, and no disguise did I have at my ready command. But by him I did sit, then take his hand, which I did gentle stroke. And I did know that satisfaction there could be in our reuniting.

My journey home did fix my mind on what is to be done. Fierce did I curse the poor nursing that my man does receive. Much more should he need if he is to have the return of his health. Well did I know 'twas my desire that death should take him not – yet what to do?

## September

Balty does say that Samuel did ask to see me. But little time is there from my work, and, too, I know not what to say if Samuel should have enough of his senses returned to speak with me. Then did I ask Eliza to be with me, but – go yourself – she does spit, and – know what you are in for! 'Tis being with child which does sharpen her tongue and her temper and no heed do

I give her. For no knowledge has she of life on one's own, and well do I know the troubles with it.

Yet most confused I be.

## September

This evening did I spend with Samuel Pepys, and tell all of my struggle of these months – though not with Captain Holmes and other small distractions which would have none of the healing medicine in them.

And Samuel does soothe me. And tell too how hard it has been for him, and not just the stone in the kidney. Though we say it not, yet do we test the waters and who should know what comes of it? But this time would I want agreement and all set down. Yet still this be no more than fancy.

Strange that Samuel did bid me adieu, and I did return to this my narrow bed, which be all I have.

## September

Eliza does call me fool, and one who learns not the simple lesson. All that I should get beyond what I have now would be the privy soreness and a beating and a brood of babes. My mother does say 'tis my decision.

## September

'Tis not a fair world, and most miserable and affrighted I be, and more besides.

This evening did I see my husband who does make slow recovery and we did gentle talk of the past and confess our errors – and he the more than me – so that great warmth was there in me as we do move to make our life together again. 'Twas with sweet thoughts on the future that I did leave him and make my way to my lodgings, and no proper notice did I give to the lateness of the hour. In truth, I did make my plans for how I should have the time to purchase the saxifrage[5] – for all do say 'tis excellent in provoking urine and in the distemper of the kidneys. And now that my husband does show improvement 'tis unlike to be a waste of monies, so do I think to put my purse to it.

Then just as I did turn from Whitehall Stairs to make my way along the King Street to the Charing Cross, rude were my fancies interrupted. This rogue did come upon me and rough handle me and hiss to take my money.

Yet did I keep my senses and call on any near to give assistance. But none did come and this scurvy knave does try to force me with him. So did I struggle on mine own to foyle him, yet did I know not what fate there should be, though no knife nor other weapon did I see. But he did seize all I did carry (though not the monies I did keep in my girdle) and did threaten more, so that I did risk to swoune and be undone. When one there was did come to my aid. A young gallant of fine figure who does step forward and much gratitude did I shew to him.

Firm voice and strong manner does he show the coquin who does act the pigeon and quick unhand me and flee.

Full care did mine unknown knight give me. And he did deep regret the loss of my purse and make to repay it – which I would not have. Then did he say 'twas not right that one so young and fair should walk alone and have such rough usage. And he did offer to be my escort to my lodgings, else to some select tavern where I should partake of strong spirits for my revival.

Clear it was I be distressed – and some dishevilment was there about me too – and I did give apology for my state, which he did waive with pretty speech on my beauty – which did help restore me.

Yet did I think to make mine own way and though he did try to fish from me where I should lodge, yet would I say not. Though no purpose he may have to use me, still it is not fitting

[5] *Saxifrage*: 'the root, herb and seed are used being all accounted excellent in provoking urine, and of great service in the gravel, stone and other distemper of the kidneys, also in expelling wind.' (From Nicholas Culpeper's *Complete Herbal and English Physician*.)

that the married woman should have such company, so I did take my leave.

Home I did come and all did make its presence felt. Yet do I shake for the danger, and could I cry for the loss of my purse for no saxifrage now there should be.

Yet am I safe, and some good fortune was there in it.


## September

One test did Samuel pass. I did tell him of the robbery against me – of all I did possess – and not only did he shew great concern, but he did help make good my losses. Near stounded I was when guineas he did give me, e'en afore I did say that 'twas for physic for him that I did plan to spend it.

Yet do I know that his purse be far from full for no errands can he do. But no complaint did he make of his impoverishment. Rather does he say that good fortune is with him now that he does get his health back – and have me.

And many a good word he had for me when I did tell how I did throw-off the knave who would take me with him. No wisdom was there in it to disclose that I did have able assistance. Samuel did give as pressing reason for his recovery that he does have the young wife to take about, and to protect. Which does please me but softens not my resolve to have all in writing and with witness, afore we do share the same roof again.

And did I purchase the new placket with lace trim and the stiff bodice too which does have the fashion in it – for no need is there now for the saxifrage.


## October

My better judgement does have it that all is well, but 'tis not sufficient. More than the sweet words I should want his time, and do I set down here what should have agreement.

The monies. Regular and reasonable amount and all signed, so no default.

That he should not leave me for long periods on mine own, but we should frequent sup together. And go about too.

And no wenches. That faithful he should be to me. And his temper should be well govern'd. No rages, no beating – no charges that I do rob him or keep the man in the closet. Some others I would want to include – but no help is it. 'Tis in vain to prohibit the farting though much could he do for discouragement.

All that I should do is put my list to him. Which does sound simple enough. But much is there in it to cause the stirring – and my legs do tremble. But naught else is there for it. So should I take my list all drawn up, and if he should sign it, it be good proof that he does turn over the new leaf.


## October

So he does make the counter conditions. And the long list it be that I must think on.

That I should order and clean our room – which is reasonable, and no trouble in it – but not his books. And no lovers should I take – which I have no intention. Not even *thoughts* of lovers he does insist, which is quite the task, but hard to stick a charge against, so no difficulties are there in't.

And a quiet tongue – though no need is there for this stipulation. And that of the monies I do have receipt, I should keep the good account.

Yet more. That 'tis my duty to be the chamber maid, and to attend – each Sunday and with no complaint – the home of his mother and father. Only worse should it be to oblige me to speak civil to Pall, which he does not put in't. And too, no breath about the nunnery, no talk of popery which in these turmoil times does leave my husband afear'd[6].

All this would he have drawn up and so should I sign as he does mine. Solemn will I think on't – though truth to tell 'tis

[6] During the Protectorate it was dangerous to profess any allegiance to the Pope or to the arrangements of Roman Catholicism. Elizabeth – who could already have been suspect because of her time in a French convent – was capable of playing on Samuel's fear and of threatening to declare herself a Roman Catholic which would have seriously damaged his career.

the chamber pot and the calls upon the tailor and the washerwoman[7] which do baulk me.

## 10 October

When I did think on't, one more condition did I put. That I should have leave to keep my journal, and that this he should provide for. And to give his solemn oath that no interest it should have for him, and that no way should he peruse it. And though he does say 'tis not done for the wife to have the secrets from the husband, and that no good does come of keeping record, and ne'er should he stoop to such charging of those around, nor show such want of sense, yet does he know my serious intent and no good should it do him to boggle at it.

And did he start to govern his choler on this condition for 'twas clear that the protest did rise up in him but mightily did he bottle it and bravely show only to me the goodly face which has no want of fine feeling in it. So do I think that he does have new measure and that some chance there is that we should sort our difficulties and find a way together.

And did it suit my purpose to win him to the rewarding ways of entry keeping, so should he know the need of stationery and give provision. I did counsel that certain I am that it would sort him to set down his days, and great satisfaction would he find in it, and not so many wild thoughts about those who would get at him.

I did offer to show how it was done and too did I promise that never I should read it – though I did say in my head to the Good Lord that only in necessity to discover whether he does keep his word, which is a fitting thing, should I want to look on it, which be not the breaking of the vow but the keeping of mine own, and his.

'Tis true that the concentration he would need if he did desire to keep the accurate record of the great doings that pass around us – and much talk is there about what rule there should be and who does take charge of the realm and dangerous talk

---

[7] *The tailor and the washerwoman*: Elizabeth's rude references to Samuel's parents.

too – for I do know the vagaries of my man who does more see what he should want to see and strike the grand pose – than he does accurate observe.

But false fears these should be. For who else would want to read his meanings? For his purpose only would he put all down and none to even know what his head does make out of the ordinary.

Though he does scoff now at the fondness of such pastime, and give out that no occupation it should be for a man to keep notes of his days, yet do such words come from one who has not tried it. Perchance the time will come when he will rate it more highly.

When I did say that 'twas true comfort for those who be alone and melancholy, then does he say that I should need it not again when we are come together which does have the test in it.

And much sweetness was there when we did solemn swear that always should we care for one another and no unkindness would there be betwixt us. And God be our witness.

## October

Eliza does have the daughter who does just miss the day of my birth.

'Tis told that a bad time she did have but now does do well. Much have I neglected her of late. Surely did she forgive my absences when I did work for my bread, but no stoic is she when I do spend my days beside my husband e'en though 'tis the truth that still he does need the steady care.

Much do I enjoy these days when 'tis Samuel's need to stay abed. At my leisure I do attend and give him comfort, but to mine own bed I do return each eve. Yet on the morrow should I go agossip to Eliza, and take a gift. While Samuel does suffer indisposition 'tis my lot to take the purse and go a-marketing, and much does this please me.

None should quarrel with my skill. All necessities do I put by yet still some little extra for mine own purse, which is right.

Each day is there discourse betwixt Samuel and me as we do

look to the settling of our difficulties, yet no common agreement do we reach, so no signatures. And too, this does have the problem in't. For when all is drawn up, and has the witness in the proper manner, where should it be for safe-keeping? 'Tis Samuel's view that 'tis the place of his father which is most fitting, but on this I should consult mine own interest. No liking is there in me for the tailor to take charge of the papers to which perchance I should need ready recourse. Unworthy though it be, yet do I have the smallest doubt that if we did lodge such agreement in the care of the Pepys family that 'tis Samuel who would have the benefit.

And what if Puss-Pall should have the perusal of it? How she would put my nose in it, and prattle to any who would listen, that I do swear to keep a cool tongue, and chaste head to not e'en let the *thought* of a lover enter in it. Too abasing would it be. Yet where else?

No consent would Samuel give to my mother – or Eliza – to be the guardian. Yet I will not forgo the signed agreement for want of a place of safe-keeping.

Samuel too does shew impatience and does talk more of sporting with me – which is testimony that his state does improve, though the weakness is still in him.


## November

Agreed. And all to be drawn up and signed and sealed. Reservations are there in me that we do put all with Mr John Pepys[8] yet no other would have Samuel's blessing, so to it I did bend. (When I did tell Eliza that 'twas my worry that Puss-Pall should see it she did hold that no good would it do her for 'tis like that dull-Pall cannot read, and this does make the mirth in us.) 'Tis also true that any one who should stop me from consulting with these papers – or who should seek to interfere with them – will soon gauge who they do reckon with and I will have my way.

E'en Eliza does put aside her mumpings and does give approval to our agreement, and my mother does hold that full

[8] *Mr John Pepys*: Samuel's father.

148

stounded she is with my daring. For while I do give consent to keep all clean and do my duty (and pay call on Pepys' brood each Lord's Day!) 'tis nothing to what I should receive in return. Kind and generous treatment, and to keep my journal, and private too, and for all, I give thanks. 'Tis the second chance and one thing only is there which does tarnish my joy, and 'tis my husband's health. Still does the stone sorely try him though every apothecary cure we do apply.

Some do counsel that wise it would be to have the stone removed. But few are there who survive such cutting. 'Tis a desperate solution and one I will not think on 'til desperate we be. Days there are when he does have the lessening of the pain, and 'tis my prayer that this does continue. Much fluid does he drink for the relief and much, much filling of the chamber pot there is, which does not please me, since I did sign to have the emptying of it, and already I do regret it, and no amount of monies is there which would compensate.


# 1 December

Two years this day since we did wed. Some hope was there in me that this day would be our reuniting and the veriest fitting anniversary. But not all is yet in order. And I do look back and think that 'tis 10 October which does mean the more to me and does seem the time to celebrate in future years.

Still there are arrangements which must be made afore we do again enter our life together. Nothing is there which would take me from mine own narrow bed and the kindness of my Palmer lodgings, till I have my satisfaction with all the papers. No dunce I am, so know I that all would count for naught if I should stay to lie with Samuel afore the papers be proper signed and sealed. 'Tis my bargain point that so full of ardour is he and in such haste to bed me, that willing does he concede what I set down as reasonable. 'Tis like when we did woo, again, but the better position now I be in.

# December

Tomorrow I do set up again with Samuel Pepys. A long time it has been since we did have our separation, and much learning has there been in it. No wish do I have to make mine own way again – not as the disobedient wife, nor as the lonely widow.

This time too are mine eyes well open. Samuel does say he does love me and now the agreement to forestall our difficulties is there to prove it, and both be beholden to it. No fine fancies do I entertain for the future yet do I know that this is right and that in it lies contentment. For which I give thanks.

# PART FOUR

# Agreement

# 1657

## December

Much there is the same. Do I want to make entry here? It did go from my memory how much the piss-pain did burn. And the abscess does come again which does make me more than melancholy.

Yet Samuel does have the tenderness in him, so are there compensations in it.

## December

'Twas the most pleasant Christmas ever I did have, forced though I was to fix my smile upon the Pepys brood, and yet 'tis true that brother John is no bufflehead, and pleasant converse I have with him. Puss-Pall does get more the gammer with the passing of the years and plentiful is the envy she does have of me when I do parade my finery, which does suit me.

# 1658

## 15 February

This time did I think that my termes should not come and I
would be with child. Yet today do they flow, and no abatement.
To my bed I should go for naught else can I do and some relief
is there in the resting.

## 22 February

Tomorrow is the anniversary of my husband's birth, and the
fine surprise I do prepare. And not just the food, though new
skills I do acquire – but not yet tested – but the company too I
do request to celebrate with him. And have I sent him forth
this eve to play upon his flageolet with his friends while I make
myself ready – which speedy I must do. All that I should need
to make complete would be the bond between my husband and
mine own family, but no liking does Samuel have for it. Much
does he complain of brother Balty who does touch him yet he
does converse with him, but not my mother or my father who
Samuel does act churlish to. Still, time should heal such
problems.

## 24 February

No celebration there be. Too ill was Samuel with the kidney
stone and 'tis like the knife in me to see him suffer so. And
does he fix on to be cut for the stone, for no other help is there,
yet such danger. So deadly is the cutting that few have made
recovery from it and most mightily do I dread it. And soon

does he want it, and not just for the relief of the pain but to have only the brief time for his mind to think on it. Which has the sense in it but this does knock me and should I talk to some about it.

## 25 February

All night long did he writhe and naught I could do to give him relief though I did try every way I know. All night I did sit by and soothe his brow and say kind words. And no more should I want to see him tried by such ordeal. But does my stomach lurch when he does declare that next week the stone should go, for no peace does he have, and no life this way.

Which does put the melancholy in me. For what if he should die now? Much more sorrow will there be in me, just when I did plan our sweet future together. Many there are who die under the surgeon's knife, and what should my life be as the young widow?

'Tis Thomas Hollier who Samuel has a mind to use the knife. His is the reputation for the most success and 'tis said that he does cut many who live to give testimony to his great skill and so we seek witness to his service and his expense.

And Samuel does want to make all in order of my lord's papers, and his own as well, and serious business has there been and ne'er a smile, as he does plan for me to be alone.

## 1 March

Thomas Hollier does agree and does tell that Samuel should have the success. Yet gloom there is upon me and no cheer have I been to Samuel, which I should remedy.

## 3 March

Eliza did say that if these be the last days we have together then 'tis better to have some joy in them, which I do agree and so should make all effort. Today I do pray that my husband should be spared to me and that the true life I would lead if he does get free of the stone and have back his health.

## 9 March

Now my husband's family have the knowledge of all and they do think to have attendance at the operation, though I should not want them. For no care would they show to me, and many problems could they make. The plodding Pall has no way to keep her wits about her, and she is likely to have the fit, for I have keen warned that much blood there will be. And the washerwoman should not stand such sight that the cutting should make, and yet do they all think to be witness to the event. But if it does have the comfort in it for my husband, no protest should I give, though no room is there here for him to have it cut and he must find a place for the surgeon and the problem there is in it.

## 11 March

Today my courses did flow which has no surprise in it for me, for strange should it have been if this last month did produce the child for no memory do I have that my husband does lie with me. Nor is it just the pain that does stop his ardour – though dampener enough it should be – but 'tis the melancholy that does sit upon us that does take out all the joy and no remedy is there, not even in the infusion of the thyme which oft I do prepare. Much should I like the diversion which should give us some cheer but no energy should I have now for I too have the stomache grippe to contend with.

## 15 March

Some difficulty should there be to find the place that should suit for the cutting of the stone and grateful are we to my husband's cousin, Jane Turner, for her house should be where all is performed.

## 18 March

All now is set for 26 March and most fearfully do I worry, yet should I try to give my husband the hope that all will be well. 'Tis the time for praying.

## 25 March

'Tis said that the start of the year[1] is propitious time for the granting of a prayer. So do I pray for the good health of my husband, for on the morrow does he have the deadly cutting for the removal of the stone from his bladder and the more knowledge I do gain on the nature of this operation, the greater is my fear. For even should the surgeon find the stone and take it, and even should my husband live, yet still is there much that can have the disaster in it, and not just that further stone can form so that all the cutting goes for nought.

'Tis said that one man is there who did have the operation from this same surgeon and such damage was there done to his cods that ne'er again could he lie with his wife. Which though it was the loss for him and he did complain, yet no great tragedy should she have it, for she did say that nine children should be sufficient sport for any man, and she did declare that had not the surgeon first taken the stretch from her husband's yard, then should she have snipped it.

But no children do I have and Samuel too would smile upon it if we should have a family, and sad we would both be if no more should his pintle rise to sprout forth its seed.

No end is there though with the talk of cut cods and flopping pintles. My mother did say that she did hear tell from one, Mrs Marten, whose brother did have such cutting that all control did he then lose of his insides and no more sense did he show than the befouling baby, but more unpleasant. And this is prospect without comfort for me. And are these the stories of the surgeon's success?

And all is risked to escape the pain. On one occasion some

---

[1] In the seventeenth century the beginning of the new year was celebrated on 25 March, the start of spring.

point did there seem to me to check the certainty that my husband did know full well all the dangers he does confront for did I think that most pain should have the preference in it to such dreadful fates that we do hear. But 'tis clear that his mind is set, so no good should it be to pass before him all that is deadly when no change of him there should be. Rather do I try to give him the diversion – to talk of his music, or his singing, or his books – but hard it is to keep the melancholy away for does he start to instruct me on who should have his books and his flageolet, if he should die and the great sadness sweeps over me.

'Tis his proud claim that all should be in order – his own affairs and those of my Lord Montagu, for these last days the management of such business has been his purpose. Yet though all should be planned, little can my husband provide for me should the surgeon cut him wrongly. For no store of money is there set by and unlikely should it be that my lord should let me these lodgings – nor should it be my wish to stay upon my own. Yet no desire do I have now to be back once more with my family, or to make mine own way at the Palmer lodgings. Such cruelty it would be to make such swift return to life alone.

From now until the morrow my part should be to give my husband cheer and well should I play it and with no fault. Long did I think on some entertainment, or some novel thing which should distract him and help to dispel the great fear, and did I have the solution. From my own supply of money did I take sufficient for the purchase of this new herb – the tay – which is held to have the medicinal as well as the pleasurable properties in it, and should I make my husband the dish of it. But not the strong infusion which does have the prejudice for those in the weakly nervous state, but the gentle Bohea tay, which is softening and nutritious and proper for inward decays, and does possess the calming quality which we should all need.

So tonight should we sit together and sip our tay and my best I should do to keep me and my husband from thinking on our fears. No utterance should I make that this might prove to be our last night, but fervently should I pray 'tis not so.

# 26 March

'Tis evening and the cutting is over. My husband does still live – thank the Lord – and quiet rest does he take at his cousin's place where he does have the soothing drug of sleep. Terrible ordeal was it and no way did I think he should survive and now most distressed I be. Yet should it be of some help to me to pass this long night, if I should find strength to set all down.

So should I start at the beginning and the pride I did take in my manly husband as we did make our way to the home of Jane Turner, for though I did know that inward he did have the sliding fears, yet outward did he stay firm and 'twas him that did give the comfort to me. More so when we did enter that bare room and see the surgeon and all those knives at the ready, and almost did I aswoune, yet I did not.

'Twas the presence of the palterly Pall that did give me fortitude for she did make such moan that it did unsettle my husband more and I did vow to add not to his vexations. So did I fix her with my stare, yet it silenced her not, so I did threaten to gouge her if she stopped not her tongue or the rolling of her eyes and she did quieten then else should I have had the riddance of her.

And no use was my husband's mother, for though silent enough yet did she wring her hands and try to pace up and down while all the while she had so much limpness in her that she did need support. 'Tis true that my husband's father did make a better show and no great grief did he display yet constant did he amutter and I did think that 'twas some prayer that o'er and o'er he did repeat to himself which did give *him* the strength, but did play upon *my* nerves till almost they did break.

All was so horrible.

It does sicken me. I know not even whether I can enter all here. Yet might I drive the awful sight from me, if I should set it down and take my distance from it. Else should it plague my rest for all my nights to come.

When my husband did lie upon that table in his nakedness then did my gorge rise as I did see Mr Hollier stand above him and in one hand did he hold aside my husband's cods, and in the other he did have the great, cruel knife and from then I know not how much of the gory sight I did see for 'twas not in me to look upon it when Mr Hollier did make the cut.

And I did hear my husband cry out and I did feel for him in his agony but I did try to still myself with the reminder of what my man did say when earlier we did make our way to Jane Turner's. That he could remember not the life without the pain of the stone in the kidneys and then in the bladder, and the making of bloody water which could no more be endured. And that the cutting of the stone was all that there could be.

Yet did I think that he did make the wrong decision for frightful did it all seem.

Merciful was it that soon my husband did lose all sense of what did occur and 'tis likely that he heard not the jubilance of Mr Hollier when he did bring forth from the bladder the most gruesome object that he did call the stone which did have the size of the large egg in it. Most venomed feeling should I have for that stone and though the surgeon would have it that the cutting was over and that the operation was the success – which did give me some small relief – yet did I think many days should pass afore I did count the good or bad of the surgeon's ways.

For no success should all this be for me unless my husband should live, have no more pain from the stone, and have all his parts that do come under the knife recover with their healing and do their proper work. And many days should that be.

No wish do I have ever again to be witness to the surgery which does have so much blood and the agony about it, and does look so awesome and fearful. And with all certainty do I swear that never should I willingly have such cutting. Rather should I die than be under the knife.


## 27 March

Still does my husband live though he does look most ill and I am afeared. Much do I pray for him, and help to clean and dress his wounds which does close to make me swoune.

## 29 March

The good Jane Turner does show my husband great care and does try to convince me that he does have the improvement in him. But vile mess is it all and I do think that all hopes for his recovery should be false and so will I not have them; for worse would it be to hope and be dashed, than to have the resignation to all.

Yet long hours do I spend by my husband's side and stroke his hand, and give him kind words, but I know not whether he does hear all.

## 31 March

Still does my husband live which all would have as a good sign and many prayers did I offer up this Sabbath for the return of his good health. Most lonely are my nights and anything should I promise to do if only my husband should be restored to me.

## 1 April

Thanks unto the Lord. This day did my husband know me and smile upon me and now should I let myself think that all might be well.

## 4 April

Daily improvement do I see and most excellent it is. Together do my husband and I talk and he does have the gratitude to Mr Hollier, but more to Jane Turner who does care for him and who he has did save his life. Now that he does think to have the full recovery he does solemn swear to hold each year the anniversary feast of the stone which he should keep with Jane Turner. And too does he fondly tempt the fate to declare that the stone should strike him again if ever he does break his vow. 'Tis well to give thanks but foolish to make such promise.

## 10 April

This day did I ask to see the healing of the cut, and strong did I hold myself, and necessary was it too. Most awful does it all look – and smell – and yet do I know that still should my husband's pintle rise when he does urge it to. Some pain did it give yet he did insist to make the test and from his scabby cods it did make its small move. And my husband did have the wink for me, though 'tis plain that the effort did hurt him and I know not whether I should laugh or cry.

More time yet does the good Jane Turner think that my man should stay abed for 'tis true that the cut and all does need much attention that I know not how to give, and that while my husband still has the pain with the passing of the water and the shyte, she does give him special gruel that I have no familiarity of.

Yet soon should he make his return here and most content will I be. And too must I remember to give thanks to God.


## 16 April

On the morrow three weeks should there pass since my husband did have the stone cut from him and now e'en I do let myself call it the surgeon's success, for does he live and though much pain is there still in it for him, yet it comes not from the stone. But caution should there be for early days is it yet, and still could the new stone form, which should be the great pity, though plain it is that there should be hope that soon will he have again his full place, which is the miracle for which I give thanks. And too, well should I care for him when he does return here – which the good Jane Turner does think should be within the next sennit.

Much work is there for me to do afore he does come hence for does the cleaning slip into disarray. 'Tis my presence by my husband's bedside which does take me from my duties and have the proper excuse in it, yet do I know that my husband should be not pleased if he should come home to such disorder, which he should not, for will I have all the neatness preserved afore then.

Yet such grand plans does my husband have now that he does allow himself the hope for the future that I do e'en wonder on the worth of all the work to make clean within, for does he tell that he has the liking for the new and better lodging where the more space there should be for the giving of dinners, and a closet for the keeping of his books. And though I do think that 'tis his books for which he does have the first consideration, I do favour the better room and table for the dinners and the sport that is in them, but not the work; for no satisfaction is there for me in such preparation for all his friends to quickly eat, and much is there to do when they do leave. And no help is my husband, except with the advice and that does nettle me.

Yet should I want the services of the maid, and not for some time hence but this very day, for much need should I have now to polish this present place.

And do I have my own vision for the dashing husband and the beautiful wife – and the fine establishment – and thanks do I give that my husband is spared to me and that we should have the chance to think on a future of good fortune.

## 24 April

On the morrow my husband should again lie upon his own bed and for both of us, much pleasure should there be in it. All is aready for him, and great is the excitement in me. Yet do I know that there should be some difficulties. Not just in the care of my husband – though truth to tell he does recover sufficient to be most querulous – but most days should he be within and have the supervision of me, which is not to my liking.

Other problems too should I foresee for no entry have I made in the house accounts pages that he should see, since afore he did go for the cutting of the stone[2]. And not long should it be till he should want to see the record of expenditure and the sternness he will have about him then, for though I do have charge of the purse and spend much while he does have the sickness, hard put should I be now to give full account.

[2] In return for her fixed allowance, Elizabeth agreed to keep an accounts book, detailing her expenditure.

And little paper is there left to make any entries – which will have the mystery in it for him. But still do I have the joy in his return, for when he did leave, little hope was in me that he should safe and sound return.

## 30 April

'Tis as I did predict that all day does my husband o'ersee me, and worse is there.

## 22 May

Great satisfaction should there be for me when my husband does have health enough to go hence for long duration – each day. 'Tis the truth that now should I make the change and give him the encouragement to go gad-about with his drinking friends, so tried am I by his constant company. For most superior does he act, and all day he does have the pose that he does know the best way to keep the house, and do the shop, and prepare the food, and wash the linnin, and make all in order, and does it boil my blood to have him lie upon the bed and give forth the many instructions. 'Tis his boast that he should teach me the qualities of the thrifty and orderly wife and yet no need should I have of his teachings, and no liking for all the chores he does set, for no point should there be in a-many of them, but for the show.

Yet do I still my tongue and think on how close he did come to death and I do try to give him the understanding, though he does push me.

Now has he gone forth to Paul's Churchyard to meet with the booksellers and much faith do I put in the purchase of the books that should hold his mind and keep him from awatching me.

# 29 May

Money, money, money. 'Tis all he does care about and sick to the death am I of all this chafing. For no likelihood is there that I did live on air when he did have his illness – which did also have great cost in it for me, for did I not take him many gifts and the good medications for to cheer him? And all this does take much more than he does allow me. And too does it take money each day for the food and more, and though I do have much from the good cookshops, 'tis only so I should provide him with fine food for his strength, and to give me more time to have the care of him.

And when he does make demand to know where all does go for no record there is, then do I say that I should show him mine when he does show me his. For how much does he spend upon the books, *and* the new breeches that he did surreptitious bring home last week?

Upon reflection, merit does there seem to be to recommend to him the keeping of the record. Not just for the chance it should give me to make the check on what he should spend – though certain it is that I should peruse his keepings, no matter where he should make it hid – and should I know the detail of the extravagance of his ways which I am sure he does have. But more value for me it should be this moment if he should keep the diurnal for his own amusement, for little does he have for the exercise of his mind which is why he does turn all his attention 'pon me, and dearly should I love to end it. To keep the diurnal – which I should willing teach him – would fill much of his day and too could it give him the satisfaction which if he did find, more sympathy should he have for me in the keeping of my record. But he does scoff at such suggestion and make the moan about the use of paper and all that expense and he does try me.

And too I do think on his limitations and the troublous 'prentice he should make. For such false judgement does he form on all who are around him and yet, as I do know, to keep the diurnal does need the entry of accurate account, and such unreliability should there be in my husband's report that no match should it be with what does take place so no useful record should it be if ever he did return to it.

But who should have the care for whether he does keep honest account? More use should it have for me if it does hold his fancy and keep him from the superintending of me for the Lord does know that I should need the rest from such watchful eye that does look in each corner, and count each penny.

## 3 June

This day should I have the turn to lie upon the bed and most welcome is it for my courses do flow and nothing does stem them nor stop the pain. And vexing is it to lie here and look upon my husband's stone which he does give the pride of place aside this bed. Most hideous sight is it and does it get into all my dreams and make the disturbance. But he will not move it for he does have it that 'tis the reminder to him that much he does have to give thanks for – which I don't.

Oh that something should be removed to put end to this women's pain within me. Yet all that should make it cease would be the getting of child, which should please me.

## 9 June

Much satisfaction do I take in my husband's talk to soon return to the regular care of my lord's business. 'Tis his wish to have the employment and the money, and 'tis mine that he should leave me to my own. Which does have the strangeness in it for always have I wanted him to stay in and ne'er did I think that I should want but my own company. Yet these last weeks past it does come to me that pleasure there can be to be alone.

Then too with my husband gone should I make the visit to my mother whom I do neglect since my husband has the sickness and though she does regular send Balty to make enquiry on the health of Mr Pepys, yet does she enter not here. For no affection is there betwixt her and my husband, which does have the explanation, but does give the sadness to me.

Yet much do I have to be grateful for. Today did we give thanks for the health of my husband and each day does he have more strength, and a fine pair we did make in the church and later when we did stroll on Lincoln's Inn Fields where the sun did shine upon us for all to see.

## 25 June

No great sport does my husband have with me for most tender still are his cods and easy is it for him to have the hurt of his pintle and little liking has he had for lying with me till late. Yet more strength and interest is there in him now and rod enough does he have to give the inflammation to me. And does the abscess weep and sting and make me most miserable and truly should I put end to this poking, but it does have the making of the child in it.

## 29 June

Once more do my courses flow and 'tis the case that disappointment and pain is the poor combination.

## 15 July

'Tis excitement here as I do look upon these rooms and mark how much longer they should serve as our lodgings for my husband does have it that soon we should move to a finer place and all this does please me. For though these last months have had the satisfaction in them – and good measure have we had as my husband does recover – yet do I always know 'twas here we did have most bitter quarrels and I did endure the misery that did make me leave.

Yet should our new lodgings have more to impress for my husband does say that 'tis fitting that a man of his position[3] should have more grand abode and no disagreement does he have from me on a finer place to live. But I do wonder whether it is the windfucker in him for sudden does this new sense of

[3] In the summer of 1658 Samuel Pepys became the Clerk to George Downing in the Tellers Office at the Exchequer – for £50 per annum.

importance seem. And though 'tis plain that those who cheat death should have the best they can from life – which still could prove to be short, yet do I think to ask my man whether he does rob Mr Downing, the Teller of the Receipt at the Exchequer, for it was but recent that Mr Pepys did say that no money did he have, for nought there was for me, yet now does he boast to have enough to make great show.

But no duty is it of mine to have the worry of where the money should come from. More my part it is to get the value for the money, which I should do well. And should I test my skill with the acquirement of the new dress that should be for the keeping of the new lodging, and the dress not all of it.

[4]New bodice too would I have and though my petticoat has nothing of the disgrace in it, yet should a new one – or a new lace trim – go not amiss. If my husband has money to furnish all he does want then some extra should there also be for me. But necessary it is that he should make some contribution for should I find the monies for finery from what he does allow me, soon would he call for the reducing of my payment. And though I put by some and have a store, yet not so much that I should want to take a cut in my allowance. And tiresome it be to keep two sets of accounts yet the wisdom – and the liberty – there is in it.

## 30 July

'Tis all arranged and the move we should make and Samuel does flow forth on how much there is for me to do, though I cannot see it. But here we do remain till all is made over at Axe Yard[5]. Brief have I seen it and much grandness is there in it. From the bottom it does start with a coal cellar and then does it rise to three floors and full of rooms. And a bedroom which does better our poor lodging[6] and a maid's room too which I did point out many times to Samuel for what a pity it should be to waste it.

[4] Translated from the French.
[5] *Axe Yard*: Samuel Pepys had taken the lease of a small house here.
[6] The bedroom was bigger than the garret room they had been living in.

For Samuel, more contentment was there that he should have a special room for the storing of his books and papers, and where he will do his work. Now that he does have two jobs and great responsibility he does think to spend time with his papers at home and for this he seeks to have a lock on his door. And too there is a dining room and a dressing room and much more too, with a garden[7].

[7] There was no kitchen or bathroom, of course.

# PART FIVE

# Maturity

# 1658

## 1 September

In Axe Yard do we now dwell and mightily do I like it and those who lodge around. Little did I think that so soon we should rise in the world and now too should I think my husband serious and not in jest when he does tell that he has the plan to be the gentleman knight and that we should have our own carriage, for did I not think 'twas but the air in him when once he did say that we should have such fair lodgings? Yet are we here.

And Axe Yard does have the grandness in it for many of importance do live alongside to keep note of the parliamentary business. And though Mr Pepys does have Axe Yard to be the fair place yet would I allow it no beauty, for some of the buildings do have the most ill setting out, and no grace in them. Yet should our house have the better standing and though do we have the near neighbours of the Beales who do keep the bottom part, yet are there many fine rooms and five hearths – which is too much for me. So each day do I tell my husband that the serving maid there should be though he attends not.

Much is there still unhung which has no place in the winter, yet do we have great plans for all and no disagreement – and no money for furnishing of all.

## 17 September

This day did I say the long prayer for the getting with child for again do my courses flow and great disappointment is there in it and pain too. 'Tis true that I do have the good fortune as some do tell me, that my husband does full recover and that we do have the fine house and usual it is for us to have the kindness to each other. Yet do I have my complaints.

For 'tis also true that I do suffer, that the toothache is always with me, that my muff does have the growing angry abscess and give the constant pain and all does go for nought when there is ill health and no children.

'Tis not that I have no gratitude for all that does get bestowed on me but that I do want more and so this day do I tell my husband – who also does desire the child – that the reason we have them not is that too much work is there for me and too many chores do I have, for desperate am I for the serving maid, and so do I think to convince him.

## 3 October

This day the gauntlet my husband did throw down when he would have it that no order did I keep in the house, and easy would it be for him to keep all neat and clean if he should have the responsibility for it, which I did wish on him and urge him to try, yet no mind did he have to show the proof or not of his claim. And he did call me the sloth, and charge that fine things are wasted upon me, for no appreciation did I have and no care for their preservation

And did this gall me and first did I think to storm at him, and then to show him unkindness, yet do I learn from the past that no change there should be in my husband if I do open stand to have my own way. So I did think on the guiling manners of my mother and did take as my purpose to put the lead strings on my husband and to have him go in my direction.

'Tis my plan for each day to do but the reasonable amount of work and to leave all else, for no drudge should I be. And soon there should be a fine muddle, when after a fair effort I have made, I do cease my labours. And much wisdom is there in this tactique. For more work is there than one maid should do though truth to tell, I would settle for one serving maid to begin. And so too will Samuel when he does feel my purpose.

Leastways I live no longer among the chamber pots, and though dearly would I want the chamber maid, yet not so pukesome is it to take the time for swilling when after, I can leave the pots and their putridness to another part.

## 10 October

This day do we now take as anniversary of our union and do I look back upon the year and find much comfort in it. For though there have been difficulties yet much is there we should offer thanks for, as my husband does survive the cutting of the stone which does have the miracle in it. True it does leave him prey to the chills and colds and regular does he suffer, yet does he say this is small price to pay for relief from the awful pain of the stone. Still too does he have some soreness from the great scar which does stand from his cods, and the making of stools does oft times cause him pain, yet in all no regrets does he have but rather should he resolve that each year he should keep celebration and show his great gratitude.

No knowledge do we have on the vitalness of his seed, and while his pintle does ready-rise, and do the dance when he does so desire, yet it could be that the life is cut from the seed and this would be the explanation for my barrenness.

Yet too could it be me. For no help is it to have the great abscess and the pain – and the inconvenience and the pungent offence – and many there are who have the opinion that 'tis sufficient for the angry abscess in the frill-folds to prevent the getting of child. And worse now it is than it has ever been and so could it be this which does have the cause in it. Which does give me sadness for what does it mean to have the husband and the fine establishment and no child to place in it?

Eliza will have it that the fortunate one I be – and not just the apartment which does cause her some envy, but brought down she is by babes and the carousing husband and life does have its twists, for now 'tis the case that *I* do counsel *her* on the advantages of the signed agreement.

Good companions Samuel and I do make each other and the bond together we did find when he did face the risk of the surgeon's knife and though 'tis not my way to make great show, yet does my husband know that he does have my affection and no necessity does he have for the doubts or the jealousy. More now do we have the life that I did think on, long ago, and tonight should we have the celebration so all do know we live in contentment.

But two things are there that give me anxiety – one is that I am without child which each day does come to me and have the sadness in it, though much hope should I still have that it be not a permanent condition.

The other trouble I do have is no great one, yet does it irk me, for as my husband does have more of his strength and his health so too does he by small degree have more of the ale and the wine and the spirits and no liking should I have for him when he does get foxed, for past the point of merriness does he go and get the surliness in him which is not the nature of him when he is without the drink. But worse than the way he does go foolish like the child, worst than the temper he does show to have his way, worst thing of all is that the drink does bloat him then all night does he take to pushing out the air – which does cross me.

Yet too should I think that this be no great disaster.

## 13 October

Today did my courses flow. Soon should I look to the physic to get with child if we have not the success in it ourselves.

## 22 October

Tomorrow is the anniversary of my birth, and all kindness does my husband show and ask what I would have to please me. And could I tell that he did think to hear request for finery, for the lace, or the kerchief, or the gloves. But no reference did I make to them. Straight did I ask for the maid. Straight did I tell Samuel that it was a maid who would bring the most satisfaction for me, and him too. And little enough is the price of it, for less than £3 per year would get one and not so much for a blackamoor[1] who does come easy and can ready be bought and sold if Eliza be believed.

[1] There was an increasing number of black servants in England during this

And he did agree that very desirable it should be, but all number of objections he did then raise to such gift. Yet do I think that he does move my way. For as I do tell Eliza, no liking does Samuel have to tangle with the linnins, and the washings, and great disorder. And though he should shut himself in his private closet to peruse his books, yet should he stumble through much that does hamper his way. And no guests should he have here for it would shame him to display such disorder. And me. But 'tis a good plan, for only one solution is there to it – and 'tis the maid servant.

## 24 October

'Tis done. I did win. And Eliza and I did laugh till our sides did have the soreness in them. For Samuel does claim it is all his idea. Which is little enough to allow him.

Yet there is a trade which does not please me. Now that I have Jane Birch[2], and no excuse, so should I have time to keep accounts, which he does mean to have regular inspection of. This does have some more of the planning in it, though Samuel has not the good head for the figures.

What chance would there be that he should read this? 'Tis part of our signing that I should keep my diary and that monies I should have for the purchase of it, and though he makes complaint about the expense, it is but his way, and no attempt does he make to stop it. Yet I know that it does tax him to have me make entry here for what record should I keep. And as I do go back over the pages, nothing should there be to put the furies in him – though some that he might not like – so no

---

period (from the West Indies). Ultimately, Pepys had at least three, including Doll the cookmaid, and technically speaking they were slaves who could be bought and sold. In 1680 Samuel Pepys actually sold a black servant and in 1688 he sent another, who was considered unsatisfactory, back to the plantation. One was the recipient of a £10 legacy and £15 annuity in Pepys' will. It is not known whether Samuel made the same sort of sexual advances to Doll the cookmaid as he did to some of the white female members of his household.

[2] *Jane Birch*: the Pepys' first serving maid.

great problem if he keeps not his word and looks upon this account keeping.

Yet to follow my design, I would not want Samuel to see. Which is enough said[3].

[3] Elizabeth kept a set of accounts for Samuel which were 'fudged': Samuel never knew whether there really were some errors in her accounting or whether she was conning him.

# 1659

(The Story of Barrenness)

Now that the maid I have, some time is there for me to do my writing, which does become a keen occupation for me. When Samuel does close himself in his room, then can I quiet sit here at my table[1] and make my musings, though some do leave me sad and melancholy. Always in my mind when I do stop from my work is my want of a babe. And though Eliza – who has had five but four there are (and how many she does wash away I know not)[2] – does urge me to think on the advantages of my state, yet do I get the mopishness in me.

Constant have I looked for the remedies for my barrenness, even without my husband's knowledge, for he has no high opinion of my mother's ways, and it is from her and the good Sarah Perkins that I take much of my advice. Sometimes I think she has great wisdom, and I have high hopes that I am with child, but then it proves to be false. I am left with the stomache grippe of mighty degree and with sick head that does add to my sorrow. Yet I do tell myself that this is a mixed blessing, for to hear tell from my mother, to be brought to bed with child is no pleasant thing. She talks of great pain like the bursting of the bowels, and many there are who die of it. And soon they are forgotten. So I am grateful to be spared all this.

But there be no other style to bring forth children into the world, and it is said that this suffering must be women's lot. Though why we should have the worst of it, I know not. Yet some there are, of course, who do not die, or talk of pain, and in truth I would hazard all the dangers for the pleasure of the child it would bring.

[1] It could have been in the dining room but was more likely a desk in the bedroom.
[2] Presumably a reference to penny-royal abortions.

This want of children is a topic between my husband and me which comes hard to speak on. Much blame can be laid, which he is quick to do when his temper is high, or he has the drink in him. It does vex me when he speaks roughly and point to my failing, for 'tis not my desire to be barren. I do not wilfully stop the getting of a child. And what do we know of the cutting of the stone which does for him?

When he has more of the wine in him, not uncommon is it for him to froth at me and make bold with his complaints. I am hurt by his cruelness but also much angered by his unfairness. He will not admit the necessity of it taking two for the bringing forth of children, and will have it that the fault be entirely mine. But there is no aid to be got by calling him unjust. He does but froth more when his manliness is challenged. So I am silent. Yet I do keep my thoughts and he does know they are with me, though not full knowledge of the event does he have.

When the effects of the drink pass, he can be most contrite, and say more of kindness to me. And yet he does always deny that he ever shows anything but the greatest reason in the matter. All this does make fair talk of children exceedingly troublesome. I do really but guess at his true thoughts, for there is such a muddle between us.

One impediment to us is the ill health that plagues me still. 'Tis no blessing to be burdened with such an abscess in my privities. It is the cause of much pain to me and does make the relations of husband and wife most impossible on occasion.

When we did have our reunion, and when too Samuel was sick then did he show more understanding for my affliction. Now he will have it some days that I deny him his full rights when I plead that the pain be too fierce. Yet not always do I make such excuse. Only when he has too much drink and I know that he will grind on and on. And if the abscess do not flame when he start, it will so by the time he does finish.

Though often he do have appetite much greater than he have strength. Times there are, when the drink do have him so much in its grip, that it does take little to do his bidding. He does but try and place himself, before he is overtook by sleep. Then it be no inconvenience to play at giving him his way. More trouble it is to move his heavy weight to one side so there is room in bed enough for me, and I too can partake of sleep.

Of recent times though he does bring the grudge that I do deliberate keep from having the child, which has no reason in it, but more proof that he does twist the meanings to his own strange ends. And what does rile me is that I know he does make this the conversation with his vulgar friends, who all manner of advice do give him and no dignity for me in this, when in the public tavern and with much jest and mirth all do toast his success and say that he should do it most in the morn, for at night there is not such success in it. And crude do they make the motion of how I should lie, and what physic to drink, and most hurtful is this to me.

And home he does come with the wine talking in him and one night in his revelries, one friend did set him the challenge that the making of the children was all done in the manner of taking – e'en to whether the child be girl or boy. And he would not rest on his coming home, till he did try to lie all ways but that of upside down. And did he put me about and poke from every place till I did feel like the puppet-doll, and about the same use of breath too, as my head did get pushed to the carpet. Cross did it make me to be used so, and the piercing pain in my private parts be on me for days after and no abating. And no child to show for it.

And I did o'ercome some of my reticence to consult with my mother on the best way to do't. And whether there be anything in certain patterns or frequency as some do suggest. And she too is of the opinion that the number be not so important as the manner and that 'tis the thought that also does count. But wishing does not make it so, as well I can prove . . .

My mother does know of my longing for the child and so with patience do cross-examine me. She too does want to know the details of my husband's manner of taking me, and I do find it hard to tell. For there be no names, or no names that I do know of, to give particulars of some that is done, and I do find this a most difficult conversation. How to say what manner he puts himself in, and where it does go, be the very devil to give specifics to. I do not relish such talk with my mother, but it be necessary.

And she do say that it be the right thing my husband does, and nothing remiss in the placing. So it must be some faults in the fluids, and there she has not the expertise. But she knows how to get it, and 'tis the good Sarah Perkins I do visit again.

My mother does accompany me to the place but great relief it was when she did stay outside the chamber, for then could my talk flow the more easily. Which do surprise me. But 'twas not so hard to list the manner of it all and to think on the questions when my mother be not there.

Held in high esteem is this learned lady and Eliza too does still give credit to Sarah Perkins though the babes do come to her at greater pace than she did purpose them. For Sarah Perkins is wide known to have the means for both bringing on the child and for keeping it hence. And when I do go to her, no recollection does she have of that time long past when I did as a maid have her recipes for the marriage bed. And no reference did I make to it. This time 'tis a different need I have and she does first want to know what it be that I do want – the getting with of child, or the getting without.

I did hope that she did well hear my answer, and clear I spoke, for I do not want the confusion. But she does say that she does understand full well, and that she does never make mistake between the two. Not even in the great houses, where sometimes she be tempted to exchange the herbs and the potions, because of the rudeness she does meet with. But she is a most proud person and does make much of her achievement, and be not known for any mistakes.

She showed me much kindness and do look at my tongue and the palms of my hands, and do want it to be known that if it be my fault, then easy is it cured, and 'tis close to me to say that some knowledge I have that it be not me. Yet no proof, and the mighty problem is there in it to think on Samuel as the reason for it. Yet Sarah Perkins does fill me with high hope and she does say that 'tis the woman who does give the sex to the new born child but the man does give it the life, and there is the sense in this.

But no liking do I have to put this information to Samuel for 'tis not his way to have the logic in him when he does think that his manhood be challenged. So should I bide my time and do what the good Sarah Perkins does recommend me. And the veriest bitterest physic she does provide – and for the making of it no instructions for this her trade potion be – and each day

I do swallow it and vile it is too, but worth it if it does the making. Which it does not. All to no avail.

My moyes do come and I am not with child and so to the learned lady I do return and some disappointment but more despair is there in me. And she will have it that 'tis the most efficacious brew she did give me and if no success there is in it, then nought else is there I can do. So must it be the man, which I did think on this while.

And I do tell that this does match my doubts and some evidence do I give her. Though enough it is to say that my husband does have the stone removed from him. More than the stone she does say should be taken and now his fluids too be out of substance. Yet still hope is there and she does urge me to provide the monies for the special brew she does make for the seed of the husband as that is all that there is now to do . . . and does she tell that 'tis her opinion that rare does it fail to do the trick. Which does help me . . .

But I do not face this fully. Twice more do I know that I am not with child before I think it must be done. And even then do I falter. But he does start to insist that it be my fault that I be barren, and that the abscess be the cause. Yet do I now know better.

All that is known to respectable women have I tried for the abscess, and the barrenness. I did take my share of the mare's milk, though it makes my stomach heave with great violence. I did drink of the sage juice yet the bitterness be almost too much to bear. And many more experiments have I tried. I have made use of the salts for bathing which do come from ale hoof, oaten and pease straw, when it does take mighty resolve to embrace it, and the stench be not for those of weak stomach. And when the wearing of cool holland drawers be recommended, I did put them on without remove for long weeks on end, and only desperate hopes would sustain such discomfort. Yet each month did I know the disappointment.

Everything tried, and to no purpose, and the learned lady – she does say that there be nothing else to try. It must be that my husband do drink of her brew to put the life in his fluid.

This has something of the problem in it. It is not possible to get him to drink it innocently, for it smell most foul. Like would he be to charge me with the poisoning of him if I do but just set it before him, and give no explanation. Not unknown it is for women to get potions to place in the food of husbands, and so they do die without any fuss. And truth to tell, my husband does sniff his food after we have argued, although there be nothing in it, and no intent on my part to cause his death. For what would I do then? 'Tis certain that he does not keep me lavishly, but I do be not kept at all without him, and I have no notion to end his days. But reason does not work on suspicion, and the risk be too great to pass off the brew in his supper. So he must be informed.

Yet he does not take kindly to my criticism, and will even less so when I do say that it be his fluid which is lacking in life.

So I do take three weeks to find the right time at which to tell him, for it counts as little to have his wrath against the benefit of a child. I do prepare him with the sweet talk and do coo at him until he does soften, and smile on me. And then I do take the risk. Not that I do tell him all. But rather that it be well known that for barrenness *both* must partake – though I never did intend to swallow the brew myself, for vile does it seem and pretence be good enough. Then by degree do I convince him and do urge him to please me. And he does suffer himself to swallow it down when I do say he must have been most brave to have his stone removed, and this swallowing be such a little thing.

Well should I have known my husband's habits though. It should have been my prediction that he would want revenge, if the success were not forthcoming. On the next month, when I did weep that again I was not with child, he do turn on me. He does declare that it be not his fault, for did he not willingly drink the foul brew? And with more force does he say that it be all my fault. And I have no recourse. For 'tis true he tried, and did drink it, and it did fail us.

## 15 February

My courses do flow with no abatement. Ah woe!

## 22 February

Tomorrow be the anniversary of the birth of my husband and fine celebration should I prepare and not just to give him the happiness but should I also want to be the mistress and to make proud of my maid and all my skills which none should know I do have for yet no opportunity should there be for me to give them display. Time now is it for me to take my place and should I think to do it well if I should give it the care.

What did have the perplexity for me was who there should be as the guests for dinner for no close acquaintance do I have with some whom my husband calls friend – and who he does sing and roister with – and too could it seem the presumption and be the blot if I do ask them without his knowing.

Would that I could give the invitation to my mother – and more of my family – but no bond is there betwixt S. and mine own. (And no bond either between me and his common-kin, and worse too since I did send Pox-Pall packing, who does steal from me, and has no satisfaction in her not e'en as a servant, which I do always know but which does have the advantage to be able to prove.) And though 'tis the source of some discontent betwixt my husband and me, yet while *my* family has not the welcome under this roof, neither should I allow his. Well might he want to make the show and parade his increase in the world to his doty father but not while I should have the strength to stand the door.

So no guests should family be at my husband's birth celebrations. And too difficult it is to make the surprise for him, so I did announce that on the morrow he should return here from the tavern with all he does call his friend, (though no more than six!) and with those he makes the music with, and I should have them all to a birthday feast. And Eliza and Richard too, though no babes. And certain it is that such prospect does please him for he does want the chance to make the grand and generous show – and this should be it. And so too do I ask for the more monies to provide all which be a different matter to Samuel Pepys, yet some he does find, but not sufficient, and this I must further attend to.

Much work it is for me, but the satisfaction too, for this is how I did think to live (though the waiting-woman well I could do with for 'tis true that now that I be older, my hair and beauty should have more attention for the improvement).

Early on the morrow should I rise to be at Cheapside market at six hours – for the best place and the best time that should be.

And have I thought well on the fayre we should have and though the chinne of beef should make fine show, yet does it have the expense in it and is like to be not fresh this time of the year, but to have much of the salt in it, and too long should it take to take the salt from it afore the roasting and the serving[3].

And all this did lead me to think on the main dish of the venison pasty which well does my husband like and too does it have the celebration in it. And easy should it be for the pasty to be followed with the boiled pudding, which should I manage to make myself upon the pot-hook yet does my husband have no liking for such delicacy and as all is done in the name to please him no sense would there be to boil the pudding but 'tis solution to purchase the fruit tart. Which does have more of the expense in it but should I do it. And then some cheeses too. And the dish of anchovies. And not all served together as is the common way. And should there be enough to eat from for I know not how many my husband should bring.

Yet should I have not the flurry but coolly make record now of what on the morrow I should do so no confusion is there in it and first do I make out the receipt for the venison pasty so I do have the certainty that all is arranged.

To make a venison pasty the best way:-
Take a haunch of venison (which I shall have from the Cheapside market) and powder well with salt and pepper (which be easy enough) and take out the bone and remove the skinny part – (which I do see once my mother do and should I think I have the know of it) and with the rowler beat in the venison to the portion of the pasty – (which should just take the strength which I think I do have) which must be made with fine flower, butter and eggs (which I should enquire of the baker for not certain am I of what quantity and no liking do I have to spoil it).
Then should the venison be laid upon the pasty mixture – which has the ease in it – and covered over, and the borders fixed and

---

[3] It was difficult to obtain fresh meat in winter – because of the lack of feed, cattle were killed off in the autumn.

garnished (which well I know how to do) then vent it on top and should it bake for four or five hours (which the baker should do) and then in pour the butter. Which is simple.

And all this can I do but the five hours for the cooking is a lengthy time and though I should hasten from the market at seven of the clock, and then take but one hour to make all preparation – which may be too short for all the labours – then should I have all to the baker by the eighth hour – or perchance the ninth – but no eating of the pasty should there be afore two of the clock. So should I say to my husband that he should come not with his friends until the hour of three.

Then while the venison pasty does bake, I should help Jane make the sack possett for no party is it without, and a great favourite of my husband's who does swear that 'tis good for his health and does soften the stone, though I do have my doubts. Yet should I do all to please him and list here all that I should have need of for it.

To make the sack possett:-
Take three pints of cream; boil in it a little cinnamon, a Nutmeg quartered, and two spoonfuls of grated bread: then beat the yolks of twelve eggs very well with a little cold cream and a spoonful of sack. When your cream hath boiled for one quarter the hour then thicken it with the eggs and sweeten it with the sugar. Then take half a pint of sack and six spoonfuls of Ale, and put into the basin or dish you intend to make it in, with a little of Ambergreece if you please. Then pour your cream and eggs into it, holding your hand as high as conveniently you can, gently stirring in the basin with a spoon as you pour it; so serve it up. If you please you may strew sugar upon it.

All this do I have to the ready but the Nutmeg, which the market should provide. Though more time should I like to sit here and make my plans – so no mistake should there be – yet do I leave these pages for more practical chore for must I check the plate and damask for order and quantity and all manner of things, some which have had not the use since we did wed and do I have the excitement and know that the grand day the morrow shall be. And should I get my rest for must I rise most early.

## 25 February

So fine was the birthday celebration and such success did I have and all do say that fortune does shine upon Mr Pepys that he should have such beautiful and useful wife who he does keep hid away. And too did the venison pasty come to perfection and though I did have the fearful moments when I did carry such great and steaming dish afore me, and upon the stairs, yet no mishap should there have been. And did my husband give me the loving squeeze when he did know that all should well proceed.

Yet did he make some show to his friends that more meat dishes should there have been – like the rabbits, or perchance the pigeons which be a favourite that I should not admit that I know not how to prepare – and did he announce that the miscalculation on my part it should be that we did have the dish short. Yet no fault should there have been in me for sufficient was there for all to eat (and drink) and much waste should there have been of it to set forth yet further dish. More like it was that my husband did play the rooster game and seek to crow of the great feast he could readily provide and no consideration to expense. So did I give him but silent reproach for his charge that 'twas *my* planning that did have the limitation in it with no variety for the guests.

Full well does it please my husband to play the generous host and to give impression that well do we live at all times, which is not the truth but no challenge is there to it. And fondly did I look upon him as he did ply his friends. Three there were, and with Eliza and Richard (who did squabble most – and no help should Eliza be, for now I have the maid 'tis her view that no need there is to give me assistance – and besides, she does claim, much comfort I do owe her. Which has the truth in it but be not the time to show it).

And Jane Birch does need to take the lessons in the serving, and to know more my bidding. But still it does go well. Just once when the gallant did comment on my beauty (and my housewifery) did Samuel show signs of his old passionateness. Yet did it pass without any great trouble and some relief was there in me for no desire did I have that all should be spoiled by his jealous sickness.

Most content was I when I did survey our rooms and note the comfort in them, and I did think that such a scene I had planned when first I did think to play the wife all those years ago. No small satisfaction did I feel when I did look upon our table and see all the merrymaking. Though I did know what extra work there would be on the morrow and no great help was Jane with the cleaning up of it for she did complain of the tiredness which did cross me.

# 1660

## 1 January

No sweet way this be to start the month for I did think with Samuel that this time it should be the making of a child within me. Seven weeks it is since my termes did flow and all anticipation I be – though other signs I had not, which does have the contradiction in it. Yet so long to go, that I did think and pray that this should be it. And Samuel too did wear his hopes high, which did touch me. For most like it should be that he does truly wish to have the child but does mask his need with gruffness on how all would be disordered and cause the disturbance, and better to be without the muelling and puking.

Yet yester-day did my courses flow. And most low does it leave me for truly did I have expectations. And when I did feel their coming, and disappointment did writt itself large all across my face, Samuel did instant recognize the cause of my affliction and much kindness does he show me. And the surprise is there in me for 'tis plain that he too does feel the loss, and yet still does give me comfort. Or the best he can do. Which is not to be scoffed at though no great help it should be to go forth for the walk, or to take the sack possett; more the broth and the warm bed and cosseting should be to my liking, but Samuel does have his own remedy for my sickness.

Yet too he did show his tenderness and grateful I am for it. Though more gratitude should there have been in me if I had been with child and gone to birth.

# 17 January

'Tis my mother's face which does come before me when I do sit here with the pen and think on those years ago and how she did tell me to keep the record of my days. And the great distance have I travelled in that period. And now I do make the long records of my doings and wonder who there should be to read them, for while 'tis true that I do make entry here for mine own satisfaction, yet too do I think that someone else there should be to have the interest in my account, though not Samuel who swears he looks not at my pages, yet do I know that the curiosity he has do drive him to avid read any part he could put his hand to, which be the reason I leave not my journal in any place where he could peruse it.

But still I do think that many there might be who would get the satisfaction from knowing my nakedness and how I do pass my days. For truly is this not what I seek when I do read the romances and have the great desire to know what way others should fill their hours?

So do I careful think on how all should appear to the stranger and this does shape my version, and for the reason that it does give some taste of my trials, and some information on my ways, I set down here the washing day of my life, which certain I am does have some of the amusement in it.

Though not of a morning. For most hard work should the washing be, and no liking do I have for it. Yet should it be done, though it does weary me, and 'tis never without the difficulty.

What else be servants for? I do ask of Jane Birch when she does complain about the early hour of rising. For 'tis not so long since all I did complete upon mine own, and 'tis sole reason for her existence and her cost, that I do have her to help me, as I do remind her. Yet do I understand her ill-nature, for bad enough it be to rise with the cock and start on't all, yet she must earlier leave her bed to go and fetch the water. And grateful I am that 'tis her and not me.

Bitter cold it was too, and the frost, when she did go forth and no help the darkness and the slipperiness. Yet must she start early else we would be *two* days at the washing, and such drudging I could not endure. Worse too, some cause would it be for Samuel Pepys to give comment to my inefficiency, and I do know my man sufficient to know his complaint that he does get for me the maid, and still I do not manage well the household and that 'tis my sloth which be the root of it all.

Yet I am firm with Jane and take no notice when she does moan that it be all too much, that it be too cold, that the water be frozen over, and will not draw, that she has the ague or the twisted ankle, for all these are but tricks and well do I know them.

I would like to chaff her and make the boast that if she would be like me then must she find herself the husband, who should keep her, and pay for the servant, and sign the agreement, which I be wise enough to do. But no furtherance is there in this. No wish do I have that she should look even closer to Samuel Pepys to see what advantage is in him, for too fond he is of making the eyes and so do I keep these two separate, though more as the precaution than the proof that there is anything in it.

And second I do not know if I do trust this new wealth which does come so readily. Too soon might it all go again, and back in the garret of my lord's house we would be, and much shame would there be in it. And too would Jane (and that Push-Pall) have the laugh on me.

So do I steer away from all announcement of my good fortune and how others should envy me – though 'tis true that I do often think it. Which is most different from S. For he does think always to make great show among his friends and does give out the public meaning that more monies he does possess, than is his private assessment. 'Tis his belief that all do have the admiration for him, which has the fondness in it, for it does just bring upon the hangers-on who do wish to have the benefit of his largesse – though not likely that they should grow round on what he does give them. More show it is.

But to my washing day, which be just passed. And to the complaints that Jane does make. And little fairness is there in them, for 'tis clear that we do much the same and I lead no life of ease. Though 'tis true that Jane and I be of agreement that when I do rise, already should she have the fire ablaze, so 'tis ready for me to start the first water-boil on the pot-hook. (And no objection is there in me that the room be the warmer for the effort.) Yet this morning, naught but a mean glow is there to greet me, and no sound purpose is there in this. For surely too Jane should find it better to have the warm flame than to let the fire go down just to spite me?

Yet I must do the chore, and stir the coals, and precious few of them there be, for my husband's show be directed more to the outer world than to solicitude for the comfort of his wife – and this does put the rattling in me that I should use my hands to set the coals, for raw enough work they should do this day without the fire making – and the common serving wench it does make of me when 'tis better that I do deserve.

And Jane does swear that 'twas a merry fire she did leave behind, when the second time she did venture out for the carrying of the water, yet I do not believe her. Good fires do not have such quick deaths, lest she did pour the water on it in a pett.

But too much time it takes to list all the things she does neglect and for me to play the scold herein. Better it is that I should attend the fire and start the water on to boil and much do I time and plan in my head and each week try to better it, so that some feeling I do have of success and not just the wearying repeat. But more oft it is that it should take longer and that all my plans do go awry which has the frustration in it. More sense to think how long each task does take and then to double it, if I do need to keep within my limit. Yet to think it should take twice the time I do prepare is more than I should live with.

Samuel does sleep on while Jane and I do start our work. Full well do we hear his noisome ways and do catch each other's eye to wonder which end the wind does blow from. And truly did I want to laugh though no respect is there in it to speak of the master's farts to the serving woman. So did I put on my severe look and call Jane to our task, and make out that nothing should I hear. Which has the difficulty. For even the deaf should be disturbed by such bellows and loud snortings.

The two wash tubs we soon have at the ready, and then for the special chamber pot which does have but the piss in it do I seek to take. Yet 'tis not outside the chamber door which is its place of keeping. And do I chafe at this for over and over again do I give Samuel instructions that the *one* pot there is for the piss for the wash day, yet it makes not the permanent mark in his head and like is he to forget this and use the wash-piss pot for his crapping. Which is to be the simpleton, and no consideration. So must I go to test the pots with no shyte in them, for no good it is to have the turds mixed in with the piss.

Always on the Lord's Day I do remind Samuel that 'tis piss only that I should see in the chamber pot aside the door, and I do fume to think that so little thought he does give to me that 'tis beyond him to keep his piss separate from his shitting, and does this ruin me.

So do I go to my husband's bed, and seek the chamber pot I did hear him use last night when he did return from roistering. And tempted I was to wake him, and to put the pot to him, and fortune it was for him that it had none of the stools in it, for mightily should he have known of them. And to the bubbling wash with the pure piss I did return for the washing to proceed.

Jane and I did mix the piss in the pot on the boil and 'tis well that it does do some good with the bleaching for the smell is not at all pleasant and perforce does make its way to every part of the room. Not all the piss I did use for the first wash and the safe store place I did find for the chamber pot where no careless step should tumble it, so that we should lose the little we did have. Yet does it seem to me that not enough left there is to do the full wash so I do speak to Jane to make good the contents, through the day, but with the piss only. But little reminder does she need for she too does take her turn at pouring in.

And much care do we take of the good linnin which does come from France, though not for long[1] and when 'tis in the pot we do have the minute-break. Miserable cold it was still, and though I know Jane does think 'tis mean of me to want the fire to give off the light to see by, and to lay aside the candles, yet do I persist. For the candles now be of great cost, for many there are who do want soap, and not enough fat there is to make both the soap and the candles, so are they scarce and the price does rise, and not so much money do I save for mine own purposes when the expense of the house does so increase.

[1] There was a move to promote the manufacture of English linen and in 1663 a statute was passed to discourage imports, particularly from France.

And though I do give Samuel the lesson in arithmetic and show how what he does lay out for the household does not go to meet what he does require, yet no reckoning does he make of the struggle betwixt the candle and the soap makers, and no more monies for it does he provide. So 'tis gloom and dark when we do stop for some bread and cheese, which is all we can take. We do want of something to keep our strength up, for the long day, but 'tis not appetizing with the steam – and the urine odour – and the thoughts on the hard day before us. Yet does it make a chance for us to have the talk but for a few minutes, though careful we are not to wake my husband, for that be another complication we have no spirit for.

We do debate on the merits of the lye and the soap; were it not for the great cost I would always be for the soap, though my mother does swear by the lye for her wash. Yet I think it is just her habit and she does not like to change to new things. For many do tell that the soap does do the better wash, which so it should given the great expense, or else the soap boilers be but a swindle. I do prefer the soap to the lye moreover, in that it does not make for such sore hands. If I were to have more monies, I would keep it in plentiful supply.

Then too, I do sometimes have the blue for the wash, but not today. 'Tis good that it does the better job than the urine and there be many advantages in its use, for it gives off no retching smell. But too hard it is to get, and do come and go in the market, depending on the country we do fight at the time so I am told.[2] There be none to be had at the Cheapside market at present, so I do save my bit of blue and do try to do it turn about with the piss. One week I have the piss at no cost and which do come in abundant supply from my husband, yet the stench do stay on. Then the next week I do try to have some new blue which do cost much and be not so abundant, but do give off no smell, and do definitely make the cloths whiter.

When I do protest at the hard work of the wash and do complain to my mother on it, full well does she say that I am spoilt, that there be nothing in it today. And thankful I am for the progress of the soap and the blue and the new starch. Yet

[2] The blue for the wash came from the Low Countries and was often not available because of wars.

it makes *me* feel no easier to hear how she did work harder and with me and brother Balty to do for as well. And I do remind her that my father had not such grand ideas as Mr Pepys who does want to change his outer clothes more like once each week, but no sympathy does she have for me.

Jane and I do just get the linnin on to boil and little of each other we can see through all the steam, when S. does rise and make such fuss about the chaos of the room. Yet how to do the washing near the fire, and to have the place too for sitting and eating and to still keep order in the way my husband does decree regular, does escape me. So he to his place of work does make to go, for 'tis true that no room there is for him and no consideration either, and he takes with him his rancour-tongue, which makes it much the better for Jane and me. Easier it is with him gone, and Jane and I do work at our own pace, and much in silence.

Six hours does it take to go through the wash until we do start on the rinse, and though our hands be sore we do keep to it. But I come almost to tears when the good linnin, which does come up nicely, and be boiling to content, is befouled by the soot which does fall straight from the chimney. I do think on my father's great invention for the chimney-cleaning and do wish it were already the great success, for I am so pushed to distraction to see the once clean and bubbling pot which does then become nothing but sooty broth and it should make me cry to see the good linnin in it which be washed, and rinsed and almost ready for the starch. And now must be done all over again.

And Jane does take revenge by great shouting at the chimney, but to no effect.

Nor should we know what is best to do with this boiling black broth for insufficient room there be herein to house it. Not pots enough there are to put it to one side and take out the linnin. I did make much at heaving it from here down below into the street, for it would have done me good to throw it violently. But 'tis not always possible to see who does pass below and as 'tis hot, then should it do the great damage. So we do bind up our hands and together carry the hot-pot down to the yard where we do tip it. And it do steam away. Then nothing for it there is but to start again, though my heart is not in it the second time, and once more I do not keep to the times I should set in my head. At least 'tis our fortune to make do with the water that is left, so no more carrying is there called for. Yet is it but me I wonder who does have such problems with the wash day or do it try all women and make them despair? Little complaint I do hear, but rather are there women who should take such pride in their wash and who would have it that but little effort it is to get it done, and much satisfaction they claim for it, but not for me.

Though my husband could well come home for nourishment, he arrives not and grateful I am for it. Yet might he go to The Green Dragon or some place and fire hisself up, but 'tis better than that he does come home for his dinner. For it would please him not to find still such confusion and nothing for him to eat of. And then, when he does expect to come home to the wife who is neat and pretty, sourly does he take on so when I am red of face and tired in spirit, and much bedraggled from the wash. For he does not know what great hardship it be. Just does he expect the clean linnin, and no thought to its difficulties, yet no washwoman am I, like his mother should be and no intention to get so common.

Yet I must finish it; by darkness we do have most in control, in spite of difficulty, and so we set the clothes afore the fire to start on drying and then to the starching of those that be left. And a high regard is in me for this new starch which does come from the low countries, and a great improvement it is on the starch which must be made from the boiling of wheat. For the wheat starch does take up a pot and the fire, which could for the linnin be, and 'tis but another thing which can go wrong, and does continual. For so much is there to think of, and too likely it be that the wheat starch does burn or get thick. When I do think on these vast improvements of the age I have some agreement with my mother who does give thanks for these modern times when all is made easier. Yet still does it feel like very hard work and much more there should be of assistance though what form does elude me.

The supper hour does pass but without Samuel Pepys, and Jane and I stop not to cook. For too much of a juggle it should be to manage the food, and the starching, on one pot-hook, and it suits me not to cook in the washing pot, no matter how well the viands be wrapped.[3] My pots do serve but one purpose a time, yet more of them I need to keep to this.

I did ask Jane whether she did want to go to the cookshop and get something in for us to eat, but she does say she is not hungry. Which well could be true. For with the suds and the steam – and the piss smell which do stay around – the appetite does leave. And no place is there to sit anyways, with all the cloths spread out adrying. But could it be that lazy she is and no liking to go out again to the cold, even to take away the food from the stalls. But either way, she goes not forth, and so I save my monies. Though it cannot be said that I do not feed my servants for 'twas there if she did want it.

So we just keep to the work and towards the midnight hour do get to the finishing with the smoothing iron. This is a kind clean job, once the hot coals be placed in the iron, which I do make Jane do for many the time do I burn my fingers on it. But then I am content to do the smooth iron. I do not mind the steady strokes of it and do gain much satisfaction when the good linnin and the cloths be arranged so smooth and neat.

'Twould be of great relaxation except that I start to feel unease that my husband be not in. Dully tired though my mind be, it does wake to all sorts of dreadful scenes that might detain him. For it be not safe to stay abroad at this hour and more so, that he does have no cunning when the drink is in him, but does make of himself much more of the ready fool for those who do seek to do him some mischief.

But from the King Street, just on the midnight hour, Jane and I did hear him come. I do curse to the devil those who do praise his fine singing voice for he does give it full range when he rolls along after much of the wine. And to the neighbours he does announce the fit hour he has for coming home, and in what state. And so he does let the world know that he be there for the taking. More disturbance he does make than the dog which does keep us wake a-nights, and which he does threaten to take of its life, and do I think there be those with similar intent towards him.

But on the foot of the stairs he does tarry and Jane and I

---

[3] There was only one fire and it seems, only space for one pot for washing and cooking; evidently it was not uncommon to wrap some food in a cloth and cook it too *in the washing pot*!

must go and pull him in for he does but stand there and focus as if he be not sure whether he does come to his own dwelling place. Easier it be though to get him inside, than up the stair, for no cooperation is there in him, and he does just rollock along. And he would be not hushed though we did try everything, and Jane did put her arms round him, while I did try to stop his mouth.

But to no purpose, and on and on he does keep with his wild, loud talk. So full of the wine was he, and did but match the fullness of his own importance, and he do tell rambling tales of his good dinner with Mr Pinkny. The detail of the excellent singing he does take part in, he does give and the beauty of his playing on the flageolet. On his fingers he does list the pints of wine he does take in at The Green Dragon on Lambeth Hill and then at The Golden Lion near Charing Cross.

Then does he lose some of his good cheer and become petty when Jane and I be not impressed with the size of his bladder that it does hold all he does drink, and with the operation too, for some there are – he does give out – who do claim this a great feat to survive the removal of the stone and still to keep so much in.

But then, as the reminder, he does find he can keep his no longer and urgently he does call for the chamber pot. Which do put me in the great fix for the nearest ones be hidden somewhere neath the linnin which be spread around. But thanks be we do get one in time, and no spillage there should be.

To push him to the bedchamber be my only design for fearful I am that he should fall down. But no assistance does he give me and his reechy breath he does blow pon me, and does he make to kiss me, which I have no mood for. And when I do try to aid him to his bed, he does go all high and make to manage on his own. And must I hold myself close together, as he does take elaborate step across the room and in great time.

Jane and I cannot plan for his weaving so we must move quick to take things from his path that he stumble not. Across the tub or the pot I have no desire he should trip, and too I do respect the clean cloths that are draped afore the fire which I want to keep preserved. For 'tis not my wish to see his great footprint pon the neat linnin, so do I remove things from his way.

But at last does he get to his chamber and to his bed and much relieved I am, though he should slump in the stupor and place his dirty boots without a care. No affection do I have for him in this state. And then he does start to moan with his head, and the sickness that is on him, and the stomache grippe, and I do reckon to empty the chamber pot that he has filled than to think on the mess when he does start to retch up the wine, and take it as a basin, which be not uncommon for his condition. Yet it be more extra work and I cannot smile on him or give of my sympathy when I do check that he have his needs. And I do tell him he do smell loathsome which do not improve him but 'tis true. And he make no more talk of my coming to bed, which I cannot, even if he were of sweet breath, for the washing be not finished.

And I do feel ill-used that I be so tired from being awake for nigh on twenty hours, and all the time at hard work while he do go forth to make merry. I am too weary to have the patience with him and 'tis too much to expect me to make pleasant when no enjoyment has there been for me this day. Yet I am pleased he is home safe and that no harm does come to him and that be quite enough.

Jane and I do try to finish up and to make tidy for the morrow as best we can. Though some things be still damp and must stay a-hanging and not all has been done with the smoothing iron. To see not all put away and order restored will not please Mr Pepys if he do come on them again in the morning. No good humour will he have from the after effects of the drink, and any little thing will serve to make him flare. For easier he finds it to have the fault of his temper laid to my cause than to cast blame on himself and his own habits. So I do resolve to rise before him and to make all neat.

Then I do notice that his noise do stop suddenly and do think to check on him before the last cloths is hung. For many an accident do befall those who have been to drinking. Yet I do reassure myself that it be no more than he has succumbed to the drunken sleep. So I do creep softly to his room for fear I do disturb him and do expect to see him fast sleeping. But no. To my mighty surprise he does sit in the bed with the very lowest of candles, and does he take to scribbling!

'Tis not my way to disturb him, yet this does have some

mystery in it. For what else should he do at such late hour? And e'en as I watch he does write and no attention to me, and downstairs the crier calls 'tis one o'clock on a cold and frosty morning.

Could it be that Samuel does take to the diary entry? Much talk have we had of late on how 'tis to be done, and while I showed him not mine own pages, yet freely did I talk about the manner of it all, and the satisfaction it should bring. But I did think that Samuel be not convinced for very great was his fear that someone should get to his pages; that if the plan should be to set one's self naked upon the page (as I did say was the best means) then 'twas the difficulty for some to look upon the nakedness. Which has the reason in't, and so repeated I did answer him that mine eyes should never stray to make the meaning of his words, and so quite safe he should be.

And so does it seem he did believe me. For certain I am 'twas his diary entry he did keep. Which does have the fascination in it. And more in my interest is it to wait till he does take his leave afore I should try to see what he does pen – though what sense he should put down in his foxed state does get the better of me. And much patience is there in me to discover his meanings.

Quiet did I leave him and come to this. And much does it amuse me to think that while he did write in there, I did keep account here, yet I would not let him know that I did fathom his ways.

So now perchance two records there are which be kept, and most amusing it should be to make comparison. Yet should it wait for another day, when less tired I be. 'Tis a long time to be at the washing, yet should it be done till the next week. And mightily now should I sleep . . . afore the cock does crow again.

## February

Who should have thought that the town would come to this? And little judgement do I have to know whether 'tis the cause for celebration, or whether 'tis wise to be afear'd. Much talk is there in the air about the coming and going of kings, till I know not which be proper or which should be open to the charge of treason. And no help is Samuel in this either.

Truth to tell he does put the worry in me. For so little discretion does he have. 'Tis his weakness that always there is the windfucker in him, so one day he does deplore all monarchs and the next does go royalist and call for the restoration of the King. Which does pass while all is confusion, but what should happen if one side does get the ascendancy, and seek to have revenge, and put end to t'other? Then should he find hisself in a pickle, and the danger in it too. For both should say that he did offend.

Caution be a better watchword. And do I tell Samuel to keep his peace – though little note does he take of the wife-woman. Leastways till the outcome of all upheaval should be made clear. For too great are the risks in choosing sides when the ending be not known.

Yesterday was like the fair. All were thronged into the streets, and the shouting and ringing did abound, and very playful too. And though the soldiers did come, and I did watch close to see which side they should be on, well did they meet in with the crowds, who did make gifts to them, and no displeasure did this give them.

Money too did pass hands, and I did think on it as the good will sign, for much time has passed since the soldiers be paid, but not so wise to sudden fill their pockets, for 'twas predictable that they should use such funds for the drink to flow. And easy it should be to praise them and ply them but 'tis when they have the drink in them that 'tis possible they should turn sour, and who then should know which way they go? For the town does go unruly and 'tis luck, not law that does keep the order.

The Bow Bells do take the lead with all bells ringing, and all through Cheapside the bonfires be lit, and 'tis said that more than forty there have been this last night, and on all was a rump roasted to mark the end of the Rump Parliament.[4] Which does have the mirth and mockery in it, but only when the Rump Parliament be without favour; and too soon to know whether it should find its strength and make return. Then those who do

---

[4] *Rump Parliament*: the name given to what was left of the Parliament after the fall of Richard Cromwell in April 1659. Roasting of 'rumps' was intended as mockery and insult.

build bonfires and roast the rumps, and make merry at the Parliament expense, could find they have no cause for mirth.

Yet should I hope this happens not, for my man does have the loose tongue and is full of spirit and crowing, and like his sex does know all the answers, though they change from day to day, and all fuss and no sense is there in him. 'Tis my hope that all else are so inclined with him, that none should note his blowings. And none there is who could tell whether there be reason to be sober or stirred, till the solution to these sore times should make itself known.

## March

Much excitement has there been for my husband's fortunes do change dramatically and mine with it, which does please me. For has he found high favour with my lord, and is elevated to the fine position of Secretary, which does bring with it, great responsibilities, and much money making too it does seem to me. Yet if there are the benefits, so too there are the detractions. For it does seem that my husband should go to sea – perchance tomorrow – on the *Nazeby*, and all the talk of meeting with the King, which I hope does come to pass and be no trick. For who does say he should be the King and how to make and keep it so? 'Twould be well to know.

If my husband does go up in the world so too I do. Yet not without the fears does this have for me. For 'tis plain that then the more wenches there will be to take note of him, and the more money he should have for the buying of baubles, which does add to his attractions, and 'twill take all my cunning to keep him from the towsing. But the compensation there is in it for me too. The fine establishment there soon could be, which does please me and is my due.

But further future consideration this be. More pressing now, his possible departure. As early as the morrow. And much more yet to be made ready for it. The only danger I do see for him aboard the ship is the sea sickness, or the sinking! And at this end, loneliness for me. For though I would say it not to him, yet do I wonder what I should do without my man.

Yet all else of consideration – e'en this journal keeping –

must I put aside to make ready for his sea-change. (Though true it is that herein I do have the space to gather my scattered thoughts and write down what preparations there should be.)

Jane and I do give attention to his wardrobe, which be set not just against his sea-going, but already he will have it that all must befit his new station. And should I look to the counting of caps and stockings and the folding of linnins, so that he should have the suitable attire which does rival that of the King.

And the solution which Samuel does put to me that I should be disposed of in the country, which I think on to avoid. Much I should prefer to bide my time with Eliza, though there is the small matter of Richard who takes not kindly to my presence, and who, since I did make amends with my husband and get the signed agreement, and the allowance, does have it that the bad influence I am on his wife and comfort.

Yet never did Eliza need me to urge on her the resistance and the making of demands. Which does just show how much the men do miss the mark and make the explanation to their own choosing and their own favour, though they must deny the very evidence which does stare them aface.

And Samuel too does show great reluctance for me to stay in town. All excuse he does give about the dangers – which he does have be political ones! – and the possibility of riot, and e'en civil war, which does seem too much to me. Yet do I know him well enough to see that 'tis the danger which his jealousy does provoke that does make him want to urge me to the country and the safety of the sober Mr Bowyers where naught does happen but the horse-bolt to make the excitement of the year.

The only other choice there be, is that I should lodge with his family, and the Pushy Pall, and all, and Heaven forefend! For if I did not die of want of nourishment, 'tis like I should die from the lowness and depression of it all. Else from the boringness, which be another mark against it.

So to Mr Bowyers at Huntsmore I go when Samuel does leave, but with no good grace. And yet when he does sail away, how should he know when I do come to town? For to have the tooth pulled or some such reasonable explanation? To visit with my parents? Or perchance to dally . . .

'Tis some freedom when he is from hence, but the apprehension too. For well do I know what it is to be on mine own, and not all a bed of roses is in it, and so I do anticipate the loneliness, and the coldness.

'Twas my suggestion – and not all playful – that if too much of the danger it be for me to be on mine own in Axe Yard, then why should my family not come and lodge with me? For surely my father do provide protection, and my mother does keep all in order. Though admittedly the problem should be what to do with Balty.

Yet Samuel does have the apoplexy at this possibility. And he does chafe that my father should prove no guarantee of safety for the household possessions, but worse. That my father should start on his inventions and find excuse to keep from exit, when Samuel does return.

'Twas almost worth the betwitting of him to serious hold this up as my plan, so easy did he make it to heat him. Yet did I fear that he should have the blood burst, so I did desist, and make recommendation instead, that he should have the blood letting, which he did. The full sixteen ounces. And no more did I speak of my father's protection while Samuel does his duty for the King, and does risk his fortune, and perchance his neck as well. Though truly do I pray that there should be no rift betwixt my husband and family, yet vain hope should it seem to be.

Yet e'en though I should be packaged off to the country, not all Samuel's way should I let it be. For I do insist on the buying of linnin for *three* smocks for me and some black silk taffeta as well e'en though it be unready by Easter.[5] And 'tis my excuse that he does make many additions to his wardrobe now that he does go up in the world, and does he not see the need for the well dressed wife to match his rise? And too I did play on proof of his affection, and his going away and the good sense there is in it for me to be occupied with the sewing, while I do pine in the country and think on him. And most convincing was it though none should be my real reason, which is that I did *want* them and 'tis my estimate that now he can easy afford it and I like not that which is less than fair.

[5] Women's fashions changed annually at Easter.

## May

'Tis a form of death this country life. And not e'en good for the complexion. Yet do I think it cannot last forever and that soon should my husband return. Yet he should find me expired from the boredom. Not one event do I have to record but that no reason there be to rise of the morning.

## 5 June

My husband does send me the good news, and the bad too. The good news that Mr Downing does now have his knighthood and my husband does think it soon should be his turn, for much good service has he done the King. And is it not fitting that Lady Pepys should keep a handsome place and have fine clothes, and eager I look forward to the prospect?

The bad news is not so bad. But Samuel does have the gloom that this time he could keep not the celebration with Jane Turner for the anniversary of the cutting of the stone. Yet not his fault it be that he is aboard ship, and no blame will Jane Turner attach to him for the keeping not of his word. For 'tis none of his doing, but the King's.

More troubled I am that he does report an accident[6] in which he does fire the gun to salute the King, but holding his head too much over the gun, he does almost spoil his right eye. And he does write to me assurances that he does recover, but no hair is there left upon his brow, which be worrying.

'Tis my hope that he has done hisself no permanent damage, though 'tis the case that if the serious injury it be, then the great fuss he should make of it. For 'tis not his way to put aside pain and always does he want the great sympathy. So I do satisfy myself.

Yet it does prove that little ability he has with the gun, which I did always know. But constant is the desire of his sex to demonstrate the manliness with the making of noise, and the

[6] Samuel reports this in his own diary on 22 May and although he says he almost 'spoiled' his right eye by holding his head too far over the gun, the injury doesn't seem to be very serious for he doesn't mention it again.

brandishing of weapons, so now my husband does without his hair, and not such a great crop he has that he can afford to lose it. Though whether it be from the top of his head or else just his brow that he does blow away, I have no ascertainment.

'Tis but the excuse for the wearing of the wig if it be the top, and no great harm. But not so ready the replacement for the brow. Though if he should be left with the scar, no doubt it should stand as the sign of battle and do good service for him.

But do I correspond with my mother and ask her the receipt for the growing of hair on the most unpromising of surfaces and certain is she to have some remedy.

Yet among all these accounts which do stand against him, and leave my husband to look somewhat of the fool, so too is there much proof of his great importance to the King. And I hope that he should return the hero and that there should be the great rewards. And no more do I have concern for the outcome of the venture. For 'tis plain now that the King does have guarantee of his return and all do welcome him and what does have the strangeness in it is that none there is to be found who did ever say themselves agin the monarchy, but always the royalists they have been.

Such quick change of heart I do think many undergo. And could it be back again. But this I should not think on.

Sweeping changes should there be, not just for the monarchy, but for the true character the King should be. 'Tis said that he be a man of fashion, and that his new styles do go much further than the mere cutting of his coat. And one reason that we should have the royals back is so all should have the chance to follow in their ways, so much haste there is to have the cloaks and gowns that do copy the King. And my husband does know all this and considerate does he send the detail of the dress of foreign ladies (though not the means for me to imitate, 'spite the fact that he does say that his store does grow apace); and I do think they have more splendid attire than what did pass in London town – from what I do recall the last time I did get there – though not so much finesse as from Paris. But I do look forward to the new fashion ways and much firmness is there in me to follow.

More to disconcert is the report that 'tis the eye for the beauties that the King does have and many does he take abed.

For 'tis certain that should he set such a fashion for making this sport, that many there be who should wish to emulate him and worse would it be for wives. Such habit, be it royal sport or no, is one I like not my husband to follow.

But all does pale when I do think that the homecoming of my husband be imminent, for 'tis wide reported that his ship should sail in any day, and I do look to it. And hope that my health be good.

## 23 June

Last evening did we spend our first night together back in Axe Yard, and much is there to be said for the pleasure of one's own roof above one's head. Though not for long. For now that Samuel does rise in the world so too does our dwelling, and to the Navy place in Seething Lane we should move and most impressed I be with the description of it, and much to look forward to and to meet Eliza and convey all, yet not to Samuel do I make known my plans to gallivant a little in the town with Eliza – for 'tis clear that 'tis at home that he thinks I should be and that does please him. Which does have the tediousness in it but only in the assurance that I wait within and that naught but the most innocent and pressing business does call me forth.

And all that does truly try me is mine own sickness. For the pleasure we do partake of does have its repercussions; once more 'tis my lot to have the burning pain and the need to piss all the while, which be no pleasure at all.

## June

'Tis a high life that we do lead now, and so far have we moved from the garret that times there are when I do find all these changes beyond my comprehension. Each day does my husband give more signs of his improved station, and does add more riches to his wardrobe. And if I were to have but my share, then all would be to perfection.

Natural it is that I should feel some cause for complaint when I do see Mr Pepys go forth as the peacock while content I must be to be poor and plain. And does it take the edge of my pride and pleasure when no finery there is for me, for no provision is made on this scale in our agreement and I do think I did too little require, for 'tis my sense that my husband does overtake me, as ne'er did I dream to have the share in such fortune as Samuel shows now. (Unless he does borrow for all this, and has not the means to pay, which surely he should be not so foolish to do.)

Yet will my turn come. For my husband is not such a bufflehead to think it be of no account how his wife should dress. 'Tis when the excitement and novelty of his own plumage do abate that my time should come. Though 'tis true that my husband does have the ambivalence in him about my attraction.

[7]For I would be known as a woman of fashion, of good breeding, and good taste. And e'en to the point of providing the polish for my low-born husband. For 'tis known that my father is the nobleman, and my mother of the great Clifford family, and many reasons are there for me to dress modish and make the good impression. The only difficulty there should be is that the more I look the beauty, the more does my husband have the dilemma. For there are those who almost open, pay me suit – like Edward Montagu, my lord's son among them, and William too, and then one who does stay my secret, and whose name I write not here, not e'en in the French. For though Samuel does know and need the fine wife to reflect upon him, yet too he does have the jealousy sickness full through him, and does it turn his bowels when he does suspect I have the suitor.

But 'tis not just with the clothes that my husband does think to have improvement. Constant does he urge me to learn more about the finesse of food, for here too be another way to make a show, which he does full intend. And no knowledge of the finer points should he get from his family, for this form of preparation and presentation.

When in the employ of Mr Downing, sufficient for him was the boiled chop, or the roasted leg from the cookshop. Yet now he does put about as Samuel Pepys *Esquire*, and goes looking for his knighthood, and he does have his own patent and

---

[7] This paragraph has been translated from the French.

perform the duties of Clerk of the Acts, and all this under his charge, then he wants not just silks and velvets to make known his position. He does wish to be known more as the epicure! Yet no manners does he have for it.

'Tis his new found knowledge that great men do have fine palates which be the match with their fine clothes, and he does urge me to make this my belief and to look for more refinement for our repasts . . . and me a Clifford!

But all this without the addition of the cook, which does have expense in it . . .

And not to my liking to be steamed in the kitchen, for while 'tis my place to preside at table, yet too hard it is to do the cooking and the serving. And does it show my husband's want of breeding that he should enjoin me to know more about the nobleness of dining (which does come to me unbidden) when 'tis the commonness of cooking that he does mean, and would have me learn, which I think not to do.

Though these be not the reasons I did put to Samuel who already does too oft call me the noble sloth. No. 'Twas my case that the cookshops be superior, for the little expense they cause and much more variety too, and the convenience to choose, and ready to take away, and no disorder either so that *I* did get convinced. And did I inquire of Samuel whether it be more pleasing for the persons of discernment to keep the cooking odours and the grease of pots outside the home?

Well argued, and nicely termed, I did present the points of view, yet does my husband find the fault in it. And do I harken to what he does say . . . for some twists there be. 'Tis his contention that the cookshops should do well for the poor in property or breeding, who have not the delicate tastes, and care not what they put in their stomachs, and do but take whatever comes forth from the ovens. But 'tis unfitting for the man who be charged with numerous responsibilities and who does have the position to keep up in the world, to carry home his dinner for all to see. For it does suggest to all abroad that he has not the means for the preparation of his own fine fare, and no willing wife to serve him. Which is the galling blow though I show it not.

No admission do I make, yet 'tis true that 'tis common to

feast from the cookshop, but few do have the provision of their own kitchen which does then become the mark of the gentry.[8]

And were the sweaty work not in it for me, so too should I prefer the private kitchen, but does it need the cook and the kitchen maid and truly then no difficulty should it be for me to make the plans and give the orders for the dainty dish each day. But though I did quizz him, 'tis plain as the day that my husband has no intention for the hiring of the cook, not even for the occasion, so rather would I have the cookshop provide. For 'tis not just the cook I needs do without; 'tis no easy task for e'en the most willing of workers and most refined of tasters to make the banquet from one pot o'er the fire, which is all I do have.

'Tis the usual fault I do find with Samuel Pepys, and too much to think that he should rid it by now from his character. Always he does want to play the grand one, but without the expense. No objections are there in me against the grandness, for much I would enjoy; but 'tis no great saving to my husband I should be. If he does want the fine food, and the good impression, then 'tis there for any who should pay for it . . . which be the whole point which does get lost on Samuel. For 'tis only fond pretence to want the show without payment for the substance – and no false payment should I be, to rough my hands and red my face. 'Tis the cook, and the kitchen maid, and the serving maid too and the kitchen besides if he does want the appearance of one who does keep the kitchen and the cook and the serving maid . . . and have the wife to plan and preside.

And perchance all this should happen, and e'en soon, for with the return of the King and the increase in my husband's coffers, nothing now does strike me as unlikely any more.

But did I think that all delicate dressed dishes should be wasted 'less my husband does make the alteration in his eating habits. For so quick does he gulp the food, and so ready to turn it to wind with the belch and the fart, that no means is there in him for appreciation of the fine flavours. E'en the colly flower, for the example, which be my delight to savour what does seem

---

[8] Until after the First World War, the majority of households in Britain were without cooking facilities/kitchens; they ate 'take-away'.

to me the most rare delicacy, but down it does go with one swallow with him, and none is there left on his plate when I do but partake of the second morsel. 'Tis all the fault of his home of course; for no manners nor marks of breeding should he learn from his own common family. Still does he expect the guest to bring their knife and spoon when all of breeding do know that 'tis more polite to provide these than to have each bring forth their own peculiar pieces.[9]

Yet 'tis more his own conduct at table which is in need of attention if he does sincere want improvement in how others do see him. Just to take the time, to keep from spitting forth and to smooth transfer the food from plate to palate with the fork[10] and not the fingers and all this should show more true sign of breeding than whether the fare does come from the cookshop or no.

'Tis not the partridges theirselves – which Samuel Pepys does now say should be the fit meat for his table – that do make the gentleman, nor the place nor the manner of their cooking. But the manner of their eating. And here he does fall short. And much does he have to be desired, but no easy way to tell this, else my husband does look askewe at me for the very littlest of criticism.

## June

Partridges. Sick I am of hearing of the birds. But nothing less does my husband order, yet so expensive. And to come from my store![11] Different it should be if he do furnish the means. But no, *improvement* be the key word of the day that he do utter, but no sound does come forth as to the payment. No justice is there.

Yet the wild thought does occur to me . . . that the pigeons

[9] Until the later part of the 17th century it was common for guests to arrive and produce their own eating utensils which they always carried with them: probably a sensible hygienic practice.

[10] Forks (of the two-pronged variety) were just beginning to become fashionable though they were still sold separately from knives.

[11] Presumably this means that Elizabeth is required to pay for them from her allowance.

and the partridges should be very similar and why should not the pigeons do? 'Tis said that with the very right cooking the pigeon be passable as the superior bird, and much cheaper too and nothing to say of the satisfaction there should be in me to have my husband fooled that he does sup on the partridge quality and show his breeding when in truth he does feed off the pigeon and show his want of taste. For 'spite his claims, my husband be no epicure and no way should he have to tell the difference and no drain would the pigeon be upon my purse.

## 28 June

Jane, my maid, does today lie abed, with the lameness which I feel sorry for. Yet no cause do I see, though certain it is that it provides her with the rest while just the opposite should it be for me. Yet do I take to her my partridge problem and seek her counsel in my plan, for though I like not to admit it, more knowledge is there in her on these matters than I do have. And she does agree. That the pigeons be very like partridges but not in the cost and they will serve well as the first test to please the new puff-palate.

## 29 June

Jane does still alie abed, which does make me sour, yet no longer do I put off my husband's call for the delicate dinner so I do tell her my resolve to purchase six live pigeons on the morrow, and to kill them here and try my hand at the cooking of them for the most economic that should seem to be. But Jane does warn against it (though gets not from her bed to give me assistance with it); enough it is that she sits upright in her bed and takes the liberty to abuse me on the folly to kill the birds myself, for much trouble and mess she does say there will be. Yet I do see her method. For she does think that the more work this should make for her and no plans does she have to do it, just to stay abed for a whiles, so little heed do I pay her words.

The live pigeons do go at more low cost than the dressed

ones, and no great expense do I want to invest in this my experiment. Many a fowl have I seen with its neck wrung and little skill does there seem in it, and do I know that 'tis not fear nor the squeamishness that should stop me. But I think to make the pigeon pie which my husband should want, without laying out . . . which is what I should want.

## 30 June

Oh that I did listen to the wise words of Jane! The worst day of my life it has been and no sympathy shown me. 'Tis true that I am the proud fool, with no sense, and I do think with shame if my great stupidity be widely known. So much for my desire to provide the fine food without laying out, and no facilities. Oh, can I bear to write it herein? And risk that all should see my folly preserved on paper? Yet some good it should do to confess and clear all from my system, for the most distressed I still be. But to the beginning.

This morning I did rise early for to go to the market at Cheapside. And Jane did *still* have her lameness, and insist she could not rise, and so I did make show to go alone and manage well. Yet 'tis true, Jane did urge me most vociferous against the purchase of live pigeons but not one bit should I be deterred.

So to market and six live pigeons did I buy, and the trouble of it has been so terrible to me. True too that the game-monger did try to persuade me to give him the privilege to cut off their heads, but when he did tell me how much this privilege should cost me, I did think that I had the cunning in me to take them live. For I did observe him well, and no difficulty did the birds give *him* when he did grasp them, and hold them up to parade their plumpness, and I did not think to be bested by a common game-monger.

Yet different birds they be when he does place them singly in my basket, for they take not to the sharing of a nest, one atop the other and the great commotion there is in them.

I did think to be well prepared for I did have with me a clout to fasten o'er my basket for to keep the birds contained within. But almost more than my strength did it take to hold down firm, and a wearisome journey home I did have of it. Much struggle was in those birds for to take again to their natural state, and my arms did ache with effort to keep them confined. No cooing and loving pigeons they be, but nasty vicious ones, that did beat and flap and make all manner of squawking, and all in the street did keep their distance from me, to let me pass with my rowdy, moving basket, which did seem to will its own way.

Yet that was but the beginning of my disaster day. I did reach Axe Yard without mishap, and six pigeons still complete, yet it did vex me what step next to take. For no cage did I have for the keeping of my birds and no way to unfasten my basket, but they should all escape and take flight. Then did I think that 'twas all too much and better it should be that I do cut my losses and abandon all desire to please my husband – and keep ahold of mine own store – and so let the pigeons go, e'en though I should lose the good monies I did give for them, and the toll it did take of me to get them thus far, and all in all it did seem that too much I did invest already and so I did determine to persevere. Which should be the great mistake and sorely do I regret such reasoning.

On I did go to get the pigeons from the packet to the pie. First did I sit firm upon my basket and make to ignore the great squalling from within as I did try to fathom how best to remove them, but one at a time, and to cut off their heads. One plan I did have to make the small hole in the side of my basket and to plunge in my hand to grab each one, but soon did I dismiss it. For though the birds did sit tame on the hands of the gamemonger, yet did I think they were primed to nip at mine, and such prospect did not please me.

Jane did come to the window and make the great face at me which did harden my resolve and though I could hear her not above the hubub of the pigeons, yet did I know plain enough what words she did utter. And more willed I was to prove her wrong, and that I could get the better of but six pigeons.

Nothing else for it was there but that I should take my pigeons inside, for no other method could I devise but that they would escape forthwith. So I did hoist my heaving basket to our living chamber where I did hear Jane make the most mighty protest but no assistance did she give. Then I did make to

215

unfasten the lid but in such manner that they should scramble forth but one at a time.

Yet they did not follow my intent. Great pressure was there against the clout when I did open but the littlest way and let in the light. Plunge out they did with mighty flapping and some did take to all parts of the room and their droppings were profuse. They did bat against the walls and make most fearful sight which did have me quake. But one did remain in the bottom of the basket and have such limpness and the appearance of death though covered was it with pigeon shyte and no pretty sight to see. Whether there was life in it I know not, but I did make certain of its fate and did hit it on the head with my mallet which did stand close by. Yet the dirty pigeon with the splutter and the shyte upon it did seem far cry from the delicacy that my husband did desire and which I did think to provide. All my will did it take to pluck it forth from the ruined basket, and set it on the board, and though never did I give over to squeamishness when I did stay at Huntsmore and watch all manner of animal be put to the slaughter, yet in mine own chamber did the spewing sickness come on me and all will did it take to keep mine own innards from coming forth.

But no time was there for the puking or the pitying thoughts, for the great pigeons did flap about the apartment, abatting their wings against all therein, and the mightiest mess they did cause and the great damage there did seem, and no easy choice would it be to know whether they or I be more afear'd. At least though I opened not my bowels, which they did without heed, and it has been my terrible trial since to help remove all trace of them which be the veriest most disgusting chore and no confidence do I have that it all be gone. 'Tis my dread that my husband do come across the pigeon shyte in some obscure place, for they did get in everywhere and the worse it will be for me if Samuel do fall upon it.

Oh such horror to tell, as it did go on and on.

The noise of all was fearsome and then too the addition of Jane, who did most oft hide beneath the covers for protection from the flying turds and did emerge only to add to the squalling and swear abuse to me, which be of no use at all. I did think on the neighbours to come aknocking, for to find the reason for such disturbance, and though it was my desire to shut myself away and give rein to my great frustration, yet I did stand firm and straight to capture these pigeons who did well warrant the fate of finding themselves made into pie. Yet now I do know what pigeons be made of, and how they do come to comprise such pie, ne'er should I partake of it. Not mine own nor anyone else's either.

Proper preparation had I made before setting forth for the market and my great chopping knife was at the ready, yet no use till the pigeon's neck be stretched beneath it, and far from it were they in their high perch. So I did climb on a chair and flap at them and wait my time, though some did stare full at me, till I did seize one that did hurl itself against the wall. Much did I struggle with its beating but held fast my grasp till it did submit and then did I lower myself and make for the knife.

Yet no swift accomplishment could I perform. I have heard tell there is but the flick of the wrist in the wringing of the bird's neck, but my wrist would make no such play, no matter how I did flick and twist, and all the while the bird did squawk and fluster on the end of mine arm, while the din of its companions did disturb me yet more.

At length did I stretch its neck upon the board and did quieten its wings with mine elbow, and I did think that all should be finished if only I did chop off its head. But the very devil was in that pigeon, and it did up and prance from the board and did flap about and menace me *without its head*. And this be too much for me, for I did sicken with fright to see the headless bird come toward me, and the blood all a-trailing. Not all my powers could put a stop to my screaming. And I did run to seek cover with my maid Jane and did fear to be followed. But when I did calm myself, with no help from Jane who did shoo me off, and did put up my head, great relief it was to find that the dead pigeon did not hover o'er me.

Yet still there were four that did. And much damage did I think they would do, yet I had no mind to catch them. But clear it was to me that some measure must be taken for those threshing birds with all their droppings could not share a chamber with Samuel Pepys.

Sorely did I regret my injunction to him to return with promise of a good dinner. So long had I been about my pigeon killing that I was afear'd that he should mount the stairs and get the unexpected greeting from the pigeon guests. And flumoxed I was with what to do when Jane does make the most sensible contribution – though still from her safe bed – and does send me for her brother Will, to catch the dirty pigeons and to take off their heads, which they do deserve.

'Twas great embarrassment to me to make haste through the streets in search of Will, for much mucked were my clothes, and hair all aflying, and I did think there were those who did point to Mrs Pepys who does shame her noble family and her grand husband. But no help was there for it. Better that I should provide amusement for those in the streets than I do confront my husband in Axe Yard which does become a pigeon loft through mine own folly.

And did I find Will, who did consent to do my bidding but at a price which should make e'en dead partridges a bargain. Yet I could not quibble for my need was pressing. And Will did return with me, and little fuss did he make in the snaring of the pigeons and the taking off their heads, for not much of the fight had they left in them when he did grab them. But the chamber did look like the slaughter house it truly be, when he did finish, and great was the distress within me.

Yet still no rest could there be. For the pigeons must have the careful soaking – to get off their feathers – which I did think to save, but no time there was to make proper preparation. And Will *and* I did get down to the business of cleaning and plucking, and a vile business it be. My stomach did heave and well did I know it that the trouble of all was not worth what it did cost me. For the smell of the slit and spilled innards did over power, and not enough was it to think on the mess, and the stink, but all the while I did have my ear set to hear the foot upon the stair, which should signal the arrival of my husband, and I did wait in dread.

And it did seem to me that the cookshop should look the very palace in comparison to our chambers.

Though Samuel be late, which is just his way, for no thought does he have for the mischief he does ever make to my plans, but this time no complaint is there in me. More 'tis relief. Each minute he comes *not* I give the Lord thanks. For the calamity it should prove to be if my husband arrives home to find his dwelling place become a pigeon house. And worse be they dead and gutted, than when they did flap and shyte about.

'Tis true that Will does well earn his money with the piling together of the slops, for who should have thought the pigeons to have so much of the muck in them?

But e'en when Will did clean the birds, and much of the chamber (though not hisself, and the stink there was on him), still no end of it was there for me. I did find myself in possession of six dead pigeons, a quantity of sodden feather, a mess of pigeon muck which does defy description, and no great will to go further with my desire to prepare the dainty dish for my man. Yet no other course did there seem to me so did I final throw their spindly flesh into the pot, with no regard for the fine or delicate culinary arts. Plain and piqued did I just cover them with the water and command them to boil swift, and then did I consider my part done and the birds could burn for all I did care. But no peace could they give me.

And I did live to curse myself for I should have known that six birds be too great a load for the pot, and no sooner did the water boil than it did bubble-up and overflow. And worse, it did piss on the fire and put it out, and could I have cried with the frustration of all of it.

'Twas all that I could concentrate upon, that soon Samuel should come with appetite and apprehensive interest, and not even the fire to greet him. No energy was there in me to do the rekindling, and I did prevail upon Will to restart the fire – while I did wish to have the means to go straight to the cookshop and make a good meal from tried and true means. But more compensation did that Will demand. That no monies should be enough to fix all and that he should only do my bidding if I did make the move on his behalf and find him employment; *and that he does want my husband for his master* and 'tis nothing short of the blackmail that he does call on me to serve this end.

So for the sake of saving the pence, on the pigeons, I must now have my husband take Will into his employ. True, no great obstacle it did seem at the time, for so desperate I was that little reason was there in me. And quick too it did occur to me that no bad thing it would be to have Will, for more use is there in him than the slothful Jane, and too, he does keep a better tongue in his head. But while it be one thing to convince Mr

Pepys that it should suit him to have the manservant to show his high state, 'tis quite another to get him to pay for the privilege.

The full force of this strikes me not until later however. (And now it does seem the bad thing that Will did so easy take advantage of me, when I did have no way to turn to.) Agreement I did give Will who did make good his word so soon was the fire re-lit, and the most of the mess was removed, and the pigeons to broth away, when the familiar tread I did hear upon the stair.

Close I was to exhaustion when my husband did come in, but affright did fast replace it when I did detect that he be not on his own . . . and I did think to hide myself but no time was there. Mr Hawley does he bring with him – and he has persuaded him home to dine well upon *the partridge*! And he does crow to his companion, which is his way, and I do dread the consequence.

All the good that can be said be that my husband made not the fuss to find Will ensconced therein, not in the presence of a guest. More does he take his stride and act the part that he does always have the man to wait upon him – though he does direct at me the quizzical look when the attention of Mr Hawley be diverted. And Will does take his cue and so does it seem that permanent he is with us. Which is how Will should think to continue.

More suspicion did my man show to the foul smell he did detect and he did sly sniff round to find its source, but not so much to disconcert his guest. But no trace does he find of the pukey muck which did earlier befoul his house, and Will and I did satisfy him with assurances that it was but the fine *partridges* on the boil which did give off such strong smell, and that 'twas the belief that the more odour they did release, the more tender the birds. And we did think to manage it . . . for I did say and Will did assent, that the sad fact be that the fine 'partridges' had not quite time enough to come to their full flavour . . . and perchance it would be wise to furnish Will with the means to go to the cookshop for some savoury treat till all be ready?

'Tis possible that without the reference to the monies, all could have been well. But no liking did Samuel show to put his hand to his purse, but did play to have the dinner served straightforward. And smiling did he say to me that Mr Hawley did the honour to grace his table but that other appointments did call him, so my kindness to place out the partridges would be much appreciated.

And no discouraging him was there.

Samuel would have it that the birds be carved immediate, for the good Mr Hawley should be kept not waiting, and he did try to make the jest that 'twould be the risk to stay two men of great appetite who were for their dinner starved. And only the small protest was there left in me – though I did swear that the birds should be in need of embellishments afore they would please men of such discerning palate. But all attempts I did make to delay to give the pigeons the decent time in the pot, were to no avail.

In vain did I discourse on what I did plan for the pretty birds; to take them when tender, to chop them with the onion, to add the anchovies and the grated breadcrumb, and to make the gravy from the yolk of eggs and the wine. Yet my husband would have it that all I did do was increase his appetite with my talk of such succulence, and he does come close to ordering me to serve his dinner without further excuse. For he does tell that the boiled 'partridge' – as he does persist to call the dinner – be a fine dish still on its own, and he has not the patience to await the delicate dressing.

And I have not the energy to withstand his coaxings and cunning. Reluctantly I did ladle the dreaded pigeons on his plate, and to Mr Hawley too, though none for myself, for I have not the appetite for the loathsome creatures, yet does this go unobserved by my husband, though not the visitor.

And Will does hold hisself straight, though I am not fooled and do see that there is much mirth in him which does come close to getting out as he does think to be entertained by the eating of the minute-cooked pigeon. And he is not disappointed.

My husband does take the first morsel and while I watch not there is no need to tell me of what happens when he does swift spit it – for which there be no excuse for the mannered man should remove behind the hand and place delicate upon the plate. Then do I look to see Mr Hawley who does apprehensive try the bird but who does attempt polite expression of disappointment but does agree that my husband has grounds for his dislike. And both do say that most awful do the partridges taste . . . (more like the raw and common unwashed pigeon, say Mr Hawley who does attempt the joke). And when I go close and examine the offering, 'tis clear that no exaggeration is there in them and so foul be the odour from the plate that I did truly wonder whether the pigeon shyte did make its way into the pot, though it came not to my attention.

Yet did I hold my head high to my husband, and his friend, so that they should think it was the very birds themselves which had the befouling. And did I disguise the dreadful blot with curses of the game-monger who did provide such poor fare, though not the poor cost. (Yet not too far did I seek to go with this line for I did not want to risk my husband's interference, with a scolding of the game-monger, or with excuse that I could not be trusted as the marketer.) And though my husband does have considerable displeasure (and unsated appetite) yet does he retain himself, and vent not his anger. But nonetheless 'tis my resolve to keep my distance when Mr Hawley does take his leave. Which be not long to wait, for 'tis my view that the man did think that 'twas my intention to *poison* my husband and that he should close be the innocent victim. This does explain his demeanour and retreat.

But my husband has it that his stomach does arumble and that he should accompany Mr Hawley elsewhere for dinner. While I do get rid of the blighted birds. Which does suit me, and Will too, which is my insistence.

Yet more clearing and cleaning, and the stupidest day I did ever live. And no more should I do it. And all my store has it cost me.

Yet more to come when my husband did return and do his bandying. And did he charge me with making the fool of him with my bird-mess. And bad enough his ill humour but he does also threat and raise his hand to me, that I must remind him of our agreement, and that I should make all public if he does strike me. Which he does not do, but much did it take from me to put up my defence, and after the ordeal of the day, 'twas not what I needed.

Bitter lesson have these pigeon/partridges been, and now

Will too to provide for, and no way should he let me drop my word. But no heart is there in me to take on this task to careful manage Samuel to see the way to pay for the work of Will. Yet there will be a reckoning soon.

'Tis my intuiting, that only the slow witted would want to be the good cook, for the small outlay, and with no good servants.

## 1 July

Today did my husband go to the cookshop for a good joint of the roast meat, and no comment does he make on the palterliness of it, nor the necessity for the model man to have the epicure cook. Yet he be not cured of his need to display his worldly rise, and his new found style of eating.

## 2 July

More clothes, but that is not all. Today did come home for my husband the fine camelot cloak with the gold buttons too. And a silk suit. And by my reckoning, 'tis worth more than my allowance should pay for one year. Which does incense me. But more besides.

'Tis true that oft does Samuel speak of his intent to keep a diary, which I treated not seriously, for the last one he is to keep record against hisself and a different matter it be from the book of anecdotes he does keep, and the romances he does scribble.[12] Yet should he keep the journal, how else but to expose that which we would oft hide, if he does put down naked on the page the very details of his life, and no other point would there be for all else is done in his many other

[12] On 30 January 1664 Pepys records in his diary that he was cleaning out some old papers, among them 'a romance which (under the title of *Love a Cheate*) I begun ten year ago at Cambridge; and at this time reading it over tonight, I liked it very well and wondered a little at myself at my vein at that time when I wrote it, doubting that I cannot do so well now if I would try'. Pepys wrote many things: letter books; his Brampton Book; Naval Papers; his 'Navy White Book' – a record of personal office matters . . . all were to some extent his attempts to 'organize' the world. No doubt Elizabeth was used to him scribbling but this was something different.

purpose pages. Yet little honesty is there in him when it does come to his own nature, for blind he be to his own state, so perchance he could make the record of his day and see not his own weaknesses, though bold unreliable should such entry be. Such false account, yet I think he does do it.

Why else this leaher-bound volume, and the secresy?

For he does furtive write away (and consult from notes) and then does keep his papers from me when I do come across him in such practice – which I make my very business so to do. Which is how he does get my suspicion, so shall I careful watch and keep check.

So yester-day when he does go to the cookshop for the good joint of meat I demur not about his new finery, make not to go with him, and seek not to take my dinner abroad, but did stay to make use of opportunity to uncover the papers he did write upon. Yet are they locked away. But the diary it should be it does seem to me. And wise it be for me to hold myself together for I do almost burst with curiosity to know what he does enter. But no way to find out to ask of him. Better the cunning and catching.

For so much there is that I would know. Does he keep account of what he should be worth, for dearly should I love such detail. Does he set down who he does dally with, though what I should do with such knowledge does have the measure of me . . . and truly do I wonder if that I do want to know . . . But what is the routine of his days, who does he know? Who does pay him and who does please him, and does he write of his affections for me? Or the complaint against me?

And how should I uncover this? Without that he should know?


## 3 July

'Tis a diary! But in code!

[13]All this day was Samuel gone from here though when he did depart I did not know it, and no firm assurance did he give me and though there was danger in it, yet did I find the book

[13] Translated from the French.

which he does lock away, and so get to it (and no problem should it be to break the lock but the code does seem more difficult) and the great excitement there was in me when I did take it down and did think to have his secrets uncovered to me and much feeling did I have about it and the danger too of discovery though Jane I did post, to tell when Samuel did come, though no reliance did I give her.

And then to find the code. And what vexation there is within me. For surely my thinking was well led and 'tis the diary – yet no language that I know of. But I should bottom it.

Yet 'tis more than I can bear. And too should I enter here, what I now think my man does enter there, and both we do it in the foreign language? And does he read mine as I do think to read his? 'Tis the puzzle and the privacy. For no liking do I have for him to cast his eye pon this page . . . and do I wonder whether this be the time for the double diary.[14]


## 4 July

No prediction can I make of my husband's arrangements and most vexing it be, for no safe chance is there to look upon his diary to take the method of the cipher he does use, and 'tis true that this is all I do think on and that it does scatter me. All my will it does take to show not my hand and ask what he does record and in what code, but though it may give the quick answer yet it should be the long term puzzle for 'tis certain I am that then he would secrete from me all that he does put down on paper. Most likely it is for me to bide my time and obtain the diary when he is from hence, and then to peruse for the code, which being undone I could then but take occasions to read at my leisure; which does have the sense in it but no allowance for my great vexation in knowing not what be within it.

And all is disorder here, for many possessions be left packed,

---

[14] *Double diary*: from such comments it is clear that Elizabeth kept two diaries, one which she didn't mind Samuel seeing (and which contained her fudged household accounts) and one which she kept well hidden. It is not always clear which set of papers are being referred to or whether they were later all placed together.

for 'tis as Samuel says that soon we do move and so 'tis the very waste of time to disturb them.

This day he did make visit to Seething Lane where we are to have the Navy House and most keen I am to know it. 'Tis excellent report that Samuel does give of all he does find but do I want to see for mine own self and who knows if we should agree on what does pass and what does need to be done and what rooms we have for what reasons, which is all to be decided, and with me.

Yet do I know not which I should want more to see: the house in Seething Lane or the leather-papers which are kept under key. E'en the prospect to play the fine lady and to think on what it should mean to go by water[15] and what to do when the weather be the tempest, does slip from my mind as I do dwell on the diary.

No day should we set yet for our departure from Axe Yard, yet much easier should it be when all is settled. Perchance more hope too for the testing out of the diary. So topsy turvy all is now that I have not even the certainty where he does keep all his books and scribblings yet I do suppose that naught is there to stop me from the examination of his effects . . . for to do some housekeeping and to see what should be left and have no place in our new establishment . . . if he should enter and should ask my purpose . . .

. . . and do I think I have success.[16] There, among the books, though more on top, 'tis like it is in regular use, is one which does have all the promise in it and which I should study with care. And e'en to be found in this new pursuit, well could I claim that 'tis my new amusement, for 'tis true that few enough I do have.

One more complication there be; this night does Will stay his first night and be the boy – which Samuel does have as his idea. But another prying pair of eyes it be that do obstruct me in my plan to get the diary . . .'tis my belief that Samuel should make the securing of his personal papers the charge of Will, and would I know if this be the case. Such things be sent to try me!

[15] *To go by water*: access to the house in the city was easier by boat.
[16] It seems that she has left the diary-keeping to go off and check among Samuel's books, and has returned to make a note when she has found the code book.

## 10 July

This day did provide the most pleasant pastime for we did attend Nan Hartlib's wedding in Goring House, and in all our finery too. Samuel Pepys did make such handsome figure in his new silk suit and many there are who do envy him and his rise. And yet my taffeta makes not so fine a show as his silk, still did all take my note, and my husband did find it fair to proclaim that 'twas his greatest good fortune to have such a beauty for a wife.

And Eliza too did make appearance and much did we have to compare for I did tell her of *A Tutor to Tachygraphy, or Short Writing* composed by Thomas Shelton Esquire which I did find upon my husband's book pile and which does answer for the code I think he does use . . . though no check do I make yet for the leather volume does keep within its secure place and no easy time has there been for me to procure it. But Eliza does gull the copy from the friend of Richard and does make her own notes and soon should we sample the journal and see what record is within . . . only then should I settle to more quiet life for much surgence is there in me while I do think to capture the diary and bottom the cipher.

Eliza does twitt me though when she does have it that so swift she is now with the short writing that straight out she could translate the page and no reference to Mr Shelton which I cannot do, and so I surmise that she does crow a bit which is like her. Yet much assistance should she be when I do get the writing of my husband to uncode.

For still he does make private record, and surreptitious too so he does hide from me what he does write.

## 13 July

Today I did cast mine eyes for the first time on what should be our new home in Seething Lane and the fine place it should be and many great plans for improvements Samuel does have, and all I do mind is how much it should cost and how all is to be paid for. Which does make me think that either my husband is the fool who does have his head turned so he does make more show than he has means to pay, which is the possibility; else he does receive a great deal more monies than he does divulge to me – which is also the possibility and the more likely too. And such question could I settle if I to his journal could have free play and find his accounts therein. For he is the very man to count his assets and keep record of the sum of his worth and not just all for order, either.

'Tis that I might snare him that I do put the sly question on Seething Lane; 'tis my pleasure that he should choose the best room for to make his library, and we to talk on where he should place his books (which now are in such disarray and which does cause him stress, but not for long) and where he should do his scribbling and all the things that do need entry now that he does go up in the world and take such responsibilities.

And while much discussion there is, no reference does he make to the diary-keeping or the code he does write in and keep from me. So no success is there in it for me.


## 16 July

'Tis the boredom and the busy-ness of my husband that does drive me to make entry here. Well known it is that my husband does play the fidget when change there is to be made, and he does prepare in advance and with over much fuss, but this be almost beyond durance.

Two days past since he did give the orders that all should be laid in readiness against our going to Seething Lane, and more hindrance than the help has he been, for must he check and then check all again, and the packing does grow out of all proportion when it must be done not once but ten times over.

And Jane has little of use in her and does complain still of her lameness – though naught do I see, and most convenient should it be to have so much illness when so much there is to be done. All does fall then on me to set aside our goods, and no easy task to put all in readiness when my husband does burrow in it for to take his own stock for he will take not *my* word that what he does make inquiry of does have its proper place at the bottom of the bundle.

And nothing damning do I find which should tell its own tale of my husband's interests and no time for me to place the code along side the entries. So no joy is there in't.

Trial enough should it be to pack all the household *once*, and with Jane's help, but perforce to do it many times, and all alone, and distressed too that all my handiwork should be constant undone, does give the cause for me to tie all together with great knots so that they should be *cut* open to examine their contents, and then do I give instructions that not before they do have delivery to Seething Lane should they be spilled. Which does stop him somewhat.

And when all this is done then does my husband tell that two more days it should be afore we do make the move . . . which does throw me. And one day he does plead tiredness and lie abed, and the next it does rain and he does rant that all should be ruined. And for all of this I do sit here amid the tight packed stores and nothing is there for mine entertainment. All that I do own but what I do stand in is trussed away so 'tis not e'en possible that I should go forth in the street for mine own amusement for 'tis my plainest clothes that I do wear for the purpose of moving and for two days must I live entire in them, all for my husband who does have no judgement with the timing.

But no constraints there are upon him. For he does come and go as does please him and but add his fussing and flustering to my unsettled state. And convenient for him to dine out and make excuse that all his goods be stacked away so his friends do press the invitations on him and all manner of hospitality, yet must I remain within. With Jane who be but full of complaint . . . and not even fit to go to the cookshop for to buy some viands.

Worse. Most galling it is to have my husband, who does do so little but make more work, to tell the world that the effort of all does strain him. From my window, where I do watch all awhile for naught else do I have to do – I do hear him inform all who would listen that the worry of so great a move be so immense that no time is there for the sleeping, so much there be to attend to. And I do watch him give hisself the great airs, and mop his brow to show the trouble of it all, yet the only trouble he does get close to is that which he does give me!

Both our tempers be frayed with the pressure and not soon

enough it should be when we do take up residence in Seething Lane. Then do I have the change of garments, the good meal, and the knowing of what it should be to play the lady.

## 29 July

So little time there has been, and so tired but some satisfaction too, and not all with being ensconced in such fine premises which do please me well, though more work it is and not enough to do it . . .

But still the fears I have of all the expense and where it all should come from. This day my worries did get to the fore and I did press my husband – who has the great reluctance to state specifics on what he should be worth but is the great braggart on his store – to make the tally and tell me true what all should cost and when it should be paid for. For does it tug at my mind and take my peace from me . . . And perchance it is that I did take him from his guard, else that he too does have the care of it, for . . . he does go to his leather-bound papers and scrutiny it and then does tell that 'tis fifty pounds he has beforehand which is a great deal, but not so much to settle all he does order. Yet much do I learn from this.

For do I keep record that he sets hisself at fifty pounds, and do I see where he does place his journal which I know not afore this. And his reckoning I should soon prove or disprove . . . when I do have my chance.

## 30 July

What insult my husband does this day offer me. For he does bring home the loud Mrs Crisp to give of her advice for the new upholstery. If she does dress her house as she does dress her person, then should her quarters be most vulgar. Much I could learn, I do ready admit, but not from her, and does it anger me that Samuel Pepys should show such common breeding to seek such counsel for his wife, who be a Clifford and should well know what does have refinement in it.

# 1 August

So soon he does fall once more to bad ways. All the assurances that Samuel does give that when to the fine abode in Seething Lane, and the comforts, then should he stay in and we should be the envied couple. Yet does a new house and soft surrounds so soon lose attraction, for this last night, late home was my husband and with naught but the cholique in him to show for his day's work. And no consideration for me, though great be my discomfort.

'Tis well known that the lobster does cause great gas in the stomach and bowels e'en when on its own it be eaten, and too Samuel does know all this but no regard does he give it. Yet much worse and the sorry thing it be to mix it with the beer, and the wine, which does but swill the poisonous brew within. And my husband does admit to the mixing of all and does suffer much from such a diet. As I do too!

Very unwell I have been and all at the time when no respite there is. My termes be due, which does bloat me, and my tooth does ache – which does also have the swelling in't – and too, there is the burning soreness in my privities, which does go with the sporting that my husband does look to since we did make the move. Too much of the fire he does have in his blood and 'tis true that no room – nor even corner – should there be which he seeks not to use for amouring (and does Jane say but with no insolence in her, that 'tis like the dog which must piss in each part to claim its territory, which should have the amusement in't, if not so much pain for me in the performance).

'Twas on account of such sickness and soreness that I did take to my bed this very night past to have the cure of sleep and peace, when mine husband did come tumbling forth and then all quiet, adieu!

His presence he did announce with the great stumble pon the bed and he did make to talk with me but so laboured his words, and so retching his breath, that no parley would I have with him. For 'twas but excuse to belch all on me.

Then 'twas melancholy which did win in him and most sorry for hisself he did feel, and on and on so. And though I be the one with the sickness yet must I endure his moans and groans, while he does hold his head and his stomach, and does put forth the fearful wind.

And all his own fault too, while my pain has naught of mine own making in it.

But a fine pair we do make as we each lie abed and hold close over our bellies for to stay the grippe. Though more cause I have, much quieter am I. All through the night does my husband issue forth loud noises and foul smells, yet without waking, which is a great grievance to me for does he keep me from sleeping.

But more galling e'en than the pain, which does wake me, and the noise and the odour, is this morn's announcement from Samuel Pepys that not one wink does he sleep through the night! Which is the greatest untruth ever uttered but no way is there to disavow him of it.

Still more pain.

## 3 August

No entry could I make yesterday for the sickness did defeat me. My monthly flow did come, which was my anticipation, and it did drain all from me. So heavy my legs did feel that I did think they had weights upon them that I should drag them from place to place, for they go not forth willingly.

And though I should have been the better served by confining myself to my bed, yet did I consent to accompany Samuel at noon to Dr Clerke's for dinner for much did it mean to him, and much did he insist that 'twould be no effort for me if we did but go by coach, and that he should look a poor figure in the world without his wife who he did give promise should attend. And what should be done with the waste food?

So I did give way, and go, though I did live to regret it.

For no great satisfaction was the meal. Nor the company neither. Misery though I had with me to start, yet did it turn to more besides when first Samuel does talk only with the wife (and does sing her praise to me as the best woman of language he did ever hear – though I did see it not – and what fine pattern she should be for me) and then he does go forth and leave me. To business he does say. And all alone and in pain must I stay.

## 4 August

Today I am resolved to stir not forth from my bed; much does it rain and the thunder and the lightning do have their play and so the best place this should be. And though 'twas my plan this week to p'ruse my husband's diary, no will do I have for it . . . no way to stand against what I should find therein if it hit me, and all my energy does concentrate on the driving pain and to be free of it. So I do lie here with mine own scribblings which be almost more than I can perform, and I do count the minutes with the hope that the fierce burning should abate. Yet it do not.

## 5 August

'Tis the Lord's Day and for giving thanks, yet 'tis far from it that I be. So great my pain that I should wonder what punishment it be, for no crime do I think on that should deserve it.

And much degrading is there in't, for constant change of linnin do I need, which does place me in Jane's debt and I know not whether I should do for her, though common trials we should share.

My husband's contribution is to send the ointment which Will does obtain from Dr Williams but no appearance from Samuel who all day is from hence.

## 6 August

No help has the ointment been. Nor Samuel neither. For he did come in and tell last night of all the places he has been from seeing his mother (which I have no envy for) to Mr Shepley at dinner and Mr Hill in Church and Mr Howe and Mr Pierce for singing, and my lord for business, and all for drinking, and very late home he is, and all the while I do lie here in fearful pain and no sympathy, and no prospect to go abroad.

And 'tis my judgement that the poultice does make all worse. Like the burning acid it did seem upon my soreness and it did make me leap with its hot sting, till the tears did just course pon my face and though I did thank mine husband for the plaister, and did promise that most regular I did apply it, yet did I lie, for no strength there was in me to try more than once and the only benefit did come when I did wipe the fearsome poultice from me and get but my customary pain, which be some relief.[17]

## 7 August

And last night does Samuel show his anger to me, and make it that I am pretending to sickness which I have not, and that tired he is of coming home to the indisposed wife, and much of this have I heard before and no liking to return to, and needs I must remind him of our pact. Though little stomach do I have for standing against him, yet it should be done, and the great anger is in me.

[18]When I do tell Eliza of his ill humour and his word that 'tis the duty of the wife to lie with the husband when e'er he so desires it and no complaint either, then she does have a mind on how to fix him, and 'tis with the herb lettuce, which previously I have no learning of . . . But 'tis well known to wise women – or so Eliza does tell – that the lettuce does have within it the way to damp the bodily lust and stay the venerous dreams, so I do think to feed my husband much of it when I find my feet again, and no thought to the expense of the herb. Yet not all by mouth. For 'tis the case that the lettuce, applied to the cods with the little camphire, does take away all thoughts

---

[17] Some of the remedies of the time would be, by contemporary standards, barbaric and ineffectual. Nicholas Culpeper's *Complete Herbal* for example, recommends the Golden Rod – 'the decoction of the herb . . . for staying the floodings of the body, body fluxes and the immoderate menses of women; and is most available in ruptures or burstings, being internally or externally applied' – among other curative properties. And this is one of the most innocuous.

[18] Translated from the French.

of sport. And this too should I use. Though Samuel should not want it, yet do I wait till he does heavy sleep from the drink that is in him, which be not long to bide my time. But what he should make of the plaister and the greens stuck upon his cods when he does wake, I know not. Though well do I know what my ayre would be. For I would feign the innocent and make inquiry what *he* does do to his cods when he does have the drink in him, and let him have the puzzle of it. For truth to tell he does often have no memory of his pastimes when he does wake from the drink and much does it worry him, and do I add to it.

'Tis enough to make me want to leave my bed, to go to market and get the green lettuce, which should be there.

Oh that my pain would pass and that I should get to see my husband's diary and what he should do while I be confined here.


## 10 August

My husband's turn it was to be ill, all night, and to vomit in the basin, and by his own hand for all the Rhenish wine he did put down did want to rise up again, and though some of my heart did feel for him, yet I did not show it, for 'twas my resolve to grant him the same kindness he did give me in my sickness. So I did offer to get him a potion, but no more, and it was of no assistance for none could his stomach take in it.

And this morning when I keep my form, and no compassion words do think to give him, then does he say that 'tis not the drink but the after effect of the stone he no longer has, that does make him ill – and no way do I have to know if there be truth in it.

Yet I do give him the benefit and rub his head for him, and his back, and say the soothing words, for whether it be his fault or no, 'tis the case that he is exceeding sick and in need of comforting, and all in all, 'tis my husband he be, and though I should seek to do for him what he should do for me, yet too I have the affection for him. And much to lose if he does die – or take e'en to his bed. So I wish him speedy recovery.

Though I do recommend the eating of lettuce as the cure . . .

and I do think to decode his diary when he does leave his bed and go from home.

## 18 August

Twice this day did I get money from Samuel for mine own wardrobe; the first of five pounds for the petticoat, but then I did see the rich lace and a most fine cloth and which does go at twenty-six shillings a yard and which Eliza says is the best and the most becoming to me. So I did return to Samuel – who should not be so free if from Eliza he thinks the counsel should come, and so I did tell that was my noble father who does know quality when he does see it – which role e'en Samuel should not dispute – who did recommend the cloth and the lace, and always it does work for me. Samuel does not think to be bested by my father, nor cut the mean figure in his company, which I do ask him in, so he does hand over the more monies and much satisfaction it does give me and the new garment too. [19]Though less I did pay than Samuel did give and more is there for my store.

## 19 August

Yesterday when I did return I did plan to p'ruse my husband's papers, and to put them aside the code, for 'tis the burning curiosity which is with me to know what his entries do mean. And all plans did I have set, only to go awry, which be the way.

'Twas my interest to have the guarantee of two uninterrupted hours and to this end I did urge my husband to attend the Cockpit play. For 'tis *The Loyall Subject* which be performed and much praise does go to the boy Kinaston who does play the Duke's sister, for 'tis said that the more lovely he be than any woman (and certain more lovely than the Duke's sister herself!). So do I honey tongue make encouragement for no such treat does Samuel have since he did come from the sea, though no great persuasion either to use his time to this

[19] Translated from the French.

purpose, and 'tis the satisfaction I have within me – and the prospect to study his entries with Mr Shelton's assistance – when he does suggest to me that the good idea of *his* it should be to make his way to the Cockpit.

Though 'tis the risk that my husband should make eyes with some puss while I be not there to keep check, yet is there the gain in it for me. For do I think to have the assurance that for two hours more he should return not.

And neither he did. But no opportunity was there for me to study his journal. No sooner did I know the play to start and see myself safe to my task, than my bitch does start awhelping and all night I must spend with her. What coincidence it should be that she should do this right when all is planned for the unmasking of my husband. Yet not e'en he could order it.

Further opportunity I should make for myself to learn my husband's secrets, though no more to send him forth to the theatre. For he did – again – come home with much wine in him, and the boast that the actors do all drink with him now that he does have a place, and he does endless sing the praises of this beauteous man who did play the lady's part. 'Tis a good time he did have of it, and all the while I did have the trouble to soothe the bitch and a most worrisome and wearisome task it be.

But did I twitt my man and tell him that 'tis wide reported that women soon do play their own part on the stage for 'tis the King's wish, and what then for the beauteous boys who do now act them? And Samuel does tell me not to be the fool, for never should it come to ladies making the public performance, not e'en if the King should wish it, which he does not – so Samuel says.

## 6 September

[20]So. He does dally with Mrs Diana. And not just in code but in the foreign language too . . . none does he want to see this! And he does count that he does have two hundred pounds in cash . . . two hundred pounds beforehand! And so grateful I

---

[20] Translated from the French.

was for the necklace of pearl which he does say should be the very ruin of him.

My rage does go right through me. Mrs Diana is what I should expect, and the money too, but no advantage should this knowledge be if I do let it throw me, or do give way that I do learn it. Yet must I do the veriest tight control to keep all the order.


## 25 September

[21]Other records do I keep against my husband for the risk this could be to keep account e'en though I make the foreign entry.

But what I do record herein is that my husband does give orders to find more knowledge about this new tay he does drink, which he has does come from Chinea and which is given out now in the coffee house and does impress him with its fine flavour, though how it should be prepared, I know not. But Eliza should determine and could I then serve it and lead the way.

[22]No more monies does he set down, nor the wenches he does do, but I should make the snare, and have him if I but bide my time and keep mine wits about me.


## 26 September

No fault it is of mine that the plasterers do make the mess of all herein for 'tis Samuel who does want all these changes and improvements and the kitchen too. So we must sleep upon the floor and the powder of all does stop up the breathing. Yet always does Samuel look to me when 'tis his own acts that do cause the problem.

[21] Samuel's diary actually states: 'From thence to Axe Yard to my house, where standing at the door Mrs Diana comes by, whom I took into my house upstairs, and there did dally with her a great while, and found that in Latin *Nulla puella negat.*'

[22] Translated from the French.

## 3 October

Each day more furniture we do add and so I do think 'tis no idle boast when Samuel does reckon his accounts as he is wont to do obsessive. Though much more must he add to pay for the purchases, and to keep his cash as well. Still does he tell me that none is there left and to think not to increase my garments, to grace mine own chamber.

## 4 October

Painters everywhere. And no sign of the diary. Where should he put it?

## 17 October

This day I did persuade Samuel that the time was right to put all the books in order, for much of the work on the house should now be complete – though still the door and other things there are that Samuel should require. And he does agree to my proposal. And his diary in the leather-bound he does take from the pile (which I could find not, though I swear that I did search the stack he does have) and all, with the diary, he does arrange in his closet. And my hands do burn to remove it from its place.

## 21 October

Now too I must have boils as well to try me!

## 25 October

Much of the miser there is in Samuel. For did I think to keep one half crown he did ask me to retain for his later use and when he did call for it, I did feign forgot where it should be, but too much to endure his protests, so I did return it for easier ways there should be for the plenishing of my store.

## 28 October

Pills and plaisters for the pain. No relief.


## 1 November

The great chafe I am in, for last night my husband does make
to baste me – by reason that I am ill! And does he count the
days since we did lie together and demand his dues soon, else
he does claim as 'tis his right to put his pintle in some other.
Which does bring out the very deep anger in me, and no way
to win me to him it is. And will I observe where his pintle does
go (and I do have my ways) and the price he should pay if it
should find other accommodation.


## 4 November

Yesterday did my lord and my lady have audience with the
King and I did ask of Samuel, who does constant talk of the
service he did render and the gratitude the King does have for
him – though no knighthood yet which I do remind him, and
mine own disappointment – that if he be in such good grace,
why do we not get into the presence of the King or Queen,
which I should look on with favour and convey to Eliza with
much satisfaction, and so does he say he will look to it, but no
great faith is there in me.

  'Tis my way that if we should gain such audience, then the
black patch must I wear, for all do it, but Samuel does have the
mark against it, though he does agree that 'tis the fashion
requirement in the royal presence. So I do don it now and in
preparation – for the practice there should be to wear it and
well does it become me – and no point to wait to the Queen
does see it on me – else I might die the old lady afore I do
patch.

# 7 November

All night does go to quarrelling. My bitch does have the trouble with her bladder, which Samuel should be first to understand. But rather he does abuse her and put her out which I will not have.

# 10 November

So. He does want Plain Pall to come and be the servant. For no husband can she get for her provision. And first I did think 'twas the worst idea I ever did hear to have that sour face to look on me each day and in mine own privacy, but then I did think that no need should there be for me to see her for she would be the servant and all orders would I give. And Jane could too. And one should be that no appearance she does put at table for two of the same family and manners should be more than I should take and still have appetite. But in all, this arrangement does have appeal to me. For much do I have to repay her.

# 12 November

When should I get to read and make comparison with the code?

This day we did buy the dozen table napkins, the first that my husband does ever possess, though always does my family have their use. And the only blight on all this great purchasing of goods should be that my husband does send his father to supervise my dealings, when he should know not a napkin from a wall hanging, the tailor though he be. Yet 'tis true he does drive the hard bargain; 'tis the family trait.

And Pall is to join us, and she does cry with gratitude for the privilege to be the servant which does show how low she does go, but further yet I do think.

## 14 November

'Tis true that the oven works not well, and no liking do I have to know its ways. Perhaps Pall should be put to cook. Then her fault it should be if the pies and tarts be burned. But not mine.

## 16 November

So do I try my translating again, though not for profit. And my husband does have pride in me. For my lady did get the French maid and no understanding is there betwixt them and so I do interpret and e'en my lord is impressed and Samuel does swell with it. Though the warning not to be too clever when once we were all alone. But a change from not to be too bold, or too free with favours.

'Tis the very substance of our conversing that Samuel should always warn me against excess, with no thought to his own. And from what I know of what he does write in his journal (which be not enough and sorely do I seek to remedy it) no sense he does have of his hypocriteness. Which he surely should have in admonishing me.

## Lord's Day 18 November

New pew. Old sermon. Pleasant supper.[23] Usual quarrel.

## 19 November

This day I did insist that Samuel should hang not two pictures which he does get cheap and would have pass for beauty, and 'tis like him to measure even the pictures in terms of expense which does show the true want of taste and breeding, and I do tell him I should choose what ornament there should be and he does agree.

[23] With Sir William and Lady Batten; Sir William the Surveyor of the Navy.

And Pall does stand there pop-eyed to hear him pulled down.
And both should know the worth of a noble Clifford.

## 20 November

[24]Last night my plans did meet with success, and while Samuel
did take to sleep, I did stay till past two of the clock, and 'twas
to wake the maid to start the wash, which I did give as my
pretext, though truly 'twas to read his diary that I did stay while
he did snore.

And the time there was when I did think to be thwarted
again, for Samuel did be up most late to play his music, so I
did fear that two of the clock should come afore he did take
hisself abed, yet he did tire, and leave me, and then quick did I
take his papers, and to start on my translating, which now I
should do with much swiftness. Yet no great distress the details
did this time cause me; so either he has done with wenching –
and account keeping – else he does have his suspicions of me
and think that I do bottom his meanings, so no more should he
set them down where I should see.

Past the time when the crier does give out that 'tis two of the
clock, I do wake the maid to start the fire and make the water
ready, while I to bed.

## 21 November

Such exciting prospect it be. We are to see the Queen. Little
faith did I have in mine husband, yet does he say that all be
arranged, and though I should wait to find whether it does take
place, and not be but the further puffing – yet do I think he has
the truth in him. Perchance he does have favour with the King
and the Queen which I did think be but ayre.

Oh what Eliza should say to this. And so much to do.

When my first joy at all did somewhat abate, then soon I did
say that not one thing was there that I should wear. And while
S. does add all manner of finery to be in royal company, yet

[24] Translated from the French.

nothing has there been for me. Or 'tis how I should see it. And though he does make the protest, yet he does see my meaning and so he does consent to addition to my wardrobe, though but the promise of future funds!

So to Paternoster Row, where I did think to have mine own way. Yet for my husband – once more – do we make the purchase. Some green watered moyre for a morning waistcoat, but nothing for the royal presence for me. And I do plan to have remedy.


## 23 November

Much there was in't. But the disappointment too. Yet do I set all down here for the record. For who should know that Elizabeth Pepys does have the audience with the Queen, and the Princesses?

First in the morning, when I did rise, I did do my toilette most careful – for I did want to leave the grand impression – and too much time it did take to don the patches, for little knowledge I did have of the wearing of them, and I did settle upon three, which I did think most becoming, and too did Samuel give assent. And there were flutters within me, for not so soon did I think to have such position, and I did want to acquit myself in the manner of the Clifford, and 'tis true that I did fuss so that 'twas almost late we should be for the good Foxes.[25] For much time and trouble did I take to frize my hair, and though Jane did give some help, yet no great use was she to make it how I did intend.

And e'en when I did make myself aready, yet some satisfaction there was gone from me and did I complain to Samuel that I should look the poor one, and all should know it, and no great credit I should be. Yet perchance I play upon a guilt part – that so much does go on his ornament and so little for me – that he does agree to the purchase of a whisk which I do say should set off all most satisfactorily, and so we do walk by the Old Exchange where I do have my white whisk. And not e'en that Samuel does get the new gloves for hisself does put me

[25] Mr Fox was to take them into the presence of the Queen.

244

out, and so to the Foxes where we did have the most warm welcome that did please me, and put me to my ease. For Mrs Fox did think it go for naught to be in the presence of the Queen, as she does oft attend, and so did I think to mimic her, though this day she came not with us but did stay within.

And so to the Queen's Presence Chamber where 'twas my place behind the Queen's chair that Mr Fox did fix me, and did I think to see much grandness which is for the disappointment to come in. For none was there in't. Though 'tis true that the Queen does eat most dainty, which I did remind my husband, and give comment on the delicate way she does hold the fork and lift it to her, which does have the art in it.

But none in her dress. For the most plain and little person she is and with no grandness in her. Many there were in the room who did better dress than she, and more money and more modish than ever did get in to her garb. And too the Princesses, though 'tis the case that Princess Henrietta does have the charm and the figure, and too did I close study her hair, for was it frized different to mine own, less on the ends and more to the centre, and so I do profit and know how to do't in future.

But soon was all over, for no great feast it should be – though served in the French manner which does have more style, and which does take longer, from the soup, and many were the pyes and sweetmeats which I know not, and were left pon the table, and which I did wonder where they do end up. But 'twas my thought when we did leave that the better table I should keep – if but the monies my husband should give me. And this too was the disappointment.

If I should be the Queen then not only the better wardrobe would there be, but the better dinner.

No time there was to look around to see all else who should be there, and who should see me. So soon was time to take leave, and we did to Mr Fox's to make our own dinner, and it too did have more in it and more delicacies than the royals did dine pon.

And then was my husband bidden.[26] So to the coach and I to

[26] Will arrived with the message that Samuel was wanted by his employer.

home where I did think on all this and wonder what it should mean to be the royal one.

Late home was my husband. And much business had there been.[27]


## 30 November

'Tis said that thieves there are about and that two nights past they did try to rob Mrs Davis, which does put the fear in me, and 'tis recommended that 'tis wise that all should stay within, which does have the presumption in it that this should keep the thieves without.

None there were who did want what we did have in our garret house but much there should be which does warrant thieving in Seething Lane. And all this does show that the more one does rise, the more risks there be; and though I do hope that the robbers should go to prison, yet do I hope that Samuel should not, for the want of paying his bills to gain what the thieves should now have their interest in. So does the world go round.


## 30 December

'Tis all arranged that Puss Pall should come to live in now, and the pretty plans I do have to do with her.

[27] Samuel had also been to the theatre, which no doubt Elizabeth would discover later when reading his diary.

# 1661

## February

Only the low frequent the public hot house, or so my husband will have it. Plain does he say that 'tis only for wantons that they be set up, and that 'tis the place where whores parade their wares for the whoremongers all to see. And 'tis in me to ask how it is that he should know all this, but no point would it be to provoke ill will betwixt us, so do I let the insult pass. And too the opportunity to make comment on the deficiencies of his bathing habits. And no matter Samuel's condemnation of these Turkish Baths,[1] yet do I go and take my pleasure, and all too for my health. And if my husband does find it such cause for complaint, then should I solve it and tell him not when I do attend.

No way other would there be for him to know, for no great attention does he pay these days to the softness or beauty of my skin, which the hot house does surely improve.

While he does make a mouth about all the disgrace that the public bath does bring, I do but bide my time. True it does mean I should forgo the temptation to shew-up the blotted nature of his mind, and his want of bathing. For what can be said of Samuel Pepys is that he does have the constant aversion to soap and water, and a strange suspicion too of any who share not his narrow views.

'Tis his contention that those who do remove all their

[1] The Crusaders had brought back with them the belief in the benefits of the Turkish Bath. At the end of the 18th century there was still a public hot house in St James's Street, known as The Turkish Head. And Queen Elizabeth's Bath – at Charing Cross – was still standing in 1831; it was a square pool with ascending stairs that bathers sat on, and it was set inside a brick vault. Health, rather than relaxation/pleasure was the main reason for taking the Bath.

clothing for to bathe, not only risk death and injury, but are of loose morals besides. So too does he close-keep about him all his garments, yet will he have it that he is clean. And times there are when he does accuse *me* of the slattern standards, when 'tis him who be almost unknown to bathe, lest it be the spa at Bath, which be very rare. Heated does he argue that those who do put off their clothes more oft than he should think fit, then is there the lecher about them and the bawdiness.

Which be his very ignorance. For well known it be that full bathing does enjoy favour with the high born and that 'tis but the low and limited – and the perverse – who do dread to part with their dress and who do see the purifying of the body as the impure.

But first mention I make of my partialness for this gentle practice, then on does my husband prate on the sin of slovenliness, which in him does equate with dirt! And both does he charge me with. And always, and unfair, will he have it that he be the one who does keep all fine and clean, and 'tis me who does despoil it. Which does have the very error, and the malice in it.

Yet 'tis because all must have order, for Samuel, that he should hold such belief. Truth to tell he should drive me to the veriest distraction with what he does see as the proper thing in the proper place – so that he does shift the chair but one part of an inch, and make moanings when each book does move a fraction out, or the littlest tilt does come to the wall hanging – and all this is how he should decide what be neat and clean. 'Tis the appearance of order – e'en though it be but the surface – which does lead Samuel to presume that all is underneath clean. Which is why he does keep his clothes upon him, and neat and of the fashion. Yet something do I know of what does go beneath, and no sweet smelling cleanness is there in't.

E'en where he did come up from the cellar – and not our cesspit[2] – but where he did lodge hisself in a great heap of surprise turds which did come from Mr Turner's place where his house of office[3] is full, and Samuel did reek of shyte, yet

[2] There was a common cesspit in the Seething Lane house which clearly did service as a place of defecation.

[3] *House of office* was the term used for faeces container, and obviously Mr Turner's overflowed more than once as Samuel refers to this first in his diary on 20 October 1660.

still did he take not off his clothes and make clean the muck of all of it.

Such dread and dislike does Samuel have of the scent-soap[4] and water that naught but his hands and face e'er find their way to this form of repair. He does even show the preference for the harsh pumice stone for to shave with, rather than the razor which does want for soap and water.

The most use Samuel should have for water upon his face is when his head does ache from the wine drinking and he does need it to stir hisself sober from a morning stupor.

But no use does he have at all for the contact of water with his other parts. Though, 'tis the case, I needs confess, that very occasional does he take the footbath, but always with the protest that he should catch his death. And 'tis only when his feet be unendurable sore from the corns that he does succumb to such rashness.

Not like me. For much satisfaction does it give me to have the cleansing of my feet, and other parts besides. And no chill is there in such hot house. So if I should hear the boy pass by and shout that the water be hot[5] then sore am I tempted to make my way, if Samuel be not privy to my arrangements. And if I do have the cost of all about me.

Though he should make strong protest about the soothing of the flesh, yet it is but his low prejudice, and to think that this be new. For it has been known for many centuries that the stews do more than make clean the outer layer; they do have restorative powers for the inner as well.

Which is why those who be born in high places do keep the practice[6] and make much of bathing. Though not in the public hot house of course, which be where I must descend to. Yet it does still have the benefit in it. 'Tis much more healthy to partake of the Turkish bathing, than not.

And no lewd things do happen there. Or none that I do see.

---

[4] *Scent-soap* came from France; there was also the popular Castille soap from Spain, made from olive oil.

[5] Young boys were sometimes employed to run through the streets and announce when the steam was ready; it could be piped from the baker shop once the bread was done.

[6] Bathing was much more common in the 15th than the 17th century and there were some 'ignorant' people who thought Turkish Baths were new, rather than an old practice.

Or my maid either, who at all times does accompany me. 'Tis the meeting place for many of discernment and much high talk does flow. For 'tis those of breeding who do know the value thereof, though many do come on hard times.

And all is kept decent with the bathers. Strict separate are the sexes kept, though not all those who work therein. For the stovers do much business, and much surgery too is conducted in the stew. 'Tis the big woman who does scrub down all the ladies – and great pleasure as well as the pain is there in't in having the outer skin removed – and 'tis said that she be bewitched, for not one word does utter from her. And many there are who feel free to talk in front of her, but not me. For other explanation do I have of her silence, and not the foreign tongue either, though this may have contribution. But much should she hear in that place where even the very discreetest could talk out and much I do think she learns to her advantage. But another matter is that.

'Tis only the bathmen who do enter to do the cupping, and blood letting, and other sundry things which the ladies do require for their health. And no mischief is there in't. If perchance some bawdy arrangements should be made – and I admit not the event, just the possibility – then no different it be from what does take place at the public *tavern*, and the far quieter it is. And the bathing be better for the health than the ale should be.

Some discourse there is on how long the benefit of the bath should last and no certainty do I have of it. But once I did know the precise time that it did have effect. For on my way home did I get messed with a pot of turds which did descend with no warning, and not quick enough was I to keep from being covered with the filth. And no means for cleaning my clothes, or returning for another cleansing, though well did my state call for it.

That night Samuel and I did talk of the shitty hazards of the town, and not just the turds that do fly, and the ordure that does pile high on each corner. But so much excrement each day does get produced and no ordered place to put it – which does offend Samuel.

'Tis our way to have the fine close-stool in the drawing room and most well does it serve as the office of the house, but e'en it be limited, and must be regular emptied. And the cellar cesspit too, which does foul up the place each time the filth be carted forth through the premises.

Much gratitude I do have that it be not me that is charged with the duty to clear it all out. If my maid do nothing else but be the stool carrier, then could I be content with her. Still the thought of the full and foul chamber pot, and the awfulness of emptying it, does wake me from my dreams.

Yet some solution to all this shyte there should be, else the great problem it could become. At home and abroad.[7]

'Tis said that some there are of high birth who do make over the special room for the taking of the turds, and too, that 'tis possible to flush all down with water and to make drains to carry all hence.[8] But too fantastic does this seem to me. So still should I settle with the sweating house and the rubbed skin, which does give me satisfaction. And the turds and what to do with them do continue to try us and our ingenuity.

## 24 April

Now the Coronacion does have the royalness in't. And the finalness too. For should all the plots and plans be put to rest now that we do have the King upon the throne and all arrangements be blessed with bishops, and all the loyal oaths and royal pardons do mark the clean starting point again.

'Twas the most pomp-day I did ever see, and should ever hope to see again, for none should there be that do come to meet this measure again (and mightily did it cost, or so my husband did tell). And the fine position I did have among the best, to see what did happen in the Hall and though I did fear to fall from such high scaffold, yet 'twas the wondrous vantage point.

And did I have the argument with Samuel on how all did proceed till I did make accusation agin him that 'twas entire

[7] *Abroad*: in this sense meaning outside, public places; not in a foreign country.

[8] This could be a reference to Thomas Povey's establishment; he had a bathroom at the top of his house and presumably had piped some form of running water.

another coronacion that he did see, for so little correspondence there be betwixt us . . . and I did think that such confusion he should have as the consequence of too much drink in him. But then too he did say that so urgent was he taken by the push to piss that he did leave all, midway before the King had done with the ceremony, and round the Abbey he did go, to Westminster Hall, so 'tis abundant clear that much he did miss, though he should not make admission.

From the early hours of morn I did stand upon my scaffold with the fine few of ladies who did have such privilege and we should see what did go on 'neath us; while others should have fair view of us, which did have the satisfaction in it. And most pleased I was with mine own gown, and well it did compare. Though not so much finery among the ladies to pale the gentlemen for most colourful they should be, and all their decorations.

And did the Abbey have the magnificence in it, with all done in red, and raised up in the centre, with the throne and footstool for the subjects and the King. And all who do attend in the veriest brightest plumage, to even the fiddlers who do sport their red vests.

And all the bishops do come in cloth of gold (which is very high and much of pomp, and some do call it popish, yet should I find it pleasing), and think that much is there to be said for men in fine dresses. And then does come all the Lords of the land, and 'tis clear that they did think to outdo one and t'other, in their great splendour, for each procession I did think to be the most grandest, only to find that the next did make them pale.

For then there was the Duke and the King – least in the coronacion that I did attend, though my husband should witness a different occasion ([9]and should I peruse his papers to see that he does so, yet much more trouble it should be now he does keep it locked from me, and with Will charged to guard it safely, yet should the day come when I do have the opportunity to make comparison and to list the faults my husband does commit. But I should bide my time, and do my watching, for clear it is that he abandons not all this wenching, spite his

[9] Translated from the French.

contrary assurances, and do I close watch him – yet this be for another day's entry).

No great liking I did have for the coronacion service, and around me all did want to get on with it, and outside ten thousand people who did impatient wait the appearance of their King, and all within the rails they did obedient stand, and most well behaved for such a mob which did have the celebration and not the violence in it.

Full singing there was which did please me, and fine musique, and then did the King get crowned and the great shout go up, and most moved I was with it. For 'tis the handsome man he be, and the royalness there is in him, and 'tis said that many the maid does not mind to be called to his bed chamber which I do understand, but think not to seek.

And then all the men do put their hats pon their heads, and come to swear their allegiance, and though I did think that 'tis not long since some o' the same did swear that ne'er a monarch again there would be in England, yet none did raise this issue. But the general pardon was read, which does put all in the proper place, and silver medals there were thrown about by one Lord, whom I know not, but who did seem to have much importance, and many did go ascramble for the silver, and no dignity in that part of the proceeding but that was all the blot that I did see and the rest should be rejoicing.

And then the coronacion does have its ending, and the sinking feeling there was in me, for when again should such event be? And so much anticipation and now the end of it. But yet more celebration after the crowning did finish.

And though I did see it not, Samuel did give his version of what did happen thereafter, though he should be in his cups and have the memory lapse as well, which does not lend substance to his claim of accuracy.

Yet did he see the King with crown and sceptre when he did go for his dinner, and under the canopy he did proceed, and held up by six silver staves carried by the Barons of the Cinqueports, and little bells at every end, which is how he does have it. And slow was the progress of the King till he did to his own table and then all else did take their seat, and the great feast did begin.

The Knights of Bath the first course did carry to the King,

and the tasters there were too.[10] And some lords there were who did come before the courses on horse-back and stay so all dinner time. Which does have the show in it.

And the King's Champion does come and throw down his gauntlet and call for any who do challenge the lawful King . . . but none there are to risk it.

But Samuel too does make too merry and now does have the sorriness for it. For 'tis his word that he does have the four rabbits, and the pullet, along with what he does drink, but 'tis my belief that more wine than food he did put in him, which does mean 'twas a very quantity of drink he does consume. As do most other people. Yet not all should be so low to fall down spewing as Samuel does, and to be messed with one's own filth, which does make me turn from him.

But then when all did have their fill and the King too did take his leave, then did occur the very strangest thing. And did it make me think what all should mean. For the thunder and the lightning and the rain there was in it, and like I have ne'er known it. And some would say it should be the blessing, and some the curse. But Samuel does say that naught there should be in it. Yet I do wonder where the King shall lead.

*Considerably more work needs to be done on the remaining pages before any further publication can ensue.*

[10] According to Samuel's diary, 'My Lord Albimarles going to the kitchin and eat a bit of the first dish that was to go to the King's table.'

# Glossary

| | |
|---|---|
| **to Act the pigeon** | to be a coward |
| **Ague** | feverish fit |
| **All the world does ride me** | everything is against me |
| **Angel** | gold coin worth ten shillings |
| **Ayery** | sprightly, stylish |
| **Baggage** | of a woman, often used affectionately, sometimes to mean impudent |
| **Ballers** | ruffians, hoods, rakes who roamed the streets in groups |
| **Band (strings)** | neckband (ties) |
| **Bandy** | strenuous argument |
| **Baste** | chastise |
| **Baulk** | stay away, avoid |
| **Bawdy** | dirty talk |
| **Bedaggled** | muddied, bedraggled, particularly the bottoms or skirts of a garment |
| **Beforehand** | (*fifty pounds he has beforehand*) to have money in hand |
| **to Bell** | to throb, swell up like a boil |
| **Bespeak the good character** | provide a good reference |
| **Betwitt** | disparage, mock |
| **Betwitted** | deranged |
| **Bicher** | bicker |

| | |
|---|---|
| **Blooming** | probably refers to loss of weight at a time when 'roundness' was considered desirable |
| **Blot** | mistake |
| **Blown up** | unmasked |
| **Boggle** | hesitate, demur |
| **to Bottle it** | to put the lid on, keep control |
| **Bottom me** | beat/defeat me |
| **Bound** | constipated |
| **Bout** | quarrel |
| **to Break one's mind** | to disclose |
| **Bubo** | tumour |
| **Bufflehead** | fool, blockhead |
| **Busy looks** | curious onlookers |
| **By-book** | note book |
| **Cankre** | ulcer, abscess |
| **Carpet** | bed covers |
| **Cataplasm** | poultice |
| **Catt call** | whistle |
| **Caudle** | thin gruel |
| **Child-play** | childishness |
| **Chouse** | swindle |
| **Close beneath the covers** | hidden in the bedclothes |
| **Close-stool** | a chamber pot enclosed in a stool or box, the forerunner of the commode |
| **Colly** | dupe |
| **Conceit** | idea |
| **Consult one's pillow** | to sleep on it, to think about it |
| **Cool-say** | speak calmly |
| **Coquins** | knaves |
| **Courses** | periods, menstruation |
| **Crumb** | savings |
| **Cry up** | praise |
| **Cut for the stone** | surgery for the removal of a kidney stone |

| | |
|---|---|
| **Defyance** | mistrust |
| **Dogged** | cowed, beaten |
| **Doty** | doting |
| **Dower** | dowry |
| **Doxy** | whore, mistress |
| **Drawers** | undergarment with draw-strings round the waist, long knickers |
| **Draw the lemon** | get a bad deal, have a sour time of it |
| **to Dry beat** | to beat without drawing blood |
| **Dry money** | ready cash |
| **Effeminate** | a lover of women |
| **Empty his stock** | empty his bladder (and bowels?) |
| **Fanfarron** | braggart |
| **Favours** | a small bunch of ribbons given to those attending marriages or funerals |
| **Fish from** | ascertain, elicit |
| **Flagelette, Flageolet** | a whistle-flute with four holes in front and two thumb holes at the back – very popular in England in the 1660s |
| **Flannel waistcoat** | vest |
| **Fluxes** | discharges, urinating etc. |
| **Fondness** | foolishness, stupidity |
| **Foule copy** | rough copy |
| **Foxed** | drunk |
| **Foyle** | to repulse |
| **French dinner** | each course served separately and in order, not all at once as was the usual English fashion. This became more popular during the Pepys' time, particularly on festive occasions |

| | |
|---|---|
| **Frill-folds** | labia |
| **Frize** | to crisp the hair, or curl it closely (French – *friser*) |
| **Froward** | peevish, petty, hard to please |
| **Full mouth** | loudly |
| **Fumbler** | unperforming husband |
| **Furrow** | to worry |
| **Fusty** | peevish |
| **Gammer** | old woman |
| **to Gossip** | to attend a new mother |
| **Grief** | this could also refer to bodily pain |
| **Gulling** | deception |
| **Hangings** | wall hangings, curtains, used to keep the room warmer |
| **Harny** | hassle, tease, taunt |
| **to Have cups** | to be drunk |
| **Hawk** | to offer for sale |
| **to Heave** | to aim with hostile intent |
| **Hector** | street bully |
| **Hog high** | pig-headed |
| **Hot house** | Turkish Baths |
| **Hot humour** | high spirits |
| **Huffe** | fit of petulance caused by an affront |
| **Hurly** | crowded and noisy |
| **Ingross** | record |
| **Jangle** | quarrel |
| **Lay out** | to spend |
| **Linnins** | bedclothes, and possibly nightgown as well |
| **Low-like** | rudely, with an absence of breeding; common and coarse |
| **Made over** | refurbished |
| **Make cake of one's dough** | to have one's plans miscarry |
| **Menses** | periods |

258

| | |
|---|---|
| **Meschants** | villains |
| **to Milk** | literally, to take from by hand |
| **Mopish** | melancholy |
| **Mors** | a bite (French) |
| **Moyes** | periods (from the French – *mois*) |
| **Muff** | genitals |
| **Mumpings** | sullenness |
| **Nicotique** | pertaining to tobacco |
| **Night-geere** | night clothes |
| **Nipped** | finished, ended |
| **No stuffing was there in me** | I had no will/resolve to do anything about it |
| **Ordinary** | eating place serving fixed-price meals |
| **Pacquet** | parcel of papers |
| **Paduasoy** | from Padua in Italy; a strong corded or cross-grained silk |
| **Palterly** | mean, stingy |
| **Parts** | genitals |
| **Passionateness** | ill temper |
| **Pattens** | wooden shoes or clogs which served as overshoes to raise the ordinary shoes out of the mud or wet . . . consisting of a wooden sole mounted on an oval ring by which the wearer is raised an inch or two from the ground |
| **Pay shot** | to pay a share of the feast |
| **Penny-royal** | a species of mint, with small leaves (*Mentha pulegium*) cultivated for supposed medicinal properties; often used to procure a miscarriage |
| **Pett** | sulks |

| | |
|---|---|
| **Physic** | medicine, often an enema |
| **Pintle** | penis |
| **Ply** | to question and challenge |
| **Portion** | dowry |
| **Possett and purges** | wine and enemas |
| **Pot-hook** | a pot on a hook over the fire in which the water is heated |
| **Pot-venison** | pâté |
| **Press** | bookcase |
| **Privities** | genitals |
| **Privy parts** | genital area |
| **Privy soreness** | genital inflammation |
| **to Pull a crow** | to quarrel |
| **to be Pumped** | to have sexual intercourse |
| **Puss** | an ill-favoured woman |
| **to Put on more of his father's air** | to grow more like his father |
| **to Quarrel with one's own** | to take it out on one's self |
| **Quire** | collection of unbound sheets of paper |
| **Rattling** | irritation, state of being discomposed, upset |
| **Roisting** | loudness, bawdy |
| **Sack (and sack possett)** | white wine (and eggs beaten with sugar and curdled milk in white wine) |
| **Salt-eele** | rope or belt used for punishment |
| **Salve up the matter** | smooth over |
| **Scandalizing** | speaking scandal of |
| **to School** | to scold, rebuke |
| **to Score** | to rebuke |
| **to be Scoured** | to be disapproved of |
| **to Scowre** | to beat, punish |
| **to Screen** | to hide |
| **to Scruple** | to have trouble making up one's mind, to have objections to |
| **Scurvy** | contemptible |

260

| | |
|---|---|
| **Second placket** | second-best petticoat |
| **Secrets** | private parts |
| **Self-charge** | self-control |
| **Sennit** | seven nights |
| **Shaded not** | not eclipsed, not outdone or put in the shade |
| **Shirker** | slow payer |
| **to Sidle** | to be ingratiating |
| **to Slabber** | to dirty in a disagreeable way |
| **Smock** | woman's undergarment, chemise |
| **to Snuff** | to speak scornfully |
| **to Speak broad** | to speak frankly |
| **Spoiling** | deflowering |
| **Sporting wife** | a wife who is sexually eager |
| **to Stay** | to stop |
| **Stews** | popular word for bathhouses; by 1650 it is also being used to mean 'brothel' ('on account of the frequent use of the public hot-air baths for immoral purposes' *OED*) |
| **Stir** | commotion |
| **Stomachful** | pride |
| **Stone pain** | kidney pain, and pressure to urinate |
| **Stounded** | astonished |
| **Stovers** | members of the Barbers' Company who performed such offices as hair cutting, shaving, cupping, blood letting and other minor operations |
| **Subtility** | cunning |
| **Surveiller** | a supervisor, close watcher of someone who is not trusted |

| | |
|---|---|
| Swoune | swoon, faint |
| to Take the wall | to walk on the inside of the road or pavement – supposedly because it afforded better protection from 'swill' being tipped from the upper storeys |
| Tansy | sweetened egg pudding or omelette originally flavoured with tansy but sometimes with spinach |
| Tattle | gossip |
| Tay | tea |
| Termes | periods |
| to Tight screw | (of flesh) to pinch |
| Tossed | confused, troubled |
| to Touch | to try and get money from |
| to Towse | to tumble a woman |
| to Truckle under | to make subservient |
| Twattlers | those who tittle-tattle or tell tales |
| Ugly | unpleasant, offensive |
| to Undo | to expose |
| Unhung | bare walls |
| Untruss | to undo one's breeches |
| Vapourings | pretensions |
| to Vaunt | to sell |
| Wencher | womanizer |
| Whisk | neckerchief or scarf, which could fall gracefully to the shoulders |
| Whitester | launderer, washerwoman |
| Windfucker | talkative braggart |
| to Wipe | to insult |
| Without aid | in a natural state |
| Without book | from memory |
| Yard | penis |

# Index